PRAISE FOR *THE POWER OF CITIZENSHIP*

"Scott Reich's book delivers a message of service and citizenship that is as essential today as it was when president Kennedy first asked what we could do for our country. Using the lessons of history, he urges our generation to invest their time and talent in the world around them and to use the opportunities we have as citizens of this great nation to help make her stronger. At a time when it can be easy to focus on the differences that divide us, Scott makes a powerful and compelling case for the values that unite us."

—REP. JOE KENNEDY III (D-MA)

"Scott Reich's *The Power of Citizenship* is the best and most interesting book written on the Kennedy presidency in decades. It is also one of the most innovative and important presidential profiles I've read—a book which distills Kennedy's appeal to its essence and presents Kennedy to a whole new generation of readers. But above all, *The Power of Citizenship* is one of the most moving books I have ever read on patriotism and citizenship, and the power of leadership to inspire both. This book will be read as a primer and a classic on the subjects it covers for many years to come."

—DAVID EISENHOWER,
bestselling author of *Eisenhower at War*, 1943–1945

"Democracies are no stronger than their citizenry. John F. Kennedy's commitment to civic duty and public service is just as compelling today as it was during his lifetime. Scott Reich has thoughtfully conveyed President Kennedy's inspiring and enduring legacy of commitment to our nation."

—SENATOR SUSAN M. COLLINS (R-ME)

"Scott Reich offers unique and compelling insights into JFK's focus on public service. Collectively, we must embrace President Kennedy's message of good citizenship and work together to strengthen our country—especially for the next generation."

—GOVERNOR MARTIN O'MALLEY (D-MD)

"Scott Reich has produced a timely look back at the meaning of the Kennedy presidency and, even more importantly, the meaning of citizenship in our democracy. *The Power of Citizenship* is a challenge to all Americans."

—RICHARD REEVES,
bestselling author of *President Kennedy: Profile of Power*

"President Kennedy's legacy inspired my generation to embrace the challenges and responsibilities of public service, whether here at home or around the globe. Scott Reich's book should move the next generation of American leaders to heed President Kennedy's noble call to unite and achieve freedom for all."

—SENATOR MARK UDALL (D-CO)

"*The Power of Citizenship* is an antidote to the pervasive cynicism and rancor that marks much of today's politics. Scott Reich captures brilliantly how President Kennedy inspired Americans—and others around the world—that public service was a noble calling and one man, or woman, can make a difference. The Kennedy spirit, he writes, lives with countless citizens today who reject the politics of fear; there will be countless more upon reading this timely book."

—ALBERT R. HUNT,
Chairman of the John F. Kennedy Profile in Courage Award Committee

"Many of us of the Kennedy era—those of us touched by the way he mobilized American idealism, shaped by the words he spoke, charged by those words to shape a world he did not live to see—have struggled with how to explain to our children why the years 1961–1963 meant so much to us. Fortunately Scott Reich has found a way to explain the inexplicable. I'm buying a copy for each of my daughters."

—DAVID SHRIBMAN,
Executive Editor, *Pittsburgh Post-Gazette*, Pulitzer Prize winner

"*The Power of Citizenship* helps illuminate the legacy of President Kennedy and his administration. Reich points out that government service and serving the public interest were once noble undertakings that might be replicated once again. President Kennedy's principles and priorities are as important today—perhaps even more important—as they were fifty years ago. This book is an important contribution to a timely discussion of the meaning and importance of the Kennedy years."

—KENNETH R. FEINBERG,
Chairman of the John F. Kennedy
Library Foundation's Board of Directors

"Half a century after his death, my uncle John F. Kennedy is a historical icon whose ideas can still teach us invaluable lessons about the nature of citizenship. Any American interested in civic responsibility and the qualities of true leadership can find powerful insights in JFK's wisdom. These insights are aptly portrayed in Scott Reich's *The Power of Citizenship*, a must-read for anyone interested in the importance of duty and citizenship in these turbulent times."

—CHRISTOPHER KENNEDY LAWFORD,
bestselling author of *Recover to Live*

"Reich's talent for capturing lessons from the past is matched here by his clarity of vision on how we can use those lessons to move our nation forward. He reminds his readers that we should ask ourselves anew—what can we do for our country?"

—GOVERNOR JACK A. MARKELL (D-DE)

"Scott Reich has written an incisive and timely account of the citizenship ideals espoused by John F. Kennedy. President Kennedy's call to civic responsibility and public service resonated with Americans of all political stripes in the early 1960s, and is especially relevant today. Mr. Reich has done a service to a new generation of Americans to whom the torch of freedom—of which JFK so eloquently spoke—is now being passed. In 1963 someone looking back 50 years might have found historical inspiration in the legacies of Teddy Roosevelt and Woodrow Wilson. Today, half a century after its passing, we have the added benefit of revisiting a Presidency where Americans were called upon to 'ask what you can do for your country.' That is the essence of American citizenship, and why JFK indeed matters to young Americans today."

—FORMER SENATOR ALFONSE D'AMATO (R-NY)

"At a time when Americans have less faith in Washington to solve big problems, Scott Reich's book is a heartening reminder of President Kennedy's ability to inspire Americans to achieve great goals, 'Not because they are easy, but because they are hard.'"

—REP. STEVE ISRAEL (D-NY),
Chairman of the Democratic Congressional Campaign Committee

"A must-read for all concerned with the current political paralysis and partisan bickering—this is a refreshing reminder of Americans' unique devotion to civic responsibility and JFK's belief that every generation can improve our imperfect democracy by engaging in collective action for the common good. The future of our nation has been passed to the millennial generation, and this book was written for them: it inspires, informs, and calls for the new action we need."

—ANTONIA HERNÁNDEZ,
President and CEO, California Community Foundation

"A fresh look at JFK from a fresh voice of the new generation to which the torch is now being passed. Scott Reich has provided a fascinating and thoughtful perspective to those of us who were participants in the search for a New Frontier."

—DAN H. FENN JR., Staff Assistant to President Kennedy, 1961–1963, and Founding Director, John F. Kennedy Library and Museum

"Scott Reich's *The Power of Citizenship* is a powerful reminder that fifty years later, President Kennedy remains an inspiration to a new generation of Americans. Reich calls on us to carry forward President Kennedy's legacy and overcome the challenges of our own time by meeting the responsibilities of citizenship."

—ADAM FRANKEL,
Former speechwriter to President Barack Obama

"Among one of our most highly respected Presidents, John F. Kennedy should be as familiar as Abraham Lincoln to every generation of Americans. Scott Reich has performed a critically important task which will benefit future generations. Upon reading *The Power of Citizenship*, one comes to appreciate Kennedy's profound impact on our American civil society. His legacy must be shared."

—REV. DR. CALVIN O. BUTTS III, President, SUNY College at Old Westbury, and Pastor, Abyssinian Baptist Church, Harlem, NY

"Scott Reich provides the hope we need to overcome our current political impasse. His astute and loving appreciation of the Kennedy style of presidential leadership sees past party labels. In this eloquent and inspiring book, he identifies a core of idealism that ennobles politics and speaks to a new civic-minded generation."

—MICHAEL A. FITTS,
Dean and Bernard G. Segal Professor of Law,
University of Pennsylvania Law School

"At a time when effective communications through multiple media remain one of the greatest challenges of the presidency, and candidates of all ideological stripes have challenged young Americans to perform acts of public service, Scott Reich vividly recreates a time when a bold, young president succeeded in both endeavors. His extraordinarily well-researched and well-written work should be of interest both to young Americans today and those who seek their support."

—ALVIN S. FELZENBERG, PH.D., author of *The Leaders We Deserved (and a Few We Didn't): Rethinking the Presidential Rating Game*

The Power of
CITIZENSHIP

The Power of
CITIZENSHIP

Why John F. Kennedy Matters
to a New Generation

SCOTT D. REICH

To my good friend, Bruce Herzog –
Whose guidance, mentoring and warm friendship
will always mean so much to me. Hope you enjoy
the book!

All the best –

Scott D. Reich

BENBELLA

BENBELLA BOOKS, INC.
DALLAS, TEXAS

First hardcover edition October 2013

BenBella

BenBella Books, Inc.
10300 N. Central Expressway, Suite 530
Dallas, TX 75231
www.benbellabooks.com
Send feedback to feedback@benbellabooks.com

Printed in the United States of America
10 9 8 7 6 5 4 3 2 1

Library of Congress Cataloging-in-Publication Data
Reich, Scott D.
   The power of citizenship : why John F. Kennedy matters to a new generation / by Scott D. Reich.
      pages cm
   Includes bibliographical references and index.
   ISBN 978-1-939529-36-7 (trade cloth : alk. paper) — ISBN 978-1-939529-37-4 (electronic) 1. Citizenship—United States. 2. Patriotism—United States. 3. Kennedy, John F. (John Fitzgerald), 1917-1963—Influence. I. Title.
   JK1759.R365 2013
   323.60973—dc23   2013023280

Cover photo courtesy of the Library of Congress
Printed by Bang Printing

Distributed by Perseus Distribution
(www.perseusdistribution.com)

To place orders through Perseus Distribution:
Tel: (800) 343–4499
Fax: (800) 351–5073
E-mail: orderentry@perseusbooks.com

Significant discounts for bulk sales are available.
Please contact Glenn Yeffeth at glenn@benbellabooks.com or (214) 750–3628.

To my parents, Jamie and Danny,
who taught me that good citizenship begins at home.

CONTENTS

Who is here so vile that will not love his country?

—WILLIAM SHAKESPEARE

The main source of national power and national greatness is found in the average citizenship of the nation.

—THEODORE ROOSEVELT

A man may die, nations may rise and fall, but an idea lives on.

—JOHN F. KENNEDY

PREFACE

I STILL REMEMBER the day I fell in love with America. It was a sunny fall afternoon in 1998, and I was a high school student in Long Island, New York. I had just arrived home from soccer practice and found myself flipping through the television channels. U.S. history had always been fascinating to me, and so when a program on the American presidency appeared, my interest was piqued.

The program was just beginning—images of presidents flashed across the screen; triumphant music played in the background; key lines from historic speeches were recited. Within a few moments, I heard the most exciting, even magical, words I had ever heard spoken: "And so, my fellow Americans: ask not what your country can do for you—ask what you can do for your country."

At age fifteen, I certainly didn't understand these words in the ways I do now. But I knew they were special—I knew they represented something extraordinary, that there was a reason I was hearing them—and that they were being replayed with the aim of eliciting some sort of reaction from the viewer. It was a special moment for me because it marked the first time I can recall that I consciously identified with my country in a serious and meaningful way. To be sure, I had learned in the classroom and at home about the Declaration of Independence, the Constitution, wars and movements, and the unique heritage we as Americans share. But this experience was different for me because I sensed a new responsibility as an American—that in exchange for the privilege of being born here, I owed something back, some sort of debt that I was obliged to return.

For the first time in my life, history truly came alive. It was no longer merely the story of things past, the actions of gray-haired men in times too distant for a teenager to truly imagine or fully appreciate. It was real. It was tangible. It had meaning, and it could have an impact on my life. All because I heard one president—who was already part of that history long before I drew my first breath—utter one line that changed my view of the world, and altered, in a mere ten seconds, my core beliefs as an individual and therefore the trajectory of my life. I may not have been able to articulate it then, but surely this experience made me love my country in new ways. To this day, I cannot help but feel it was destiny that I should live in the land where those words were said.

Soon after, I began reading about the speaker of those words— and, to no surprise, I learned that he was a beloved president who seemed to elicit similar reactions from others: my parents, teachers, historians, and so on. Moreover, the same line that had sparked my interest seemed to be the very line that anyone with whom I conversed had memorized and was able to recite. All this confirmed my inclination that there was indeed something special about those words and about that president. It made me curious to learn more.

In many ways, this book traces its origins to that fateful day—a day that sparked a lifelong belief in the importance of public service and a fascination with the president whose words so fittingly captured this spirit. Like others before me, I was captivated by such visceral and evocative words as well as what they encapsulated. But I was also left with questions I've been seeking to answer ever since: Why do I find these words, and ultimately John F. Kennedy's presidency, so inspiring? How can we account for his iconic appeal? What do the themes of his presidency mean to us today? And, perhaps most germane to the study that follows, why should Kennedy's words and the concepts they embody have significance for new generations of Americans with no living connection to his era?

. . .

A PERUSAL THROUGH the many books on JFK reveals two truths: JFK's story thus far has been written largely by people who lived through his presidency; and there is little connection drawn between the meaning of his presidency and how it relates to a new generation born in a new era and in a world dramatically different from the one he inhabited. Yet half a century later, the latter point is what I believe matters most today—assessing why a rediscovery of this unique time in history offers constructive value to a new generation in modern times.

This is not an easy task. Fifty years is a long time, and the country has changed dramatically since 1963. Drawing meaningful connections between then and now would suggest that there are certain elements of the Kennedy story that might resonate in any age and place—if we can identify them.

I began considering these ideas in earnest as a college student. I took classes about presidential history and about the 1960s. I visited the John F. Kennedy Presidential Library and Museum in Boston. One of my professors introduced me to the late Theodore Sorensen, JFK's principal speechwriter, who was kind enough to spend time with me and listen to some of my early interpretations of Kennedy's legacy. Likewise, a friend introduced me to Dan Fenn Jr., a Kennedy White House aide and the founding director of the JFK Library, who shared valuable insights and encouraged me to pursue my studies further.

For me, someone born two decades after Kennedy died, the Kennedy presidency was a blank slate of sorts. I did not live through the times and gain firsthand knowledge of the intellectual currents that shaped contemporary public discourse or what behind-the-scenes forces framed the interplay between politics and public policy. Yet this meant I was not a prisoner of experience either: I did not see the 1960 election develop. I did not vote for a candidate or support a campaign. I did not live through the ensuing presidency and form opinions about the events of the day and how they were handled, for better or worse. Instead, I could approach the subject as any future historian will—not as a witness or participant, but with an eye toward understanding a familiar story in a new light and in search of truth.

As I have pondered these aims, I have grown more fascinated by the idea that there was a central theme underlying Kennedy's speeches and each of the initiatives he undertook as president. The deeper I have considered this theme, the clearer it has become. I stumbled upon it almost by chance when I came across a speech from ancient times that transported me back to 431 BCE, when an Athenian statesman named Pericles delivered a mass funeral oration to his fellow citizens amidst a war with Sparta. In Pericles's speech, I immediately saw the classical expression of the ideals famously accentuated in JFK's inaugural address and during his time in office—devotion to one's community, the need for collective action, and focus on individual responsibility—which in turn had a profound impact on my views of the meaning of Kennedy's presidency.

My research had turned a corner as the new theme of citizenship emerged as a central facet of the Kennedy ethos, in which the dogmas of public service and civic activism were emphasized as critical features of national progress. The connection between these concepts and the underlying idea expressed in the line that first drew my attention to him was unmistakable. Now I had *new* questions I hoped to answer: How did Kennedy define the concept of citizenship? How did this definition influence his actions as president? Why should this matter to us? And how can we embrace his brand of citizenship in useful ways that make us worthy of the republic we inherited?

It is difficult to separate this intellectual journey from my own coming-of-age story, and perhaps those of others in my generation. As my focus on classical precepts was borne out in Kennedy's presidency, the world around me was changing in ways that forced me to crystallize my own beliefs about government and politics and to wonder how those very concepts might morph and survive under different leadership and in different times.

The events of September 11, 2001, occurred during my first week as a college freshman. Soon after, we found ourselves engulfed in two wars in distant lands. New nuclear threats contributed to new geopolitical realities. Globalization continued to shape our national economy and dramatically shifted entrepreneurial profit centers both onto the Internet and abroad. Natural disasters literally and metaphorically shook the foundations of many nations, including our own. American dependence on foreign oil remained high, as did our trade imbalance with Asian manufacturing countries. Growth of online social media changed the ways we relate to one another. Generations of technological advances seemed to occur annually. And the country was consistently—and bitterly—divided along partisan and political lines. It was a unique time indeed to be formulating one's philosophical dispositions.

In some ways, these experiences served both to illuminate aspects of the Kennedy story and to highlight some of the contrasts with modern events. Yet they also provided a construct to view the similarities and place emphasis on the enduring impact JFK has had in the way we view new challenges in different circumstances.

• • •

ANNIVERSARIES OF HISTORIC events offer fresh opportunities to look back and remember. This year marks the fiftieth anniversary of JFK's death, and for some, this presents one such occasion. But the condition in which we find our country today warrants much more than mere nostalgia—it demands critical analysis of who we are as a people and of the nation we hope to be.

We live in an age of interconnectivity unsurpassed in the history of civilization. Yet in some ways, we've never been so disconnected. We e-mail or text instead of calling or meeting someone; we choose to read a tweet of 140 characters before delving into an op-ed or reading a newspaper; we multi-task more than we focus, distracted by buzzing BlackBerries and iPhones day and night. And our public discourse is just as worrisome. Our elected officials talk past one another and communicate via self-serving sound bites; we choose which television station to watch on the basis of which network supports "our" views and critiques those of the "other" side; we attack people instead of principles when we disagree with them, paying more attention to issues that divide us than to those that unite us.

The present state of affairs begs important questions: Are we fulfilling our obligations as citizens? What kinds of actions are required to satisfy such responsibilities? How can each of us direct our efforts toward the common good?

In the first televised debate between JFK and Richard Nixon in September 1960, Kennedy expressed dissatisfaction with the America he saw. For all its greatness, Kennedy noted, there were many reasons for concern. "This is a great country," he said, "but I think it could be a greater country."[1] The same is true today.

At the fiftieth anniversary of JFK's death, the need to look at how Kennedy resolved to make our country better has never been more urgent—and the Kennedy story should be retold today regardless of any event we might commemorate. The challenges of the twenty-first century are fierce, and we must commit ourselves to meeting them in serious and fruitful ways. In both his words and actions, Kennedy mobilized Americans to meet the trials of his times; he offered us passion, energy, and wisdom that still advance a vibrant and universal model of citizenship that we can embrace today—one that cuts across the distinctions of political persuasion and other factors that divide us.

Fortunately, there is no more universal force than the can-do spirit of the American people, and we can answer the call to service once again. I believe we still want to be challenged and inspired to live meaningful lives. We still want to make our country better. We still want to prove ourselves worthy of the nation we love. To do these things, we must revive the get-up-and-go sentiment Kennedy offered until his presidency abruptly ended on a sunny November day in 1963. It is time to dig deeper, to be inspired, to consider how each of us can act and be good citizens. It is time for a new generation of leaders to emerge and bring about the progress we seek.

In reviewing Kennedy's urgent call to service, we are reminded of the special obligations that come with the privilege of American citizenship. Regardless of our age, background, or station in life, we can all serve our country—the only qualifications are a patriotic spirit and a willingness to accept the sacrifice necessary to help a nation in need of our best efforts. In accepting this obligation, we begin anew the quest to improve and make a better life for our children.

It is up to the new generation—those of us born years after Kennedy died—to carry the torch forward; to prove ourselves worthy of our forebears who heroically fought to secure a better future for their children, regardless of the consequences; to determine whether we shape history or history shapes us. In doing so—in living up to our responsibilities as citizens of the leading superpower of the world—we honor a legacy that reminds us of our potential, of our sacred duty to remember, and that brings us closer to a time in which this union is more perfect and more just. And when that day comes, we may take sober satisfaction in knowing that we embodied that immortal creed: "Ask not what your country can do for you—ask what you can do for your country."

PART I

THE MAN AND THE MISSION

JFK is photographed at his desk in the Oval Office for the first time, January 21, 1961.

CHAPTER 1

The Kennedy Promise

"Don't let it be forgot
That once there was a spot,
For one brief shining moment
That was known as Camelot."

—from the 1960 musical *Camelot*

HALF A CENTURY ago, a charismatic young president challenged Americans to be good citizens. He spoke of the need for a new generation to take up the torch of progress and lift the nation to new heights of greatness—daring Americans to be better, to reject the status quo, and to shape a bright future. He envisioned a country and world of increased cooperation, of collective responsibility, where anything was achievable if people saw past their differences and worked together. It was a time of excitement and adventure and promise—a New Frontier, he called it—a time for Americans to be bold and courageous.

At the peak of it all, the voice that inspired so much was silenced, leaving the country and future generations wondering what might have been. Yet rather than lament the past, we have the opportunity to look closely at the man and his mission—specifically, the ideals of citizenship he promoted and his belief that there were new horizons for Americans to explore—and to consider how we can revitalize that same quest for greatness today. In a word, Camelot—the quixotic name we give to John F. Kennedy's presidency and that unique time in our collective past—did not have to end in 1963. We can bring it back today.

The familiar story goes that Kennedy's bold rhetoric swept an entire generation of Americans into careers of public service and government, marking a historical turning point when the prestige of government itself increased and a more robust spirit of service permeated public discourse and action. It was a time when people seemed inclined to pursue careers serving the public interest—when civil service jobs were appealing and engagement in public affairs was deep.

To be sure, informal historical accounts by nature tend to gloss over certain details, and perhaps our collective memory of the trumpet's call to service during the 1960s is too rosy, overdone, and enhanced by the romance of Camelot. But the seeming contrast with modern times nonetheless begs reflection on contemporary understandings of individual responsibility in public affairs and the manner in which our civic discourse seems to have veered so far off course.

To understand the mission, we must first look at the man.

The King of Camelot

John F. Kennedy was not a great president in the traditional sense. His presidency boasted no sweeping legislative achievements. He won no wars. The economy did not boom under his leadership. The soaring rhetoric at times did not match the actions actually taken or offer a true reshaping of the status quo that might vault him into the traditional pantheon of presidential greatness that includes the likes of Washington, Jefferson, Lincoln, and the Roosevelts. Yet when we recall his not quite three years in office, we think of the term the media loves to use for him: Camelot.

When Jacqueline Kennedy first brought to mind the imagery of Camelot in an interview with the journalist Theodore White shortly after JFK's death, this was perhaps a young widow's attempt to secure for her late husband a place in the rich history of the country he loved. It was also, undoubtedly, a conscious endeavor to cement in the public view the notion that the early 1960s were a magical, transformative time for America and the world under Kennedy's watch. In some ways, her tying Camelot to him was the beginning of the shaping of his legacy—a legacy that has ebbed and flowed with the passage of time but that nonetheless remains a point of fascination for men and women of all ages.

The world loves to remember JFK. Schools and streets have been named for him; parks, buildings, and an airport bear his name. Children are named after him. He is quoted in speeches. His words rest on plaques and refrigerator magnets and bumper stickers. Images of his face adorn book covers, posters, and the walls of college dorm rooms, offices, and people's homes. He is one of only a few figures in American history known simply by his initials—no further identifying factors are needed.

In Washington, D.C., millions of people have visited his grave set high on a hill at Arlington National Cemetery. Indeed, many children have had perhaps their first conscious interaction with Kennedy by visiting the grave and receiving an explanation of the importance of this man with the eternal flame over his final resting place. To hear such explanations offers a telling glimpse into the ways in which Kennedy endures. Some speak of his tragic death; others emphasize aspects of his life; and still others wonder, sometimes aloud, what things might have been like for the country and the world had he lived longer and served a second term.

Near the grave is a low memorial wall inscribed with quotations from the president's historic inaugural address. Here, for all time, are words chiseled into granite to offer generations of visitors a chance to bear witness to the guiding principles of the Kennedy presidency. Seeing such beautiful prose on the wall—including lines such as "Let every nation know, whether it wishes us well or ill, that we shall pay any price, bear any burden, meet any hardship, support any friend, oppose any foe, to assure the survival and the success of liberty," and "The energy, the faith, the devotion which we bring to this endeavor will light our country and all who serve it, and the glow from that fire can truly light the world"—makes one wonder: if, over the centuries, our whole civilization were to disappear but for that wall, would it alone tell future historians enough about who we were as a people?[1]

A short drive from the cemetery is the performing arts center that bears his name, which honors the arts in ways commensurate with the manner in which Kennedy promoted them. Not far from the performing arts center is the White House, where the most famous portrait of Kennedy—the painting with the president looking downward over his folded arms—hangs prominently on the first floor.

And still, Kennedy is remembered in other ways. He is honored by the presidential library dedicated to his memory in Columbia Point, Boston. His birthplace in Brookline, Massachusetts, has been designated a national historic site. There is a museum in Dallas near the fateful place he was shot. Items that belonged to the president regularly fetch large sums at auctions (in February 2013, for instance, the president's Air Force One bomber jacket was sold for $570,000).[2] Films and television miniseries such as *JFK*, *The Kennedys*, *The Missiles of October*, *Thirteen Days*, and others have depicted his life, aspects of his time in office, and his assassination. New books are published about him every year. Teachers recite words that he spoke. His name enters the national discourse during every political convention and amidst coverage of almost any presidential election debate. The media hovers around Kennedy as subject matter on every five-year anniversary of his birth, death, historic election, and inauguration.

Year after year, we seem only to increase this longing, this devotion to learning more about Kennedy—we want to see him again; we want to understand him from a different angle; we want to be reminded of this time in our collective past. He is, undeniably, an

American icon embedded deeply in our national consciousness. But why? Why this man?

The Power of Television

There are several explanations for why Kennedy remains as pervasive in American culture as he does. Television, among other media, powerfully captured the essence of Kennedy's presidency in ways that perpetuate our collective remembrance of this period by means not available to most presidents who preceded him.

The swelling of television ownership during Kennedy's presidency transformed—almost overnight—the manner in which citizens interacted with their president. Just as radio helped connect presidents and citizens in prior years (think Franklin Roosevelt's "fireside chats"), television brought this interaction to a whole new level that invited a different kind of presidential dialogue and a more personalized view of the president. Rather than read about the news or listen to it, individuals could watch it from the comfort of their living rooms and see their president in action. Television shrunk the gap that separated the news from the viewer, in turn making the president seem more accessible and more concrete.

Kennedy understood this newfound power, and he wielded it in constructive ways. He used the new medium as a tool to bolster his initiatives and bring his case for a host of issues directly to the American people. This effort included regularly televised press conferences and major speeches captured live with audiences customarily in the millions. These changes enabled him to communicate more effectively with the American people, giving him a forum to convey to the public at large whatever messages he wanted—meaning he could, for example, publicly accept blame for his mistakes (such as in the wake of the failed Bay of Pigs invasion), which would ingratiate him with a sympathetic electorate; convey the refined tastes and style of the First Lady (such as her televised tour of the refurbished White House), which would add to the perceived sense of nobility many had begun to see; and put the weight of his office behind a particular issue (such as the way he handled his landmark civil rights speech), appearing very "presidential" while so doing.

Television had other consequences, too. It meant that the "middleman" role played by the media was altered to become at times simply the medium of delivery rather than a curator of the message. Instead of receiving condensed versions of speeches and positions articulated by a president in newspaper articles and radio broadcasts, viewers could formulate their own opinions about presidential action more directly, more basically, and more immediately. This ability permitted a more intimate exchange between the president and the average citizen—leaving room for a more personal interpretation of the president's message. Kennedy therefore became a tangible figure to the electorate—perhaps the first truly tangible president in the sense that his image was regularly broadcast into the homes of Americans, and, in consequence, he became universally recognized in his role as president, his image cemented in the minds of viewers in ways images of other presidents had not been.

Though we revere men such as Washington, Jefferson, and Lincoln, we do not feel the same connection to them that we feel with modern leaders—those who have joined us in our living rooms. We don't know what these great men of the past were truly like or if they were even likable. What we know about them is based on what others have told us about their words and deeds. They remain impersonal; relics of history whose impact on our lives no doubt remains strong but nonetheless distant.

The prevalence of television also dramatized the Kennedy assassination and its aftermath in ways that fortified public perception of the late president. Television enabled the news of his death to spread faster than any other bit of news had been relayed perhaps in history up to then. When Walter Cronkite's live early afternoon broadcast relayed the sad news from Dallas, it was so momentous, so earth-shattering, that as the message was conveyed, an entire generation of Americans' lives stopped and became frozen in time forever. Indeed, news of the assassination shocked a generation the way the bombing of Pearl Harbor had done and the way another generation would be so heavily affected by the events of September 11.

Two days after JFK was killed, Americans watched as Lee Harvey Oswald was murdered live on television by nightclub owner Jack Ruby while being transported from a Dallas police station to a county jail. Events were spinning out of control and seemed so far-fetched, so foreign, that they bordered on the imaginary.

In the wake of the assassination was the state funeral for the slain president—intricately modeled, at the First Lady's request, after the state funeral conducted for Abraham Lincoln—broadcast live for the country and world to see, allowing all to agonize with the young widow (Jackie was thirty-four) as she marched with the late president's surviving brothers; to cry when the president's three-year-old namesake famously saluted his father's coffin as it passed him by, a salute captured for all time by the rolling cameras; to grieve for the young daughter, just shy of her sixth birthday, who seemed on the cusp of understanding at least the permanence of the tragedy, that her father would not be coming home. The country was heartbroken, and these somber images were seared deeply and eternally into the American consciousness.

Later, the existence of the famous Zapruder film—which caught the assassination live on camera from the amateur hands of an innocent bystander—became public, and soon Americans could actually watch the haunting images of the murder: the slow progression of the presidential limousine, the gunshots, the president clutching his throat, the chaos surrounding the motorcade, Jackie climbing onto the back of the car to retrieve what was apparently a piece of her husband's scalp, and Secret Service agent Clint Hill sprinting toward the

First Couple and hitching himself to the car for the ride to Parkland Hospital, where they hoped that emergency medical assistance would prevent the dreaded fears from becoming reality. Even fifty years later, viewers of the film are instilled with the impossible desire of somehow stopping the motorcade—wishing that they could only press "pause" on the videotape, or speed up Kennedy's car, or avoid the turn onto Elm Street, or offer a warning, or cancel the trip to Dallas altogether— a trip Kennedy made only begrudgingly in an effort to assuage tensions that had arisen among warring factions of the Democratic Party in Texas.

Then the conspiracy theories spread, as countless people questioned the claim that Oswald had acted alone. Was it the enemies the Kennedys had made in the CIA? Hoover's people at the FBI? The Soviets? The Cubans? The Italian Mafia? Oil interests? A disgruntled civil rights opponent? Some sort of "divine retribution," as Lyndon Johnson put it, for allegedly condoning the murders of foreign heads of state (Rafael Trujillo of the Dominican Republic and Ngo Dinh Diem of South Vietnam)?[3] The subsequent release of the Warren Commission's report seemed dubious to many, generating a whole new slew of theories. All of these events had the collective impact of securing a certain kind of immortality for Kennedy that may never fade.

The Kennedy Mystique

While television captured images of Kennedy, including the assassination, it also highlighted the youth and vitality he and his family exuded that in turn created an aura of royalty for them. At forty-three, he was the youngest person ever elected president (Theodore Roosevelt became president at age forty-two by virtue of William McKinley's death). By nature of his age, he remains one of the few presidents who had very young children in the White House (even the children of Bill

Clinton and Barack Obama were not quite as young as Kennedy's were at the time). Images of Kennedy playing with his children in the Oval Office—including John Jr. hiding underneath his father's desk and Caroline skipping around the perimeter of the room while the president clapped his hands and encouraged her—resonated deeply with an adoring public, as did Americans' fascination with Jackie's chic styles and sophisticated taste. Likewise, there was the Kennedys' enormous wealth, their good looks, and popular images from the family estates in Hyannis Port and Palm Beach, where they played games of touch football and sunbathed.

One element of this aura is the profound sense of tragedy associated with the family. Before Kennedy was elected president, he had lost two siblings in plane crashes, and another was kept out of the public eye after a botched brain surgery left her incapacitated. Nearly five years after Kennedy's death, his brother Bobby was killed, and shortly after that, his youngest brother, Ted, was engulfed in the disaster remembered as Chappaquiddick. Later was a failed presidential run for Ted in which he challenged a sitting president in a primary. One Kennedy cousin was accused of rape in a high-profile case that brought many family members to court. Other cousins died in accidents, including a drug overdose and a ski crash. Then John Jr.'s plane went down, so the prince of Camelot was gone, too. Were they cursed? All this reinforced the notion that there was something romantic about this family; it all deepened the public's curiosity.

Yet another component of the Kennedy appeal is the nostalgic feeling Americans have for the era that ended in November 1963. The military build-up in Vietnam was already underway, but it was not yet the issue that would tear the nation apart. The wave of assassinations that began with Kennedy, which later included Malcolm X, Martin Luther King Jr., and Bobby, had not yet begun. Watergate was in a distant future. In the wake of the relative peace and prosperity of the 1950s, Americans felt good about where they were in the early 1960s.

It was a time of movement and action—an almost ineffable sense that America was on the threshold of better times, when a president regularly invoked patriotic motifs like American uniqueness, great national purpose, individual empowerment, and a generational imperative. There seemed to be a kinetic, restless energy offering big goals, common aspirations, excitement, adventure, and pride—a spirit of collective progress that reminded us of our potential, that we can do better—all believable because of Kennedy's seemingly effortless ability to persuade. His death left people aching for a continuation of these themes, searching to capture this unattainable essence in ways that have kept him in our orbit.

Kennedy's death was indeed a transformative event. As we look back at this era, the assassination is an exact time we can pinpoint as the culmination of one epoch—an era of peace, progress, hopeful optimism, and American prestige—and the beginning of another—one of war, destruction, reignited racial conflict, and perceived American decline. It was the end of people's trust in government and general faith in "the system," and the beginning of distrust, disbelief, and disappointment. The idea of American greatness morphed from a feeling of collective invincibility that united citizens into a cheapened campaign slogan that divided them. Politicians spoke to voters' fears rather than their hopes. America became a different place.

Americans who lived during this turning point therefore recall Kennedy with fondness—not only fondness for a fallen leader who inspired them, but also fondness for where the country had been and seemed to be going—fondness for the sense of innocence that, after JFK's death, seemed lost. To these individuals, a political candidate's promise to return to better days implies some sort of homecoming to Camelot—a world where the strong are just, the weak are secure, people are safe, and everyone can partake in national advancement.

The Kennedy Brand of Citizenship

To Kennedy, at the core of national advancement was the age-old notion of citizenship. Like our Founding Fathers, he sought political inspiration from ancient models—such as those established by the Greeks and the Romans—where engagement in public affairs was not merely an opportunity to participate in one's community but the most basic realization of one's citizenship. Individuals living in the same community had common concerns and therefore needed to act in certain ways not merely for the benefit of their community but for the very preservation of it. Citizens understood that to look after the affairs of their country was to look after their own at the same time, and that serving in public office represented the greatest trust bestowed upon citizens and was viewed as an honor and a privilege—in fact, the highest privilege in society.

Kennedy eloquently gave voice to the modern expression of this concept. In the process, he developed a brand of citizenship that underscored the role of individual citizens in society and the related responsibilities that they must fulfill.

This may seem like an intuitive concept, but to Kennedy, this notion of citizenship was so fundamental and critical that it needed to be emphasized in fresh and practical ways to reshape the means by which individuals thought about their country. Citizenship, in theoretical terms, connotes belonging to a wider community; in concrete terms, Kennedy reasoned, this reality is borne out in the actions individuals take to advance the interests of that wider community. Hence, individual action forms the basis of collective progress, and a leader's job, in part, is to summon the action needed to meet national imperatives. In turn, Kennedy recognized the importance of articulating an inspiring call to service that would encourage people to be good citizens.

In classical times, fulfilling the obligations of one's citizenship meant taking part in commonsense things like defending a community from external threats or ensuring that food was adequately distributed to all in search of it. In the 1960s, Kennedy endeavored to transform the abstraction of service into a mode of living that went beyond the basics of preserving community life. He challenged Americans to consider what role they could play in the quest for communal advances, and, on a more fundamental level, to recognize the interrelatedness of their existence—that the actions of one can affect those of others, that there are indeed issues of common concern, and that being a good citizen requires us to do something for someone else.

This brand of citizenship was based both on the well-established rights of the citizenry—the right to vote or the right to free speech, for example—and on the obligations that come hand in hand with those rights. In other words, in return for the privilege of being a citizen, one must live in certain ways and fulfill certain prescribed responsibilities. This means that being a good citizen is not merely having a job or taking care of one's family; it is about taking action to help others and improve one's community or even the world. We are more than individuals who live in the same place; we are people with collective hopes and dreams with obligations to one another. The Kennedy era was a time when we felt this way, a time when the popular culture could, without embarrassment, extol the qualities of courage and public-mindedness that in ways large and small were not uncharacteristic of the era.

The Citizenship Gap

In recalling Kennedy's emphatic inaugural declaration that "the torch has been passed to a new generation of Americans," we may consider starkly different sets of values between that generation and this one in terms of how we view the role of government and public servants generally. Today we live in an era that almost devalues these elements of a successful democracy. Our discourse lacks civility, and we regularly seem to fail at having a genuine, constructive debate without keeping political tallies and seeking to destroy those who don't share a particular view. We mock people who seek public office; we are suspicious of their motives and often appear eager to read about their failures. In fact, to call someone a "politician" is undoubtedly an insult intended to suggest insincerity and an affinity for quid pro quos of some kind. We seem to define who we are on the basis of whom we vote for. We've lost some of that sense of "all for the common cause" that Kennedy stressed. Our discourse suggests in many cases that we do not actually see one another as equals—that someone's views, if disagreeable, can make him or her of less value to society. At times, we seem nearly blind to our common humanity, ignoring the uniting factors that should define us, such as our hopes and fears and common concerns as people who compose the same community.

Our politicians have helped foster this environment with their fanatic loyalty to party and seeming inability, or unwillingness, to compromise or even hold a dignified exchange of ideas. But we seem also to have let this spirit permeate other aspects of public life that highlight our differences and promote a "me first" mentality we cannot afford in these challenging times—when individuals place private comfort above public gain, people resent the beliefs and values of others, and we are less interested in the plight of our neighbor. In short, we have a "citizenship gap" that speaks to the difference between who we are as a people and who we aspire to be—it is a distinction between the values Kennedy expressed and the values we actually promote.

We can do better. We can refocus our efforts and retool our creative energies and refashion our commitment in favor of a renewed national purpose. We can revive the prestige of government and increase emphasis on the critical need for public service. We can nurture individual achievement without sacrificing our devotion to public betterment. We can change the tenor of our political debate. We can harness what Martin Luther King Jr. labeled during the Kennedy presidency as "the fierce urgency of now" to cultivate a new national spirit.[4]

We sometimes hear that these efforts will be hopeless so long as our perceived adversaries do not adopt more enlightened positions. A more civil discourse will promote such enlightenment. But by the same token, each of us must also look inward and assess our own positions—to see if we, too, can be more enlightened. For every thoughtful citizen who cherishes what America stands for and what America aspires to be has an obligation to look beyond the prism of the present and assess what he or she can do to further national progress—and this effort begins at home.

What we need is a rededication to the tenets of good citizenship. It requires individual responsibility and accountability; it demands courage and sacrifice; it asks for much more than it promises. But it can be done. In fact, fifty years ago we had such a rededication, and many people have already embraced this spirit today. In studying this effort—in interpreting its foundation and meaning—in seeking to understand what impact it had a generation ago—we will be armed and inspired to seek a better and more hopeful world. Looking back at Kennedy in this way is not hero worship or demagoguery; it is a framework that can be used to help us regain the great national purpose remembered as the New Frontier. Then we can reclaim our rightful place as heirs to the greatest national legacy ever bequeathed in the history of the world, and we can usher in a new era when words such as "patriot" and "citizen" will again be the vernacular of the American people—a time when we each accept the nation's responsibilities as if they were our own—a time when we each play a role, however small, in building something bigger and better for the next generation to inherit—when we all feel we are doing something to advance the cause of our country.

It may be hard to imagine that the factory worker or the bus driver or the salesman or the attorney approaches his everyday affairs with his president in mind or thinking that he is doing his country's work.

Harder still is it to picture an individual who seeks merely to provide for his family thinking that he is bearing the burden of his citizenship each time he enters his office. But there was a time, perhaps, when we felt that way. Or perhaps we want to believe that there was a time when we felt that way, because it means that we can feel that way again—and we need this spirit.

The Kennedy ethos suggests that such action—such ordinary action—collectively provides the thrust of necessary generational movement, and it is this thrust that brings us closer to perfecting the ideals present at the birth of the republic.

Atticus Finch

The notion of everyday heroism is personified artfully by Gregory Peck's Academy Award–winning portrayal of Atticus Finch in *To Kill a Mockingbird*, a story about tolerance and racial injustice, which was released during Kennedy's presidency. Finch is a small-town lawyer with little money but ample courage and a strong sense of duty. When told by the local judge that he is considering appointing Finch to defend Tom Robinson—a black man wrongly accused of raping a white woman in 1932 Alabama—Finch does not hesitate, despite the inevitable threats and intimidation he is sure to endure from the local white community. When reminded by the judge of the steep sacrifice that would lie ahead, including risk to his reputation and therefore his livelihood, Finch responds without hesitation: "I'll do it."[5]

Atticus Finch is in many ways a worthy representation of what Kennedy was asking Americans to do. He was asking people to place the public good above self-interest—he was asking people to embrace a code of honor and morality that spoke to their sense of community. This is the concept underlying his famous call to action; the idea that service could be an everyday aspect of life. And in this regard, ordinary people can do extraordinary things.

Atticus Finch's decision to defend Tom Robinson is emblematic of how a person with an everyday job can play his part in the pursuit of progress. When citizens behave in these ways—when citizens place the public interest ahead of private comfort—they pave the way to achievement and improvement and live up to their responsibility to ask what they can do for their country.

In the film, Atticus Finch voices justification for his actions that fulfill the necessity of service highlighted by Kennedy. In teaching his daughter about justice and equality, Finch instructs: "You never really understand a person until you consider things from his point of view—until you climb inside his skin and walk around in it."[6] In other words, as Kennedy would later say in another context, "Who among us would be content to have the color of his skin changed and stand in his place?"[7] We are all connected, this idea implies. We should treat others as we would wish to be treated. Our freedom and future are bound up with the fate of those who surround us. Therefore, we serve the public interest.

As president, Kennedy did not claim authority over everything in daily life, but he did ask people to accept responsibility over their own lives and to direct their efforts in productive ways. Such was the depth of the need for citizenship in those times, and Atticus Finch serves as a heroic reminder of the citizenship qualities that Kennedy sought to elicit.

A Generational Imperative

A key element of citizenship, the Atticus Finch story makes clear, is embracing the burden of these responsibilities, particularly in the context of generational change. Previous generations earned the country we inherited at great expense, including the sacrifice of their comfort, their pleasures, and in many instances, their blood. Brave and selfless men and women in our generation have done the same. Such efforts have not been for the self-indulgence of ensuing generations, but as part of a growing foundation upon which future improvements can be made.

This is why, in his inaugural address, Kennedy instructed that the torch had been passed to a new generation. He was sounding the trumpet's call not as a declaration of newfound privilege but as one of newfound responsibility. He was reminding his fellow citizens, as he said later in the speech, that "the graves of young Americans who answered the call to service surround the globe," and therefore, the country he and his fellow citizens loved required their best efforts. "We shall pay any price, bear any burden."[8]

This doctrine—this brand of citizenship—is the most fundamental element of the themes of Kennedy's presidency and the initiatives he sought to advance. It is the underlying premise upon which all of his actions were based. All can contribute—all are expected to participate in ways that benefit the wider community.

These ideas advanced a related point: that there is a distinction between what is legally permissible and what is morally justified, and that to fulfill the duties of citizenship—both at home and abroad—individuals and nations must meet both of these standards in their actions. Hence, the quest for civil rights at home during Kennedy's presidency was about more than changing the law; it was about accepting a higher law that reflected moral truth. Those displaying prejudice breached the law *and* their duties of citizenship. Similarly, in a global context, the construction of the Berlin Wall was not illegal, but it reflected a violation of the moral code underpinning world order, signifying a failure of the Soviet Union to fulfill its obligations toward the international community. In effect, Kennedy was crafting a new American social contract that inspired citizens to fulfill a calling higher and more encompassing than their legal obligations. This thrust would be used to guide individual thought and action.

This meant that Kennedy's aim, as leader of a free society, would be in part to summon these efforts, but also to create a social climate filled with patriotism and pride. One must feel pride in one's country in order to be inspired to serve it. One must be proud of national efforts in order to support them. One must love his country to accept sacrifice on its behalf. Sending a man to the moon, as Kennedy pledged, would elicit such pride. Restoring the White House would make citizens feel proud of their nation and their leader. Forming the Peace Corps, or protecting democratic interests abroad amidst the Cold War, or helping other nations escape poverty, made people love being American.

When Americans love their country and feel good about its future, Kennedy's paradigm suggested, they are more inclined to do good deeds—they are more likely to accept responsibility in their own lives that will increase their pride and increase their willingness to make personal sacrifices. The promise of better days ahead, based on these efforts, invites an atmosphere of shared optimism, a desire to cooperate, a sense that we can work together to make this world better. Hence, we treat one another with more respect. We are more willing to hear a different point of view. We are more tolerant. We are better positioned to achieve individual and national success.

A study of the major episodes of the Kennedy presidency reveals the depth of these themes, which he began articulating to the American people in his bold election campaign in 1960. But the concept of citizenship as a focal point in his life had been evolving for Kennedy for some time—before he was elected to public office, and even before he served heroically in the Navy in World War II. People and events molded the man we remember—experiences that clarified the mission he would seek to achieve.

As we proceed further into the twenty-first century, we grapple with new challenges and new problems scarcely envisioned during Kennedy's time. Yet in studying his presidency—in learning what it meant to be a pioneer in the New Frontier—we can perhaps increase our own understanding of citizenship and what contemporary standards of such citizenship require from each of us in our daily lives. In turn, we might replicate in our time some of the patriotic verve that made the Kennedy years seem so adventurous half a century ago. This country is ready, indeed poised, for a revival of the themes that have always made it great; it will be up to the new generation of Americans to make this happen.

JFK graduates from Harvard in June 1940. A month later, he would publish his first book, *Why England Slept*, which became a bestseller and brought him wide acclaim.

CHAPTER 2

Becoming JFK

"Public life is regarded as the crown of a career, and to young men it is the worthiest ambition. Politics is still the greatest and the most honourable [sic] *adventure."*

—JOHN BUCHAN, *Pilgrim's Way*

A STUDY OF a president's formative years provides hints into the leader we remember, offering a window into how a mind and persona developed and what inspiration formed the basis for the path ultimately taken. For John Kennedy, this is particularly true, and a review of the experiences and circumstances that shaped the man he would become confirms that journeys intellectual and physical were the foundation upon which a self-invention of sorts could be achieved. Put another way, "Before Jack Kennedy could make himself president, he first had to make himself Jack Kennedy."[1]

Anticipations

Growing Up Kennedy

John Fitzgerald Kennedy was born on May 29, 1917, in Brookline, Massachusetts, the second of nine children of Rose Fitzgerald and

Joseph Kennedy. Rose and Joe had met as teenagers, got married in their mid-twenties in 1914, and moved out of the Irish-American area of Boston in which they were raised to the posh, Brahmin suburb of Brookline. While the Fitzgeralds and the Kennedys had enjoyed success in their predominantly Catholic world, the move to mostly Protestant Brookline reflected Joe's ambition to seek success on a larger stage, and the young couple would raise their children with this aspiration in mind. Within a year of marriage, their eldest son, Joe Jr., was born, and the climb began.

Both Rose and Joe came from families that had politics in their blood. P.J. Kennedy, young Jack's grandfather, had been a saloonkeeper who used the bar scene to grow acquainted with many of Boston's Irish business and political leaders, and he parlayed these relationships and his good-natured appeal into a political career of his own. He served in the Massachusetts State Legislature and became a political boss who traded on his reputation and connections to secure jobs and patronage for friends. He also used his bar profits to invest substantially in both a liquor-importing company and a bank, which improved the family's financial status and further built his network of relationships that would be key to his family's rise.

P.J.'s one son, Joe, inherited his father's political ambition and brought a new intensity to the family's financial affairs. After graduating from Harvard, Joe used his father's contacts to become president of Columbia Trust, the bank his father had previously invested in, at age twenty-five. Joe understood the idea that perception could be more important than reality—a lesson he would later teach his politically savvy sons—and so he endeavored to portray himself in ways that would enable perceptions to shape the realities in business and politics he sought. To this end, he became a public relations mastermind, including regular promotion of his unconfirmed claim that he was the youngest bank president in America, with the aim of creating certain beliefs about his wealth and power. In short order, Joe dramatically increased the size and number of accounts at the bank, and as the size of his own bank account increased, so too did his status in Boston society.

The Fitzgerald family was even more well-entrenched in politics. Rose's father, John, was a member of Congress and later the first Irish-American mayor of Boston. Nicknamed "Honey Fitz," Rose's father was a natural politician beloved for his gregarious personality and talents as a public official. Honey Fitz later ran for U.S. Senate and lost to Henry Cabot Lodge Sr., whose own namesake grandson was the incumbent senator Jack would beat in 1952 to avenge this earlier family defeat (Lodge would also be Richard Nixon's running mate in 1960).

Given their fathers' involvement in politics as well as Joe's own rising ambitions, the union of Rose and Joe had the makings of a political dynasty. P.J.'s back-room dealings and behind-the-scenes political machinations, coupled with Honey Fitz's power and vote-getting prowess, gave the young couple a promising start toward realizing the outsized goals of Joe, whose financial success would provide the means to transform abstract political goals into realities.

As the size of the Kennedy family expanded, the growth of Joe's rising business empire kept pace, including larger profits in his liquor business (rumors swirled about his alleged bootlegging during Prohibition), acquisition of movie production enterprises (which included an affair with Hollywood star Gloria Swanson), and stock speculation that helped him reap huge profits during the booming 1920s and avoid losses in the market crash of 1929 (in an age before insider trading laws that under modern standards might have invited criminal investigation).[2]

Joe traveled relentlessly, often leaving Rose alone with their growing brood. Rose, a devout Catholic, attended Mass regularly, and perhaps as an effect of the constant burden of parenting such a large family, she regularly spent long periods in seclusion and away from home. Jack resented her absences: "Gee, *you're* a great mother to go away and leave your children all alone," he once complained to Rose at age six.[3] He may have had similar distant feelings for his father, who, when he was around, exhibited the most pride in his eldest son, Jack's brother Joe, upon whom his dreams of fame and success had been conferred since birth.

Already feeling neglected by his parents, Jack looked up to his older brother and kept himself in Joe Jr.'s orbit whenever possible. In part, this behavior reflected a younger sibling's natural inclination to emulate his big brother; it also revealed Jack's sense that in order to receive the parental attention he craved, he needed to be around Joe—even competing with him in order to prove his mettle and convince his parents that he, too, deserved their devotion.

Such efforts would prove somewhat futile given the stark contrast between the brothers in appearance, personality, and ambition. Joe Jr. was tall, athletic, handsome, and outgoing, with dreams of large-scale success in business or politics—everything his parents wanted in a son. Jack was thin, shy, introverted, and chronically sick.

Despite these differences, and perhaps because of them, Jack maintained a fierce rivalry with Joe in his attempt to live up to his father's maxim: "We want winners, we don't want losers around here."[4] They competed for attention at the dinner table, at school, and in athletic pursuits, including racing each other in sailboats, on bicycles, and on foot. Jack was so determined to challenge Joe that he would even have bicycle races with him around their neighborhood block in opposite directions to prove he wasn't scared of crashing into his brother (though he usually paid the price when they collided).

Despite his efforts, Jack was no match for Joe in the eyes of his parents. In fact, his sister Kathleen, whom the family affectionately called "Kick," recalled that it was "heresy" in the Kennedy household even to imply that Jack might do anything better than Joe could.[5] Conversely, Jack was a cause of perpetual concern given his habitual health troubles, which ranged from scarlet fever at age two to anemia to hives to colitis to other undiagnosed afflictions that regularly seemed to puzzle physicians and required lengthy stays in health clinics that took him away from school. The protracted nature of his problems often kept his weight very low, further diminishing his ability to compete with Joe or anyone else in physical endeavors—a cruel mix of reminders that he was in fact second fiddle to Joe.

Studying Greatness

Jack's compensation for a sickly childhood took the form of certain unforeseen benefits. Naturally he didn't like being forced to stay inside, but while there, Jack could spend more time than he might otherwise have reading and learning in ways that expedited the intellectual journey to come. Indeed, in recalling his voracious appetite for reading as a child, Rose later told Harvard president Nathan Pusey that Jack's reading habits developed so rapidly because he had spent such "long periods in bed, often on weekends when the others were out playing."[6]

As a child, Jack read such favorite books as *Billy Whiskers*, *The Arabian Nights*, and *King Arthur and His Knights*—a collection of stories that signaled an early penchant for excitement and adventure.[7] As his intellect matured, he discovered a great passion for history that led him to the works of ancient philosophers such as Plato and Aristotle and the classical historian Thucydides. As Jack's interest in history grew, he was increasingly drawn to stories of heroic figures who loved their country and defended it in one way or another—usually by risking their lives, fortunes, or both. He read stories about ancient Greek generals who led their troops into battle. He was inspired by the life of the British Duke of Marlborough, John Churchill (an ancestor of Winston Churchill), who sacrificed his private comfort to become an eminent statesman and military commander. Thomas Macaulay's *Lays of Ancient Rome* became a personal favorite, in which the character Horatio courageously risks his life against seemingly insurmountable odds to defend Rome from an invading army.

Common themes in his reading began to emerge that can easily be identified in his later rhetoric: bravery, sacrifice, patriotism, activism, and adventure. There were also common story lines: when confronted by challenge, leaders delivered inspiring speeches aimed at eliciting action from others, seeking to persuade and reshape previous conceptions. Individuals embraced their responsibilities in the name of important causes. People coveted honor and glory.

From his reading, Jack learned of the interplay between rhetoric and action, the relationship between the individual and the community, and the sense of interconnectivity one might feel between one's actions and those of others. These were important lessons to be learned by an aspiring young leader. All would be vital features of the call to action he would later voice as president—all of these elements helped form the foundation upon which his understanding of citizenship continued to develop.

The stories of activism led him to understand another basic point: that the characters of which he read were people in the arena of public life, they were individuals who desired to be involved in public affairs, and they wanted their lives to count; in short, they *mattered*. This might seem self-evident in the political context, but it is nonetheless an important connection to make, because it implied that to be heroic meant in some sense that there was a public or communal element to achieving heroism. To be a hero meant doing something that advanced the public good—often, as it turned out, by giving up one's own comfort. Therefore, one who strives to be heroic, and one who seeks to make a difference, must by nature identify with causes larger than oneself. Out of this conception, a more nuanced understanding of the meaning of citizenship is possible, and hints of Jack's subsequent inclination to promote the themes of civic obligation and public service begin to appear more visibly.

An insatiable hunger for reading had an added benefit: it would ingratiate Jack with his father in new ways that balanced the scales of his father's affection toward his two eldest sons. Joe Sr. was a man very much involved in public life vis-à-vis his extensive business and political connections, and he had certain political aspirations of his own. As Jack's interest in public affairs deepened, this erstwhile sickly boy could converse with his father on topics of interest at the dinner table in ways that enhanced their relationship. Jack also could partake in conversations that previously had been reserved mainly for Joe Jr., thereby providing a forum in which he could actually compete with his older brother. Jack had some potential after all.

A Global Perspective

Jack's formal educational pursuits concurrently broadened his world-view. After the family moved to New York in 1927, Jack was sent to private school at Riverdale Country School and then Choate, the preparatory school where Joe Jr. matriculated and where Joe Sr. hoped his boys would gain an advantage in life by befriending the other privileged children who went there. Though he wasn't a particularly strong student in terms of his grades or the seriousness with which he approached his studies, Jack nonetheless continued to have a strong enthusiasm for unassigned reading that sharpened his intellectual curiosity. For most of the students, a central purpose of attending the school, in addition to the social networking that transpired there, was the advantage it gave them in gaining entry to an elite Ivy League institution. And indeed, Harvard accepted Jack, where Joe Jr. had begun studying two years earlier. (On a historical side note, evidence suggests that Jack may have borrowed the famous "Ask not" inaugural line from Choate headmaster George St. John, who purportedly told the students, "Ask not what your school can do for you—ask what you can do for your school."[8])

Though Harvard had accepted him, Jack chose to study first at the London School of Economics. Shortly after he arrived in London, however, his stomach problems flared and he was forced to return home, whereupon he enrolled at Princeton. But before he could get comfortable at Princeton, health problems forced him away from there, too. Lingering stomach trouble and asthma attacks sent Jack to the Mayo Clinic, where his ailments remained undiagnosed and he stayed under the watchful eye of his physicians. After missing an entire year of school, he then went to Harvard as initially planned.

While he was at Harvard, and with the world around him changing as Europe inched toward another war, the Kennedy family's political status was rising. After serving as the inaugural chairman of the U.S. Securities and Exchange Commission, Joe Sr. was appointed to serve as U.S. Ambassador to Great Britain in 1938 (a visible confirmation that Joe had succeeded in entering the Brahmin world of upper-class, highbrow socialites that he had long coveted). Jack took a leave from Harvard to research a thesis and, along with his siblings, moved to London to accompany his father and enjoy the privileges of British high society.

Living in Britain afforded Jack a front-row seat to history and gave him entrée into the world of foreign affairs. He was there when Neville Chamberlain returned from Munich to declare that he had achieved "peace for our time," and he was swept up by the ubiquitous public debate concerning the future of Europe.[9] He was also there for Winston Churchill's rise and witnessed the bold, soaring rhetoric at the beginning of the war that became the stuff of legend; Jack would later emulate it.

Jack capitalized on the opportunity to study diplomatic relations during this period. In 1940, his first book was published, titled *Why England Slept*, a twist on the popular title *While England Slept* written by Churchill two years earlier. Jack's book grew out of the thesis he authored at Harvard and sought to address the failures of Great Britain in the lead-up to the Second World War.

Though the faculty admired the intellectual thrust of the thesis—it explored Britain's failure to prepare for the war, reflecting a departure from his father's support for appeasement policies—it was not considered to be particularly noteworthy. Nevertheless, Jack's father enlisted his friend Arthur Krock—an influential columnist for the *New York Times*—to help get it in publishable form. Krock assisted with a rewrite of the manuscript, including giving it its catchy title.[10] Krock later conceded that he "may have supplied some of the material as far as [the] prose" was concerned—a practice Jack seems to have accepted again in his later collaboration with Theodore Sorensen on his book *Profiles in Courage*.[11] Henry Luce—another family friend and the famous publisher of *Life*, *Fortune*, and *Time* magazines—agreed to write a flattering introduction. Several publishing houses rejected *Why England Slept*, but perhaps with promises of financial success from Joe, a small publisher, Wilfred Funk, finally agreed to publish it. The book sold eighty thousand copies and became a bestseller, and Jack began to emerge as an intellectual standout in his generation with a solid grasp of public affairs.

A Defining Influence

While Kennedy was in London in 1940, John Buchan, a British Member of Parliament, wrote a book that would prove vital to the man Jack was becoming. *Memory Hold-the-Door*—or *Pilgrim's Way*, the title of the American version—was a collection of the author's reminiscences of his famous contemporaries, profiles that were intended to inspire and create in the reader a desire to admire and emulate the lives of those portrayed. Jack read the book closely and discovered that Buchan's profiles offered similar themes to those he had long admired in his reading. He saw outlines of men he wanted to be like, and for the rest of his life, he would urge anyone who wanted to understand him to read this book.[12]

Jack must have seen himself in many of Buchan's colorful passages, specifically those that discussed youth and "the ordinary high spirits of young men delighting in health and strength."[13] Jack had a spirit of adventure, leading British Prime Minister Harold Macmillan later to find it enchanting how traveling 1,800 miles for a luncheon seemed perfectly normal to the debonair American president.[14]

Jack's favorite passage in the book was Buchan's portrait of Raymond Asquith. Raymond was the privileged son of British Prime Minister

Herbert Asquith, who during World War I courageously rejected a job as a staff officer (where he would be safe) and requested that he be placed on active duty. It didn't matter that he was wealthy, highly educated, or from a famous family; what mattered to Raymond was that he fulfill his responsibilities as an individual, regardless of the personal risks he might undertake. He later died bravely in battle while leading an attack on enemy soldiers.

Buchan glorified Raymond, highlighting the depth of his sacrifice. "There are some men whose brilliance in boyhood and early manhood dazzles their contemporaries and becomes a legend," he noted. "It is not that they are precocious, for precocity rarely charms, but that for every sphere of life they have the proper complement of gifts, and finish each stage so that it remains behind them like a satisfying work of art."[15] For some of these people, "the curtain drops suddenly, the daylight goes out of the picture, and the promise of youth dulls into a dreary middle age of success, or, it may be, of failure and cynicism."[16] Others are different. Indeed, "for the chosen few, like Raymond, there is no disillusionment. They march into life with a boyish grace, and their high noon keeps all the freshness of the morning."[17]

At this point in his reading, like any other young person whose mind might be flickering with aspirations of greatness, Kennedy no doubt drew comparisons to himself, or at least the kind of person he hoped to be. In particular, he knew he could consciously seek to adopt certain traits embodied by Raymond as his own: courage, selflessness, and a willingness to risk whatever might be necessary for the country he loved. Yet at the same time, to embrace these qualities required a meaningful departure from the beliefs his father had tried to inculcate in him.

Though Jack had coveted his father's attention as a child and yearned for his approval, with age and experience he indeed grew more independent and more willing to reject his father's views. After World War I, Joe had said that the young British men who died in the Battle of the Somme, as Raymond did, died "for nothing," and that they had given their lives for a "delusion."[18] In other words, Britain's fight for global freedom was not worthy of the ultimate sacrifice paid by so many of its loyal sons. This idea was in direct conflict with everything Jack, and his hero, Raymond, had come to believe as a logical extension of one's patriotism and sense of duty. Though Joe may have espoused the concepts of service and sacrifice in the abstract, Jack made these themes the core of his existence. He understood that with privilege and opportunity comes great responsibility, including the need to place the national interest above one's own private comfort.

For years after reading *Pilgrim's Way,* Jack would continually quote various sections of Buchan's portrayal of Asquith in notes to family and friends, particularly in condolence notes to the families of fallen servicemen (including in a note to Kick, when her husband died on the battlefront in 1944).[19] "I remember [Jack] saying over and over that there was nobody in our time who was more gifted [than Raymond Asquith]," remembered his close friend, David Ormsby-Gore, who served as Britain's ambassador to the United States during the Kennedy years. "Whether Jack realized it or not, I think he paralleled himself after Asquith"—meaning that Jack aimed to embrace Asquith's sense of duty and live in ways that underscored his commitment to this goal.[20]

Reading Buchan's book came at an opportune point in Jack's life. He was twenty-three—mature enough to comprehend the messages Buchan intended to impart, yet also at a point in his life when he was particularly attuned to considering what kind of life he wanted to have and what kind of contributions he wanted to make. The book confirmed his belief, as Buchan wrote, that "[p]ublic life is regarded as the crown of a career, and to young men it is the worthiest ambition. Politics is still the greatest and the most honourable [*sic*] adventure."[21]

The Call to Duty

The bombing of Pearl Harbor thrust America into the war that had already engulfed Europe. Despite physical problems and failing a medical exam, Jack, now twenty-four, was determined to serve his country and enter the service—a vivid illustration of his rejection of his father's conceptions of citizenship. Whereas Joe sought to avoid serving on the front lines of battle during World War I, Jack would seek the opportunity out a generation later. In short order, after pressing his father to help him overcome the physical exam, Jack joined the U.S. Navy and became the skipper of a PT boat—a sleek, torpedo-armed craft employed to sink enemy destroyers.

After being commissioned a lieutenant, Jack was deployed to the South Pacific, where he patrolled the waters with a small crew, and he quickly saw action. Late one night in August 1943 in the Solomon Islands, a Japanese destroyer rammed into Jack's boat, PT-109, causing the deaths of three crewmen and serious injuries to two others. The boat was cut in half and went up in flames, and the survivors struggled to evade enemy fire while searching for land. Jack's heroic leadership included locating an island a few miles away and pulling an injured crewman to shore by keeping the man's life jacket clenched in his teeth while towing him to land—mostly under the darkness of night.

Seeking to avoid enemy detection, Kennedy's squad hid on the island, surviving on coconuts, hoping Allied forces would find them before the Japanese did. A few days later, after wondering if they would ever be found, they were discovered by local island natives sympathetic to the Allies. Kennedy engraved a message requesting aid in the shell of a coconut, which the natives delivered to a nearby American base that sent a rescue party. (The coconut was subsequently returned to Kennedy as a souvenir, and he later put it on display in the Oval Office.)

Jack's gallant display of courage earned him great praise at home, not to mention a Purple Heart and the prestigious Navy and Marine Corps Medal.[22] A writer named John Hersey picked up the story and informed readers about the suspenseful endeavors of the PT-109 crew in a piece that ran in both the *New Yorker* and *Reader's Digest*, significantly raising Jack's profile. When given the opportunity, Jack had fulfilled his duty, and in the process, he crystallized his vision of what it meant to be a citizen serving the interests of his country.

JFK aboard the PT-109 in the South Pacific, 1943. He became a war hero when his boat was at-tacked and he saved the lives of many of his comrades.

A New Man

After the war, Jack took a job with the Hearst newspaper chain and wrote columns about postwar issues from the perspective of an American G.I. that underscored his burgeoning political acuity. A particularly revealing article he wrote covered Churchill's postwar defeat in Great Britain, which seemed so shocking to many Americans unfamiliar with British politics in the wake of Churchill's gallant leadership during the war. Jack noted that during the campaign, Churchill had made the same promises he had successfully made in 1940, offering Britons "nothing but 'toil and sweat.'" But the British people had been on a "diet of toil and sweat for the past five years. The British people will take that diet in an emergency but they feel the emergency has passed."[23]

This article reveals an important insight Jack learned that he would carry with him as he embarked on his own political career the following year in his first race for Congress: the right leader at the wrong time will not be elected. Timing and message are central elements of a winning campaign. It was this foresight that enabled him to craft the right theme in 1960 in which he pledged to "get the country moving again," recognizing that the 1950s had been no forced diet on the American people. He understood that there was political capital available for use—Americans could again be asked to make sacrifices because America in 1960 was primed for change, primed for a government willing to take action, primed for citizens to respond to the government's call for action.

In the wake of his coverage of the British elections, Jack took the opportunity to travel through Europe, making political and social observations in a diary along the way. Jack's diary entries reveal a great deal about how his political beliefs continued to evolve in the aftermath of the war. "The best politician," one quote began, "is the man who does not think too much of the political consequences of his every act"—the very theme of his book *Profiles in Courage*, published just over a decade later.[24]

He also noted lines from Dante—"The hottest places in Hell are reserved for those who, in a period of moral crisis, maintain their neutrality"; Thomas Jefferson—"Widespread poverty and concentrated
wealth cannot long endure side by side in a democracy"; Edward
"Colonel" House—"The best politics is to do the right thing"; and
Daniel Webster—"A general equality of condition is the true basis,
most certainly, of democracy."[25] One wonders how many of our current politicians have considered these truths.

The diary entries also accentuate the depth of his evolving perspective. He was thinking seriously about political issues, and he continued
to find inspiration in the prose and stories of individuals of action.
Around the same time, he endured tragic personal experiences that
permanently shaped his views on life.

His older brother, Joe—his rival, his idol, his companion—died late
in World War II when his plane exploded during a heroic attempt to
destroy German military installations. The loss emotionally destroyed
Joe Kennedy Sr. and, as historical accounts suggest, catapulted Jack
into his father's limelight as the heir apparent.

In 1948, his younger sister Kick also died in a plane crash, causing
Jack terrible insomnia and depression.[26] Jack's close friend Lem Billings
remembered that Jack couldn't sleep for a long time after her death.
Each time he felt sleep coming on, "he would be awakened by the
image of Kathleen sitting up with him late at night talking about their
parties and dates. He would try to close his eyes again, but he couldn't
shake the image. It was better, he said, when he had a girl in bed with
him," enabling him to fantasize that the girl was one of Kick's friends
and that they would all meet for breakfast in the morning.[27]

"The only thing that made sense, he decided, was to live for the
moment, treating each day as if it were his last, demanding of life constant intensity, adventure and pleasure," Lem Billings remembered.[28]
He was drawn to Alan Seeger's poem "I Have a Rendezvous with
Death," and from Andrew Marvell's poem "To His Coy Mistress" he
liked the lines, "But at my back I always hear / Time's wingèd chariot

hurrying near."[29] He would chase greatness during his time on earth, however brief that might be.

Coming Into His Own

Joe Jr. had planned to enter politics after the war and fulfill his father's ambitious dream to put a Kennedy in the White House. With Joe Jr.'s unexpected death, however, a void developed, and the oft-repeated story goes that the father's hopes and aspirations were transferred to his eldest surviving son, Jack, who, the story continues, was an unwilling political combatant thrust into a new obligation created by his brother's death and his father's orders.

This narrative seems logical, but it oversimplifies matters. Jack had become a young man very much interested in public affairs who was "political to his fingertips," one British economist who knew him recalled.[30] Lem Billings, seeking to address this story in subsequent years, noted that "[n]othing could have kept Jack out of politics. I think this is what he had in him, and it just would have come out, no matter what…even had he had three older brothers like Joe."[31] His interest in public affairs had grown too deep to avoid it; his overwhelming desire to be a good citizen fueled his ambition.

In 1946, Jack's chance came. James Michael Curley, the colorful incumbent congressman in Massachusetts's Eleventh Congressional District, decided to resign his seat in Congress to seek the mayoralty of Boston. Shortly thereafter, Jack was on the primary ballot in a crowded field with the catchy campaign slogan, "The New Generation Offers a Leader." Despite loose roots in the district in which he ran—Jack first registered to vote there shortly before the election, amidst carpet-bagger claims—Joe's money and influence helped carry his son, the war hero, to victory in the primary and then the general election. Jack's swift political rise was underway.

Working in Washington afforded Jack new perspective on the public affairs he had long studied. With postwar problems to confront, and a renewed focus on domestic affairs on the horizon, there was a great deal of work to be done that invited fresh ideas and fresh thinkers to political debates—a new era was dawning, and if it were approached correctly, Jack could play an important part in it.

To do so required a union of sorts between the political ideology he had developed over the preceding decade and his ability to create perceptions about himself that would shape his image in certain ways in the minds of voters and other leaders alike. In other words, as his father had taught him, the perception of what his leadership was like would help reinforce such leadership in the first place. It meant, as the heroes of Jack's reading understood, that "life is really a performance...[a]nd he knew what every performer knows—you can go only as far as your audience allows."[32]

Indeed, Jack would come to understand the role of the audience in permitting politicians and statesmen to achieve the progress they seek. His close study of classical speechmaking, in particular—familiar stories from his earlier intellectual exploration—afforded him the opportunity to dissect the complex intricacies of the rhetorical techniques used by ancient orators, which in turn enhanced his performance and enabled him to capitalize on the role the audience plays in any public address.

Out of his interest in the lives of great leaders grew a man who sought to emulate the behavior of those he read about. With Jack, "There was always the aura of adventure," the idea that he was

> seemingly beckoned by some distant and restless overture to the stage where the likes of Winston Churchill and Charles de Gaulle and Franklin Roosevelt had stalked history. He coveted the company. He was perpetually enticed by events, exhilarated by maneuver, admiring of brilliance, bemused by human absurdity, angered by failure, and subdued in moments of triumph.[33]

Kennedy's study of great men and women, his sense of adventure and duty, and what he observed about the brevity of life in Joe Jr.'s and Kick's early deaths all strengthened his idealistic inclination toward service and sacrifice—not owing to some feeling that it was romantic to die young, but to the notion that our time on earth is limited and we must therefore do what we can with it, that it is people's deeds that live on after they die, and that we are all part of a larger community.

This "outliving one's life" concept certainly wasn't new. In ancient Sparta a tomb was built to forever honor women who had died in childbirth and men who had died in battle—both had sacrificed for the higher causes of Spartan independence and freedom, which would carry on in part because of their efforts. Jack determined to live just as nobly and for similar ideals. He chose to risk his life in the Pacific, and then he chose to risk his career and reputation when he entered into public affairs with the noble aim of serving his country at home.

Like many other young individuals in search of heroes and inspiration, Jack, through his reading, had envisioned the man he wanted to become—one who would lead a life of service, not because it was expected, but because it was right, because doing so served as a testament to his national loyalty, to his willingness to sacrifice on behalf of a country he loved. And so his presidency would become an attempt to spread the age-old ideals that he learned and which he embraced as an adult, enabling him to frame his rhetoric in ways that would resonate meaningfully with voters. The adventurous spirit he exuded, in which he made Americans feel like their actions could truly bend history, made his idealistic vision seem that much more achievable. In turn, this reinforced Americans' sense that they were indeed on the cusp of better times—if they would embrace the responsibilities Kennedy outlined. What made his rhetoric unique was that the underlying values Kennedy promoted were timeless and not subject to the changing tides of public opinion. No matter what the issue at hand might be, his message of service—his aim of creating a climate of collective action and accountability—could be applied and had appeal. The perceived newness of the Kennedy style was in fact a set of old truths presented in new light. "As he had liberated himself from the past," noted Arthur Schlesinger Jr., "so he had liberated himself from the need to rebel against the past."[34] For the statesman Jack became, this liberation meant accepting that the past would influence the future—yet the past was not to be feared; it was to be embraced and used as a lesson to guide the future.

Modeling Citizenship

As a public servant and as a progressive, therefore, Jack represented what it means to be a free individual in a free society—self-sufficient and self-reliant, independent and liberated. These personal ideals gave him the ability to express the postwar fears of the free world, in part because his war service legitimated his ability to make such claims, but just as much because he had survived the war and come home to find that life in the new world could still be good. He understood the distaste postwar Americans had for empty rhetoric and was determined to change prevailing conceptions by offering a new kind of message—one that was intended to inspire as much as it was to relate to individuals looking for guidance and stability in a world that lacked these elements.

This idea of using the past to look forward allowed Jack to voice the cravings of his generation—the quest for peace, the search for stability, the desire for adventure—and he did so by harkening back to long-standing principles that have always guided free societies. Jack's emulation of the heroes he read about laid the foundation for his modern articulations of the ideals for which many of them had fought. He made the unsurprising discovery that, in turbulent times, citizenship and interdependence are to be most valued in societies emphasizing freedom and self-sufficiency, and these timeless concepts are what lie at the core of national progress.

Accepting the past and preparing for the future are two different tasks, but neither can be done without the other. Like many of his contemporaries, Jack detested the pretentiousness that had dominated much of American rhetoric for years before he entered the national political arena. That is why he sought to avoid the trap of catering to an audience's needs but rather appealing to the *nation's* needs by defining national objectives and conveying how they could be achieved. It is common for politicians to seek the applause of public opinion, but citizens do not look to their leaders merely to do what is popular.

Citizens look to their leaders for vision, for a view of where the nation is going and for what their role is in reaching that destination. Among the most important tasks facing leaders is choosing the right destination. Citizens want to hear the hard and bitter truth from their leaders because it is part of their realization of citizenship. They want to hear that things ahead might be difficult but that the causes for which they fight are worthy and deserving of their best efforts. They want to know what lies ahead so that they can prepare for it and accept whatever responsibilities may come.

Jack understood these principles in the context of the generational imperative to perform service that had inspired his heroes before him. He did this not as an observer but as a son of that generation, as one who recognized that the times were turbulent and who sought to meet the times rather than recoil from the tasks at hand, however difficult.

To appreciate the evolution of Jack's thinking, one must look no further than the household in which he was raised. Joe Kennedy was among the most vocal isolationists in the lead-up to both world wars. Indeed, he was "vehemently opposed" to U.S. involvement in World War I; he believed that America "had not been attacked, and it was his conviction that one ought to fight only to protect one's life, family or possessions—not in the name of abstract ideas like democracy."[35] In other words, he valued self-interest over the public good.

The manner in which Jack volunteered to serve in World War II offered the sharpest contrast: though he suffered from a variety of physical ailments and failed physical examinations, he pressured his father to use his political influence to get him into the Navy. Though so many of that generation also volunteered, few, perhaps, had as much to lose. His decision to participate, to matter, represented a commitment to the ideals for which Asquith and other heroes had fought. Jack knew his duty and he accepted it; he resolved to serve because it symbolized his love of country and because he felt an obligation to do so. This was not a man who fought solely for his life or possessions—this was a man who fought *specifically* for freedom and democracy, the truths that made possible all he hoped to achieve, and who fought to fulfill his obligations of citizenship.

Jack's service during the war undoubtedly represented a refutation of his father's conceptions of citizenship, country, and patriotism. Of equal import, it demonstrated that he could define the person he wanted to be notwithstanding the shackles of his father's influence. This breaking free was a conscious endeavor on the part of a young man who journeyed through books and stories in search of heroes and identity, and it served as the catalyst to a continual making and remaking of himself as a free citizen in an interdependent world. What remains clear, as we look back at this progression, is that Jack stayed true to the classical ideals of citizenship that had inspired him as a young boy and later in early adulthood. In these classical stories, Jack saw reminders of what individuals can contribute to a nation in a world of interdependence and collective responsibility; in his heroes, he saw figures who had elicited and made the best contributions.

In the end, the words that a grieving Jackie offered to Theodore White just a week after the assassination were very true: "History made him, this lonely, sick boy.... History made Jack, this little boy reading history."[36] Soon he would become part of that history and advance the tenets of citizenship that defined him.

A Classic Tradition

Out of Jack Kennedy's coming-of-age period grew certain understandings about the role of the individual citizen in public affairs. From the ancient Greeks, a people that firmly espoused the tenets of civic responsibility, Kennedy recognized and understood the idea that at the root of a nation's power is its commitment to a common cause, and that this is the foundation of citizenship.

The Athenian statesman Pericles gave masterful expression to this notion in a mass funeral oration he delivered in 431 BCE, which influenced Kennedy deeply. Rather than lament the dead, Pericles spoke of the principles underlying Athens's greatness by emphasizing how individuals embraced the responsibilities of their citizenship. A country can be great if its citizens act in ways that build and justify that greatness, he suggested. Implicit in this truth is that each generation must answer the call to service because national greatness must be continually sustained.

In the national setting, this implied that a great nation should strive to serve as a model to other nations. In the individual context, it meant that people were challenged to embrace the virtues of good citizenship so that their great nation was worthy of its distinction. To embrace such virtues—to live nobly and to advance national strength—required participation in public affairs and a belief that the interest of the wider community must be emphasized over individual gain. All citizens can, and are asked, to contribute. "No one is held back by poverty or because his reputation is not well-known," Pericles said, "as long as he can do good service to the city."[37]

At the core of this commitment was the attribute of courage—a willingness to place public gain before private comfort. In certain situations, this meant the kind of physical courage Kennedy read about in his favorite historical passages and then embodied in the Pacific. In other contexts, it meant the courage to behave ethically and honorably according to certain nonnegotiable principles, no matter the cost. In the arena of politics, this kind of courage was rare—and continues to be.

Men of Valor

After being elected to the Senate in 1952 (the year he met Jackie, whom he married the following year), Jack gained an enhanced appreciation for acts of senatorial bravery that became the basis of his bestselling book *Profiles in Courage*, which won a Pulitzer Prize in 1957. *Profiles* recounted the stories of eight U.S. senators who, in Kennedy's judgment, had exhibited a remarkable degree of political courage in their leadership in public affairs.

Each of the senators profiled in Kennedy's book defied public opinion and placed the national needs ahead of all other interests amidst major issues that confronted the nation. The reward for these acts of courage was widespread unpopularity and even electoral defeat by voters who felt betrayed by the courageous actions their leaders had taken.

The stories of these eight men share an overarching theme: commitment to patriotic ideals and a fundamental sense of justice, including a noble disregard for personal consequences—real-world examples of the kind of courage Atticus Finch had exhibited. Kennedy showed how the true citizen—and hence the ideal leader—stands up for what he believes is right for his country no matter what the cost. According to Kennedy, the basis of our actions—like the real-life protagonists in his book—must rest in the idea that we act not out of convenience, but out of patriotism and because our citizenship demands it. Reading Kennedy's book today makes one wish that our current elected officials were more willing to take political risks in the name of moving our country forward. The very idea makes one wonder: who among our national elected officials would appear in an updated edition of the book today?

Profiles in Courage was not written merely to display stories of political courage. It was also written to invite appraisals of individual life and the kinds of contributions that form the basis of national progress. Along these lines, Kennedy's book raised important questions: Why were these displays so heroic? What messages did Kennedy seek to impart in his reader? And why did Kennedy choose these individuals as his models for good citizenship? A brief review of the episodes he explored provides special insight into the kinds of examples that Kennedy felt should guide the leaders of a republic. Similar action in the average citizen's life would be just as meaningful.

Here is a look at a few of the men he profiled.

JOHN QUINCY ADAMS

John Quincy Adams was a leader of the Federalist Party, but after his Federalist friends in the Massachusetts Legislature voted to elect him to the U.S. Senate (direct election of senators was a century away), Adams proved more controversial—and less loyal to party—than his allies had expected. Adams broke ranks with his party to vote in favor of the Louisiana Purchase orchestrated by President Jefferson, and his continued distaste for voting strictly along party lines simply for the sake of political expediency made him very unpopular in Federalist circles.

Adams again joined the Republicans during the fierce battle over the 1807 trade embargo proposed by Jefferson to deal with British attacks on U.S. ships. Adams predicted that he would lose his seat if he voted for the embargo—such a restriction on trade would devastate the New England economy, including the huge shipping industry in his native Massachusetts. "[B]ut private interest," Adams remarked to a colleague, "must not be put in opposition to public good."[38]

In the end, Adams resigned his seat. In Adams's case, his reputation would recover and he would later rise to the U.S. presidency. But it was clear where his principles and loyalty lay. In a diary entry during debate over the trade embargo, Adams recorded his guiding force: "I implore that Spirit from whom every good and perfect gift descends to enable me to render essential service to my country, and that I may never be governed in my public conduct by any consideration other than that of my duty."[39]

DANIEL WEBSTER

Daniel Webster of Massachusetts displayed a similar sense of public duty that cost him his hard-earned reputation. The issue was the Clay Compromise of 1850, which was intended to avert war amidst the burgeoning national crisis over slavery and states' rights. A lifetime opponent of slavery and the Senate's leading abolitionist, Webster was skeptical of Henry Clay's scheme that would save the union. Though the terms of the compromise called for California to be admitted to the union as a "free" state, the Wilmot Proviso (which prohibited slavery in new territories) would be reversed, and a more stringent Fugitive Slave Law would be implemented in the North. People in Massachusetts hated the proposed deal.

Just before the debate over the legislation, Webster had reassured a friend: "From my earliest youth, I have regarded slavery as a great moral and political evil.... You need not fear that I shall vote for any compromise or do anything inconsistent with the past."[40]

Yet when Clay asked Webster for his support, he gave it. Webster ultimately believed that the preservation of the union was more important than any sectional interest or personal reputation, and that the national concern is always the supreme interest that all citizens must serve. "There is one sort of inconsistency that is culpable: it is the inconsistency between a man's conviction and his vote, between his conscience and his conduct. No man shall ever charge me with an inconsistency of that kind."[41]

With this in mind, Webster rose slowly to the Senate podium on March 7, 1850—knowing full well his reputation was about to plummet. "I wish to speak today," he began, "not as a Massachusetts man, nor as a Northern man, but as an American and a Member of the Senate of the United States.... I speak today for the preservation of the Union."[42] Webster couched his support of the compromise in terms of national and public duty—despite knowing the consequences he would endure. After three hours of speaking—which garnered no applause—a period of criticism began, personal and political, that would last long after his death just two years later. In his mind, he had done his duty, and today he is remembered as a great American.

SAM HOUSTON

Sam Houston similarly had the national interest at heart when he opposed the controversial Kansas–Nebraska Act of 1854, which provided that popular sovereignty would dictate if slavery would be permitted in each of these new states. Amidst vehement support for the antebellum legislation in his home state of Texas, Houston viewed the act as a threat to the union. His guiding principle was articulated in a speech he delivered years earlier in support of the Clay Compromise: "I call on the friends of the Union...to sacrifice their differences upon the common altar of their country's good, and to form a bulwark around the Constitution that cannot be shaken.... They must stand firm to the Union, regardless of all personal consequences."[43] In return for his display of national loyalty above sectional interest, he was dismissed from the Senate and defeated in a race for governor because of this vote.

The Essence of Courage

The pattern continues throughout the other profiles and underscores the basic point Kennedy was making: patriotic duty inspires a willingness to put the collective interest above individual concern—even if the personal costs are undesirable. It takes courage to do so.

Profiles in Courage makes clear that JFK's notion of good citizenship is blind to age, background, and circumstances. The good citizen recognizes that his individual welfare is inextricably linked to that of the nation in which he lives. Therefore, he must take care of his country partly as a rational means of taking care of himself, but more basically because the rights and privileges of citizenship cannot be separated from the responsibilities that come with them.

The individuals whose stories were presented in *Profiles* displayed these basic truths in their daily lives. More important, they displayed them in times of crisis and challenge—times when the tides of history and popularity might have made other routes more individually appealing or convenient. Such was their courage.

In presenting these stories, Kennedy sought to impart specific messages to his reader that extended beyond the historical characters and episodes he chronicled. For every virtue extolled in these individuals, there were corresponding actions that could be taken by ordinary

Americans in their daily lives that would advance the cause of citizenship. Though the impact of an individual's courage might be more profound or receive more attention on the national stage, it is the common
citizen's commitment to the same ideals that reinforces these tenets.
And by no means, Kennedy made clear, were these opportunities limited. As he noted in the concluding paragraph of *Profiles in Courage:*

> To be courageous... requires no exceptional qualifications, no magic
> formula, no special combination of time, place and circumstance. It
> is an opportunity that sooner or later is presented to us all. Politics
> merely furnishes one arena which imposes special tests of courage.
> In whatever arena of life one may meet the challenge of courage,
> whatever may be the sacrifices he faces if he follows his conscience—
> the loss of his friends, his fortune, his contentment, even the esteem
> of his fellow men—each man must decide for himself the course he
> will follow. The stories of past courage can define that ingredient—
> they can teach, they can offer hope, they can provide inspiration. But
> they cannot supply courage itself. For this each man must look into
> his own soul.[44]

As president, Kennedy would seek to transform Americans' perceptions of their roles in society. Key to his success in this effort would be
the promotion of certain traits that reinforced the ideals highlighted in
his public addresses, and chief of these traits was courage, the virtue
most needed by Americans seeking to confront the great national challenges of the times. And while Kennedy was looking for a different
kind of citizen, Americans were looking for a different kind of leader.
America in 1960 was disoriented, yet not exhausted; it was ready and
poised to revive Athenian virtues and looking for leadership that embodied those virtues. Kennedy endeavored to provide just that.

Photograph by Frederick Shippey/John F. Kennedy Presidential Library and Museum, Boston.

JFK campaigns in Ann Arbor, Michigan, one of the many campaign stops where he said America needed to get moving again.

Photograph by Abbie Rowe, White House Photographs/John F. Kennedy Presidential Library and Museum, Boston.

The President and First Lady Jacqueline Kennedy arrive at an inaugural ball on January 20, 1961.

CHAPTER 3

A Bold Candidacy

"Some would say that those struggles are all over, that all the horizons have been explored, that all the battles have been won, that there is no longer an American frontier. But I trust that no one in this vast assemblage would agree with that sentiment; for the problems are not all solved and the battles are not all won; and we stand today on the edge of a New Frontier—the frontier of the 1960s."

—JOHN F. KENNEDY,
acceptance speech at the Democratic National Convention,
July 15, 1960

JOHN F. KENNEDY'S vision for the country was predicated on the virtues of citizenship he had admired and come to embody. But before he could make this theme the underlying premise of national progress, he had to convince the American people that the path he envisioned was in fact the change that the country needed. His campaign would have to articulate the transformations he sought; and it was during the campaign that his mission would most forcefully develop.

Kennedy's bold 1960 campaign is noteworthy in many respects— including his handling of the so-called "religious issue" concerning his Catholicism, the reconstruction of the New Deal coalition that had put Franklin Roosevelt and Harry Truman in the White House, and the way in which he leapfrogged more experienced candidates to capture the Democratic nomination to battle Richard Nixon in the general election. Perhaps most notable is the emergence of the Kennedy brand of citizenship on the national scene, which began to take shape in ways that hinted at the themes that would underscore his presidency.

The campaign trail also served as a testing ground of sorts—a forum for Kennedy to put forward new ideas and assess the kind of public reaction he received in reply—to see if people welcomed the ideals of which he spoke. Early enthusiasm across the country, especially among young people, reinforced his sense that the country was ready for changes not only in terms of politics but also in terms of the perspective with which individuals viewed public affairs generally.

With this foundation in place, Kennedy could begin to voice the challenges he had in mind. He began speaking regularly of the need to "get the country moving again" and of his desire to usher in a new period of action, growth, and collective advances. His speeches were filled with vibrant imagery of Americans doing good deeds and accepting the responsibilities that came with their citizenship—the idea that in return for the privilege of being a citizen, each person owed something back. He dared individuals to think bigger and be part of something special. All this was part of a larger imperative to rededicate the country to the principles that had made it great—everything of which he spoke flowed from this basic idea.

This meant challenging audiences to consider their role in society and to ponder whether the condition of America was one of satisfaction or disappointment. Could America be doing better? In Kennedy's mind, yes. Individuals and the country were not living up to their fullest potential. He felt America could surge ahead if individuals embraced the rights and obligations that their citizenship required.

Setting the Stage

The 1960 national campaign traced its origins, in some sense, to 1956, when Kennedy had vied to become his party's vice presidential nominee after Adlai Stevenson unexpectedly threw the nomination open to the convention. Behind the scenes, Joe Kennedy had been against the move. Jack's Catholicism would be blamed for the ticket's defeat in the general election, he thought—it had the potential to ruin his career just as it was taking off.

But Jack had become his own man, and he rejected his father's counsel. He went for it, reflecting a pivotal moment in his career on two counts. First, it had become apparent that not even his own father was going to stand in his way of seeking the prize he wanted. Second, he demonstrated his commitment to the idea that in life, we must strive to fulfill our potential—nothing is handed to us; we must seek opportunities out. We must be active and engaged and regularly be considering what we can be doing to further our objectives—a basic element of the civic duty on which he would soon expound.

Jack indeed felt he had the potential, and so he put his hat in the ring. Estes Kefauver, a senator from Tennessee, was initially the favorite, but with the Kennedy operation moving swiftly, Jack's support rose dramatically and brought him just shy of the nomination on the second ballot of delegate voting. Kefauver ultimately received enough votes on the third ballot to secure the nomination. But Kennedy had made impressions: he was a fighter, he had appeal; he had a future as a star, much the same way many Americans looked at Barack Obama at the Democratic National Convention in Boston in July 2004.

Kennedy's receipt of the Pulitzer Prize for *Profiles in Courage* further enhanced his profile, and in 1958, he was overwhelmingly re-elected to a second term in the Senate. With this major victory, he set his sights on the White House. By January 1960—after years of informal campaigning—his pursuit of America's greatest prize was formally underway.

Offering His Leadership

Kennedy declared his candidacy in the Senate Caucus Room in Washington. "I believe that the Democratic Party has a historic function to perform in the winning of the 1960 election, comparable to its role in 1932 [when FDR was elected]," he declared.[1] The issues were clear, he indicated: how to control the arms race and combat Soviet advances, how to assist new nations seeking democratic independence, how to improve American science and education, how to bolster domestic farms and prevent urban decay, how to expand economic growth and regain economic stability, and "how to give direction to our traditional moral purpose, awakening every American to the dangers and opportunities that confront us."

For eighteen years, he noted, he had been serving the United States, first in the Navy and then in Congress. While in Congress, he had traveled around the world. "From all of this," he concluded, "I have developed an image of America as fulfilling a noble and historic role as the defender of freedom in a time of maximum peril—and of the American people as confident, courageous, and persevering. It is with this image that I begin this campaign."

The call to action was not yet apparent, but he was carefully introducing his ideas—laying a foundation upon which the specifics could follow. If Americans are "confident, courageous, and persevering," then surely they can appreciate the need to sacrifice for the common good and meet the challenges of their time. Soon, too, he began employing a rhetorical strategy that would reinforce this point: he would ask questions intended to provoke meaningful thought—not only about his candidacy, but about the wider imperative of national improvement and how citizens needed to reconsider the very essence of what national pride entailed.

Later that month, speaking at the National Press Club, he noted that the question in 1960 was this: "What do the times—and the people—demand for the next four years in the White House?"[2] Did the times require innovation and fresh approaches to the problems of the day? Did they require energetic leadership and changes in the public discourse? He implored Americans to discuss not just the issues that the next president would face, but also "the powers and tools with which we must face them."

In essence, he was seeking to reshape the national psyche. The election of 1960 was far more than a political race; it was a question of ideology, of motivation—of what constituted progress and how the human spirit could inform and shape issues. This question required critical thought that was deeper than asking voters to choose among candidates. It was asking individuals to choose the country they wanted and what kinds of efforts would be necessary to realize such aims.

Later in the campaign, he struck a similar chord in a speech at the University of Michigan: "This university is not maintained...merely to help its graduates have an economic advantage in the life struggle. There is certainly a greater purpose.... Therefore, I do not apologize for asking for your support in this campaign. I come here tonight asking your support for this country over the next decade."[3]

How individuals would choose to act became a centerpiece of this effort. Would they improve society? Would they choose to help their communities? Would individual action comprise the "powers and tools" needed to "get the country moving again"? He was prompting questions we might still ask today.

On to the Convention

As Kennedy continued to tailor his message heading into summer, his campaign picked up steam. He traveled extensively and built a national organization, enlisting support among as many delegates as possible. Seeking a party nomination involved the same mechanics used today—a candidate needed to receive votes from enough delegates to secure placement on the ticket. Kennedy's organization endeavored to line up the necessary support, and the family political machine, which included his parents, his siblings, and many others, was in full operation.

All this backing provided the forward momentum he needed, and by July, it was off to the convention.

Contrary to the coronation ceremonies that modern conventions have become, conventions in Kennedy's time were different. Candidates were actually chosen at the party gatherings, and delegate votes had more significance. Often, at the beginning of the convention, it would be unclear who would emerge as the party nominee just a few days later. There was an aura of excitement, of raw political operations that involved back-room deals in the smoke-filled rooms we read about in our history books. The whole process required candidates and their campaign teams to have tenacious grit and determination.

Kennedy's victory was not assured. Though he had won a string of primaries that garnered considerable support, he still had not secured the number of delegates needed to clinch the nomination, and there remained meaningful obstacles. The party establishment was keen on nominating an individual who could reunite the Roosevelt coalition of big labor, farmers, the elderly, and urban voters that had been broken in the wake of Truman's presidency. It also sought someone who could instill new energy in a party that had been in the political wilderness for nearly a decade—someone who could invigorate the base but also attract support from independents. There were natural selections these leaders had in mind, and Kennedy was not at the top of the list.

The reasons for his party's lack of support were manifold. First, Kennedy's faith irked the Anglo-Saxon establishment and invited concerns that he would answer to the pope before serving the needs of his country. Second, his perceived inexperience and his young age were considered significant negatives. Though he had served in Congress for fourteen years, and in the Navy before that, Kennedy had assumed no leadership position in Congress and was not responsible for any major legislation. His ambition, the thinking went—not unfairly—was focused on moving up the political ladder, and at times he avoided controversial votes in the Senate, such as his notable absence for the censure vote of Senator Joe McCarthy. (Recovery from back surgery provided a superficial excuse. The reality was that McCarthy had been a family friend for years, and McCarthy had helped Kennedy in 1952 by not endorsing his Republican colleague, Henry Cabot Lodge. Kennedy therefore felt he could not vote for censure, but political realities also precluded him from voting against it.)

Third, Joe Kennedy had grown very unpopular. People loathed not his wealth but his positions on issues. He had opposed American involvement in both world wars, endorsed British appeasement, and been at odds with Roosevelt on other aspects of foreign policy in the progression toward the second war. He was also ruthless in his business affairs and therefore despised by many who dealt with him. Fourth, it was not Kennedy's "turn," so to speak. Others had toed the party line for years and been waiting for their chance, and Kennedy, while promising, would have a chance if he would only be patient. (Does this sound like the Democratic Party in 2008?) Moreover, party elders such as Harry Truman and Eleanor Roosevelt, each of whom still held sway over party loyalists, vehemently opposed a Kennedy candidacy and made their views public. They hated Joe Kennedy, and they were not impressed with his "playboy" son in the Senate.

In addition, Lyndon Johnson's camp raised issues about Kennedy's health, spreading the accurate rumor (though forcefully denied by the Kennedys at the time) that Jack had been suffering from Addison's disease, a deficiency of the adrenal glands that required regular cortisone shots and other medical treatment. (The effects of cortisone shots and steroids that were prescribed to relieve his colitis added weight to his thin frame and gave his skin a tan complexion, which together ironically reinforced his image of youth and vitality.)

The concerns raised by the party establishment complicated matters for Kennedy, but they also offered opportunities that underscored critical elements of his appeal. If the party was serious about bringing forth meaningful change in the wake of the Eisenhower years, a youthful candidate with good looks and an ability to speak well about the need to bring about such change could be a major asset. Similarly, his religion could help in many important Democratic areas across the country, and it could have the added benefit of promoting the fundamental notion of tolerance that infused the party's platform with respect to the lurking issue of civil rights—and perhaps other issues abroad. In some ways, then, Kennedy truly personified what the party was looking for, and each of these components of his candidacy would be used to bolster the themes of citizenship and community engagement he envisioned.

Nonetheless, the institutional leaders had other candidates in mind. Hubert Humphrey, the senator from Minnesota, was in the race. Humphrey was a bona fide liberal who earned good marks from party regulars who appreciated his loyalty to key Democratic platform planks. Estes Kefauver, who had earned the gratitude of Democrats for running with Stevenson, appeared to be in the mix. Lyndon Johnson, the Senate majority leader and a force in the Deep South, had expressed interest and was expected to make a run. Stuart Symington, a Missouri senator, was also interested. And Adlai Stevenson, though not formally seeking a third shot at the presidency after twice losing to Eisenhower, seemed to be prowling beneath the surface of the nomination struggle, somehow waiting for an opportunity to pounce if the convention could not coalesce around one candidate. In fact, a "Draft Stevenson" movement, tacitly approved by the former nominee, was in the works.

In a marathon effort of making deals and promises at the convention, the Kennedys ran a masterful operation securing support for Jack, finally giving him enough votes to obtain the nod. Now he needed to choose his running mate, and then the general election campaign would begin.

Conventional wisdom suggested that Kennedy should choose someone who could placate the wing of the party with whom he had recently fought. In Kennedy's case, that would mean making peace with the more liberal wing that was dominated by organized labor. During the convention fight and before that in Congress, Kennedy had been a reliable but somewhat unenthusiastic supporter of the unions, and he was not their preferred choice. Labor liked Symington or Stevenson. And the Stevensonians still comprised the intellectual and moral leadership of the party. Henry "Scoop" Jackson, a senator from Washington, was also considered. No one wanted Lyndon Johnson. In fact, the labor wing emphatically opposed the inclusion of Johnson, who also remained unpopular with black leaders because in their minds he was not progressive enough on civil rights. Kennedy's advisers made numerous promises to labor leaders and black leaders: it would definitely not be Johnson.

But then the Southern leaders put pressure on the Kennedy camp. Johnson, as majority leader, deserved the spot, they said. He would bring geographical balance to the ticket. Moreover, despite their pleadings, he probably wouldn't even accept the vice presidential nomination anyway—couldn't Kennedy ask him out of deference, and then go choose someone else so that Johnson wasn't offended?

On Thursday morning of the convention, after wrestling with the selection for hours on end, Kennedy extended the symbolic offer to Johnson. But in an unexpected twist, Johnson accepted—he actually *wanted* to be on the ticket. Now Kennedy was in a bind. He truly didn't want Johnson as his running mate, and he knew the pick would infuriate the liberals he had been cultivating so carefully. So Kennedy employed Bobby to go back to Johnson and try to talk him out of it. Johnson met with Bobby, and when informed by Bobby that his selection probably did not make sense in the scheme of the political realities of the party, Johnson, in a display of his unique ability to show any emotion needed to win over an adversary, began to cry! Bobby didn't know what to do. With tears in his eyes, Johnson said, "I want to be Vice President, and, if the President will have me, I'll join him in making a fight for it."[4]

The maneuvering continued. Party insiders began calling Jack, instructing him that he had to take Johnson now; it was too late to turn back and insult the Senate majority leader, which would make passing legislation that much more difficult if Johnson were not brought along. So despite overwhelming opposition and his own misgivings, Kennedy decided to sleep in the proverbial bed he had made. Johnson would be his running mate, which would at least have the benefit of removing him from the majority leadership position in favor of Senator Mike Mansfield, a Kennedy ally whom Jack trusted. It would also strengthen the party's appeal in Southern states whose constituents largely opposed the more liberal portions of the party platform, including civil rights. It is curious to consider if Johnson planned this outcome all along.

The Kennedy Vision

With the ticket in order, Kennedy addressed the convention in the Los Angeles Coliseum in front of a huge outdoor crowd, an atmosphere Barack Obama sought to emulate in his 2008 acceptance speech in Denver. Though Kennedy had already been traveling extensively around the country for months and introducing his ideas, the acceptance speech offered the first major national opportunity to present his vision to the country.

He was happy to have a unified party, he noted, but the next task would be convincing the American people that the Democrats offered a better image for the country than the Republicans did. He needed to demonstrate that his vision—based on the concepts of shared sacrifice and mutual cooperation—would be the solution to the "eight years of drugged and fitful sleep" that had prevented movement and action in the 1950s.[5]

He aimed to unify the American people in thought and purpose by highlighting the need for change and departing from the traditional lines of partisan warfare. "I think the American people expect more from us than cries of indignation and attack," he said. "The times are too grave, the challenges too urgent, and the stakes too high, to permit the customary passions of political debate." The country needed strong leadership; it needed a return to the ideals upon which national greatness was based.

A new generation would be responsible for bringing about this change. It was their future, their obligation, their purpose. It was the rite of passage previous generations had fulfilled. New perspective was required; new focus on the recognition of the interrelatedness of their existence was needed. "Today our concern must be with the future. For the world is changing. The old era is ending. The old ways will not do," he said. Ingenuity and resourcefulness in spirit could revitalize the American dream of upward mobility and progress and collective efforts to help the common good.

All of this formed the basic construct within which he could promote the traits of citizenship. National problems required communal solutions. People needed to focus on their communities before themselves. Individual advances were valued, but they meant little if the country was not moving in the right direction as a whole.

"The changing face of the future" is "revolutionary," Kennedy said. "The New Deal and the Fair Deal were bold measures for their generations, but this is a new generation." The challenges remained vast, as he had noted in the speech declaring his candidacy: farming issues, crowded schools, urban decline, racial discrimination, health care, and the existence of "a change—a slippage—in our intellectual and moral strength." He spoke of "the expense account way of life" and "the confusion between what is legal and what is right." "Too many Americans have lost their way, their will, and their sense of historic purpose."

It was all on the line. The essence of American life was in disrepair, in tatters, in jeopardy. Kennedy was not speaking about corporate profits or the urgent need for new legislation—he was talking about the very fiber of American existence and community life. People were not living up to their responsibilities, he suggested. They were acting out of convenience and a desire for private comfort, often at the expense of the public good. They were writing proverbial checks that would have to be paid by future generations—they were "passing the buck" on their obligations as citizens. There was a difference between that which was legally permissible and that which was morally right. Citizenship, in Kennedy's America, required individuals to lift their sights toward a higher purpose—Americans were special, and they indeed had a "historic purpose" that meant more than following the law. It meant striving to make things better and directing personal and national efforts with this aim in mind.

If these themes sound familiar, it is because our times resemble what Kennedy saw. If he were here now, he might address us in similar fashion. But we can also ask these questions of ourselves: Is our generation accepting its responsibilities? Are we "passing the buck" sometimes when we should not be? Are we merely complying with the law, or are our actions fulfilling the deeper calling of which he spoke? These questions cut past party affiliation and political ideology—they speak to the very essence of who we are as a people and the country we want—indeed, the country we should demand.

Kennedy had answers for these questions. "It is time, in short, for a new generation of leadership—new men to cope with new problems and new opportunities"—people "who are not blinded by the old fears and hates and rivalries—young men who can cast off the old slogans and delusions and suspicions." It was time to move forward, to put the squabbles of the past behind them, to focus on rebuilding the spirit that had created American greatness. We are at the same precipice now.

Kennedy stood at the podium facing west, he said, on what was at one time the last frontier. The land that stretched behind him had been filled with sacrifice and progress. These individuals "were not the captives of their own doubts, the prisoners of their own price tags. Their motto was not 'every man for himself' but 'all for the common cause.'" They fought together to overcome the hardships and win the battles they confronted.

"Some would say that those struggles are all over, that all the horizons have been explored, that all the battles have been won, that there is no longer an American frontier," Kennedy instructed. "But I trust that no one in this vast assemblage would agree with that sentiment; for the problems are not all solved and the battles are not all won; and we stand today on the edge of a New Frontier—the frontier of the 1960s."

The New Frontier was different from Woodrow Wilson's New Freedom and Franklin Roosevelt's New Deal. It was not a set of promises, but a set of challenges. "It sums up not what I intend to offer to the American people, but what I intend to ask of them," Kennedy noted.

The real choice was not between two candidates or two political parties—it was "between the public interest and private comfort, between national greatness and national decline, between the fresh air of progress and the stale, dank atmosphere of 'normalcy.'" America could be doing much better. Individuals would be asked to think differently and to act accordingly. They would be challenged. We should be challenged.

At last, Kennedy had painted his image of America—a nation of progress, energy, promise, and strength. Individuals and their actions formed the basis of this New Frontier. Citizens devoted to the collective good made everything achievable.

The Religious Issue

After the convention, Kennedy continued to traverse the nation to spread his message. Yet he still had to confront a major issue associated with his candidacy: the so-called "religious issue." Such efforts epitomized the flavor of citizenship he had been framing and offered a harbinger of things to come in a Kennedy presidency.

The issue was simple: Kennedy was Catholic, and no Catholic had ever been elected president. People were prejudiced. New York

Governor Al Smith, a Catholic, had received the Democratic Party's nomination for president in 1928 only to be clobbered by Herbert Hoover in that year's presidential election. Many felt that the same discrimination would endure again and cost Kennedy the election.

Unable to eradicate concerns over his religion, Kennedy determined to meet the issue head-on by appearing in Texas before the Greater Houston Ministerial Association to assuage their fears and those of others listening around the country. There, Kennedy reiterated his support for the separation of church and state and swore allegiance to the country and the president's constitutional duties to protect it. He was not the Catholic candidate for the presidency, he said—"I am the Democratic Party's candidate for president who happens also to be a Catholic." Kennedy did not speak for the Church, he said, "and the Church does not speak for me."[6]

He then leveled a bold claim at his audience and the country at large. "If this election is decided on the basis that 40 million Americans lost their chance of being president on the day they were baptized, then it is the whole nation that will be the loser, in the eyes of Catholics and non-Catholics around the world, in the eyes of history, and in the eyes of our own people." In other words, to deny the country the potential leadership of such a large swath of its citizens was detrimental on many levels, and those who used Kennedy's faith as the barometer of his qualification to be president were bigots. This was a bold suggestion: that a defeat for Kennedy in November implied some kind of national bigotry inconsistent with the founding ideology that certain truths were forever understood to be "self-evident." Of course, such bigotry would be impossible to prove, but regardless of the circumstances of the campaign and the issues advanced by the candidates, a Kennedy loss equated to this unsettling proposition. And the conclusion of his speech provided striking imagery: with his hand raised, he recited the oath of the presidency, offering a vivid illustration that he in fact could be sworn into office without issue.

Whether or not Kennedy could answer the "religious" question had broader implications. If a Catholic could be elected president, perhaps other progress could be achieved in areas like civil rights, where the same obstacles of narrow-mindedness and intolerance loomed large. A Catholic president could influence relations with Latin American nations—countries susceptible to communist infiltration and whose populations were predominantly Catholic. A Kennedy victory could therefore signify a changing tide that would bode well for new efforts in each of these arenas, and perhaps others. The idea of tolerance, Kennedy suggested, was a central facet of the New Frontier and an underlying need in the quest for a better understanding of citizenship.

The Famous Debates

As the election campaign rolled forward, Kennedy continued to emphasize these themes. He and the Republican nominee, Vice President Richard Nixon, conducted four televised debates on various subjects. Accounts of these debates—particularly the first one—suggest that Nixon may have edged Kennedy slightly on the substance, but that Kennedy's appearance and style looked more presidential. The familiar story goes that those who listened on the radio thought Nixon won, but those who watched on television thought Kennedy won.

What is important to our study is noting how Kennedy continued to frame the issues they debated. While the specific issues were important, he still focused on the mindsets and perspectives he was seeking to influence vis-à-vis his brand of citizenship. In the first debate, on September 26, 1960, six weeks before the election, Kennedy spoke first:

> In the election of 1860, Abraham Lincoln said the question was whether this nation could exist half-slave or half-free. In the election of 1960 ... the question is whether the world will exist half-slave or half-free, whether it will move in the direction of freedom ... or whether it will move in the direction of slavery. I think it will depend

in great measure upon what we do here in the United States, on the kind of society that we build.[7]

The question before the American people came down to this, Kennedy said: Is America doing everything it can do to be the nation its people desire?

> I should make it very clear that I do not think we're doing enough, that I am not satisfied as an American with the progress that we're making. This is a great country, but I think it could be a greater country....I'm not satisfied to have fifty percent of our steel-mill capacity unused. I'm not satisfied when the United States had last year the lowest rate of economic growth of any major industrialized society in the world....I'm not satisfied when we have over nine billion dollars worth of food—some of it rotting—even though there is a hungry world, and even though four million Americans wait every month for a food package from the government, which averages five cents a day per individual....I'm not satisfied until every American enjoys his full constitutional rights....I think we can do better. I don't want the talents of any American to go to waste.

The tone of his remarks was masterful. "There wasn't a word of his opening presentation that anyone could have argued with, not a sentiment that his fellow citizens couldn't share," Chris Matthews noted in his book *Kennedy and Nixon*. "No, the country was not meeting its potential. No, we were not the same nation of doers who had ended World War II. Yes, the country *could* do better. And, yes, we needed to 'get the country moving again.'"[8]

Kennedy expressed similar themes of dissatisfaction in the ensuing debates, and the choice before the American people was clear: they could choose to continue the Eisenhower years under Nixon's leadership, or they could embark on a new journey of unknowns but with an inspiring vision outlined by a charismatic challenger—a vision that hinted at key hallmarks of the presidency to come, including the idea of a Peace Corps, advances in space, promotion of civil rights, and the need to forge new understandings with the Soviets. He had laid out his vision—a vision that remains insightful still, half a century later. It was time for Americans to choose their next leader.

Victory

Polls compiled in the days leading up to the election reflected the dead heat that the contest had been all along, but on Election Day, Kennedy prevailed. Of the more than 68 million votes cast, Kennedy's margin of victory was less than 0.2 percent, a stunningly close race despite the wider margin in the Electoral College of 303 to 219.[9] Republicans accused Democrats of voter fraud in Chicago—a heavily Democratic city controlled by staunch Kennedy ally Mayor Richard Daley—and in different parts of Texas, which was controlled by Johnson's people. In return, Democrats claimed that Republicans stole votes in the suburbs of Illinois and the parts of Texas that they controlled. But Nixon sent Kennedy a congratulatory message, as did Eisenhower, signaling that the results of the election would not be contested. Kennedy could turn his efforts toward planning for the presidency.

There was a great deal of work ahead before the inauguration. A cabinet had to be chosen, a White House staff organized, and a legislative agenda established—and of course an important address needed to be written. In his first public remarks as president-elect, Kennedy concluded his brief speech by noting that he and Jackie, who was pregnant, were now preparing "for a new administration—and for a new baby."[10]

The Historic Inauguration

On the eve of John Kennedy's inauguration, a snowstorm descended upon Washington, leaving the nation's capital a wintry white for the historic ceremonies. The 7.7 inches of snow threatened the inaugural parade, and traveling to and around Washington proved difficult. Former President Herbert Hoover had planned to come for the inauguration, but after his flight circled the capital for more than an hour in the hope of landing amidst the storm, his plane turned around and went back to Miami.[11] Cars were abandoned on the George Washington Parkway. Hundreds of government workers took to the streets to begin shoveling, even while the storm continued. But no amount of snow could prevent the inauguration from proceeding as scheduled, and the president-elect, as one might expect, was raring to go.

On four hours' sleep, Kennedy began the day by taking a bath to ease the chronic pain in his back and rehearsing his speech. He was already happy with the content, and he wanted to focus on mastering his delivery. This was not a minor concern. Kennedy had been unhappy with his performance at the national convention in July, which included flubbing some planned lines; and at a handful of campaign events, his delivery did not always match the quality of the rhetoric. In part, this difficulty was due to the fast pace at which he ordinarily spoke—a bad habit he had throughout his political career.

As a historian, Kennedy understood that his performance in his inaugural speech would be compared with those of other presidents and would have the more meaningful impact of setting the initial tone of his presidency. It also had the potential to create indelible images in the minds of viewers in Washington and at home, for those living and for those not yet born who would later view it.

To complement her husband's youthful vigor, Jackie would provide finishing touches on the First Couple's regal appearance with her fine taste and style—all part of her effort to transform how the president would be viewed. For the inaugural occasion, Jackie wore a dress from Bergdorf's that had a sable collar and matching muff, along with a Halston pillbox hat.[12] When gusts of wind flew around her on the morning of the historic day, Jackie reached for the pillbox hat to keep it on her head, and by mistake, her gesture put a small dent in it. Women and designers interpreted the dent to be an intentional component of the design, and henceforth it became common for manufacturers of such hats to include the dent in their finished products.[13] The president-elect would wear a formal suit with a pearl vest and silver tie and long underwear beneath his suit to combat the cold. He did not wear the hat he brought with him during the ceremonies (which many famously believed was what destroyed the men's hat industry in the United States).

The weather was frigid as the ceremony was set to begin, but the snow had stopped, the sky was clear and blue, and the air was crisp. Shortly after noon, Eisenhower and Nixon walked onto the platform on the East Portico of the Capitol to the tune of "Hail to the Chief," and a moment later, Kennedy took the same path. Five past, present, and future presidents were on the dais: Truman, Eisenhower, Kennedy, Johnson, and Nixon.

Marian Anderson, the gifted contralto singer, commenced the ceremonies with a stirring rendition of the national anthem. Religious benedictions followed, and then Johnson took the oath of office as vice president. At Kennedy's invitation, Robert Frost read a poem. And within a few moments, Chief Justice Earl Warren—who had marshaled the landmark *Brown v. Board of Education of Topeka* case through the Supreme Court and who would later chair the notorious Warren Commission that investigated Kennedy's assassination—gave Kennedy the oath of office, and Kennedy, the Catholic who had stirred such angst on the campaign trail simply because of his religion, took the oath while placing his left hand on a Fitzgerald family Bible. He then came to the podium to begin his speech.

Transforming Vision to Reality

Kennedy's inaugural address was historic on different levels. He was the youngest man ever to deliver one. The speech contained lines that instantly became famous. And its significance actually seemed to transcend the pomp and circumstance of the day and usher in a new climate of optimism and possibility. Moreover, its timelessness still rings clear.

To watch the Kennedy inaugural address today—it is worth watching, not just reading, and it can be found on YouTube—is to experience a kind of energy nearly indescribable, and the words that follow do not do it justice. It elicits an emotional response no matter how many times one has seen it, or if one has never seen it before. It is the formal expression of everything Kennedy stood for, everything that formed—and forms—the basis of citizenship in America, and it was a harbinger of more words and action to come. It resonates deeply today.

"We observe today not a victory of party, but a celebration of freedom," he began. The occasion symbolized "an end as well as a beginning—signifying renewal as well as change."[14] It was the beginning of a new era, to be sure. Though his campaign had centered on the need for change, the change he sought was in fact a renewal of sorts—he sought a revival of old, even ancient motifs.

"We dare not forget today that we are the heirs of that first revolution," Kennedy declared. Americans owed a great debt to their forebears for giving them the country they so loved; this debt took the form of responsibilities in both private and public life. It was time for a new crop of citizens to take the reins and live up to these tasks:

> Let the word go forth from this time and place, to friend and foe alike, that the torch has been passed to a new generation of Americans—born in this century, tempered by war, disciplined by a hard and bitter peace, proud of our ancient heritage, and unwilling to witness or permit the slow undoing of those human rights to which this nation has always been committed, and to which we are committed today at home and around the world.

The thrust of the colonial revolution, Kennedy suggested, was still present in contemporary America, and it was a guiding force to be harnessed in all national endeavors. As with his campaign rhetoric, the imagery of generational change is clear. The mention of the words "at home" signaled the only reference, albeit a vague one, to the growing civil rights struggle.

"Let every nation know, whether it wishes us well or ill, that we shall pay any price, bear any burden, meet any hardship, support any friend, oppose any foe, to assure the survival and the success of liberty." These were Kennedy's pledges. Americans had greatness in them, and as faithful citizens, they would elicit this quality from one another and contribute to national prestige.

Kennedy also promised to be a good friend to America's traditional allies. To new nations that had more recently become free, he pledged American help. And to the poor people of the world "struggling to break the bonds of mass misery," Kennedy offered American aid too—"not because the Communists may be doing it, not because we seek their votes, but because it is right. If a free society cannot help the many who are poor, it cannot save the few who are rich."

Here was the crystallization of Kennedy's call to service. While all are asked to contribute to a nation's greatness, there are certain citizens who must go beyond the standard call for sacrifice. It is these individuals—the individuals who have received good educations; the people who have the ability to obtain good jobs, whether high-paying, of societal importance, or both; the folks who do not wonder where their next meal is coming from; in short, the citizens who *have* as opposed to the citizens who have not—whose best efforts are especially needed to secure the sacred goal of national progress.

To Latin American neighbors, Kennedy offered "a special pledge: to convert our good words into good deeds, in a new alliance for prog-ress, to assist free men and free governments in casting off the chains of poverty. But this peaceful revolution of hope cannot become the prey of hostile powers." The Cold War implications were clear, and Kennedy specified "that this hemisphere intends to remain the master of its own house." Looming showdowns in Cuba would offer Kennedy the chance to convert those words to deeds.

To the United Nations, Kennedy offered renewed support, ex-pressing hope that the world assembly would expand the scope of its influence. And while American efforts would always be in support of peace, Kennedy offered to American adversaries "not a pledge but a request: that both sides begin anew the quest for peace, before the dark powers of destruction unleashed by science engulf all humanity in planned or accidental self-destruction." The present course was not comfortable for either side. "So let us begin anew—remembering on both sides that civility is not a sign of weakness, and sincerity is always subject to proof. Let us never negotiate out of fear, but let us never fear to negotiate." Kennedy was voicing the new world order he sought:

> Let both sides explore what problems unite us instead of belaboring those problems which divide us. Let both sides...formulate serious and precise proposals for the inspection and control of arms....Let both sides seek to invoke the wonders of science instead of its terrors. Together let us explore the stars, conquer the deserts, eradicate disease, tap the ocean depths, and encourage the arts and commerce.

On the surface, of course, these comments rather plainly referred to the Cold War rivalry and the need for cooperation to achieve mutual goals. But as Kennedy's presidency was borne out, they could perhaps resonate in other ways, too, which we will explore.

"All this will not be finished in the first one hundred days," Kennedy said. "Nor will it be finished in the first one thousand days; nor in the life of this Administration; nor even perhaps in our lifetime on this planet. But let us begin." Progress would not be easy, the president suggested. But nothing worth doing would be easy. To accomplish great things required great effort. And while a generation may not see the ultimate fruits of its labors, it was in fact a generational imperative to begin the work—to bring it closer to fruition, to secure a better chance at success and leave a country and world to the next generation better than the ones they inherited.

"Since this country was founded, each generation of Americans has been summoned to give testimony to its national loyalty," he declared. "The graves of young Americans who answered the call to service surround the globe." Past generations had met their national duty. And as the generational imperative required, it was time for the new generation to prove its worthiness. He declared, "Now the trumpet summons us again...[in] a struggle against the common enemies of man: tyranny, poverty, disease, and war itself."

"In the long history of the world, only a few generations have been granted the role of defending freedom in its hour of maximum danger. I do not shrink from this responsibility—I welcome it." His emotion peaked. The steadiness of his delivery thus far began to change in favor of passionate fist-pumping and near-shouting:

> I do not believe that any of us would exchange places with any other people or any other generation. The energy, the faith, the devotion which we bring to this endeavor will light our country and all who serve it, and the glow from that fire can truly light the world. And so, my fellow Americans: ask not what your country can do for you—ask what you can do for your country. My fellow citizens of the world, ask not what America will do for you, but what together we can do for the freedom of man.

A "good conscience" would be the "only sure reward, with history the final judge" of their deeds, but Americans would need to remember that "here on earth, God's work must truly be our own." It was time to convert good words to good deeds. It was time to live up to the greatness of generations past. It was time to realize this vision and make it a part of everyone's lives.

A Stirring Response

The reaction was strong and immediate. Sustained applause and cheering filled the air. The new president shook hands with the dignitaries around him. The energy in the atmosphere was tangible. People knew they had just heard a rare, almost timeless speech. Words like "revolution," "shield," "deadly atom," "trumpet," and "beachhead" all evoked scenes of combat, and Americans were ready to march into battle with this man.

"We seemed about to enter an Olympian age in this country," wrote David Halberstam, looking back on that time, with "brains and intellect harnessed to great force, the better to define a common good."[15] William Manchester noted that "our history fosters the belief that we can do anything, and quickly, too," in ways that could exploit the "impatient energy" possessed by each generation of Americans looking to make its mark and fulfill its potential.[16] The can-do spirit of Kennedy's words seemed to breathe new life into this fundamental truth.

The response from the news media was lavish and seemed universal. The *Milwaukee Journal* wrote of Kennedy's "great inspiration and dedication" and his "poetic elegance."[17] The *Los Angeles Times* observed that the new president "complimented his fellow Americans by assuming that they would rise to their civic occasion."[18] Arthur Krock of the *New York Times* (the same man who helped edit Kennedy's book *Why England Slept*) predicted that the methods and measures of Kennedy's concept "of national and world leadership may prove to be as different from General Eisenhower's as forecast by the new President's personality, age, campaign speeches, and...the 1960 platform of his party."[19] William Randolph Hearst Jr. confirmed that Kennedy's inaugural "was great. Gone was all the political downgrading of the preceding administration that had characterized Kennedy the candidate. Gone were the promises of all things to all men in the Democratic platform which were so hard for me—and half the nation—to swallow."[20]

Mike Mansfield, the new leader of the Democrats in the Senate, described the speech as "magnificent, great." Hubert Humphrey, assistant to the Senate majority leader, felt that the speech portrayed "the American message to the world" and painted "a true picture of our country."[21]

Even congressional Republicans thought it was a great beginning. Everett Dirksen, the Republican leader in the Senate, dubbed the speech "inspiring" and "a very compact message of hope." Charles Halleck, the minority leader in the House, "was much impressed."[22] Gone from the public discourse was the competitive campaign that had so closely divided the country; gone were the "crabbed reminders that his margin over Nixon" had been so close.[23]

Kennedy's mission was now apparent, and the work—the implementation of this methodology as a key framework for progress in the New Frontier—was set to begin. After a period of perceived decline, in Kennedy's view, the country was poised for a fresh start. The particular Robert Frost poem he liked to recite on the campaign trail, "Stopping by Woods on a Snowy Evening," now had new meaning: "But I have promises to keep, and miles to go before I sleep, and miles to go before I sleep."[24]

Important Lessons

Kennedy's campaign offers meaningful takeaways for us in the twenty-first century. Though his vision was intended to shape the 1960s, the themes he stressed and the rhetoric he used have an enduring quality to them, suggesting that we can embrace his spirit of exploration and adventure in our time. We can make the fundamentals of citizenship our national ethos and use this framework to approach new problems and new challenges in constructive ways that heed his message—even if the issues are different now.

Shared needs, Kennedy suggested, invite mutual cooperation. We are stronger and better when we work together and focus on issues of collective concern. The answer to times of challenge is not partisan bickering or pointing the finger of blame—it is recognizing the role we each play in society and assessing how we can each contribute. It is re-dedicating ourselves to the principles of civic activism he advanced. It is creating a spirit of compromise that unites people and demonstrates that we are not all that different from one another.

At the core of these efforts must be a thrust of enthusiasm from the younger generation that recognizes its role in bringing about change. If service is a generational imperative, as Kennedy defined it, then it indeed falls on a new group of teenagers and twenty- and thirty-somethings to fulfill these natural obligations. The strength of our republic is reinforced by these efforts.

This is true in any time of great challenge and great opportunity, notions which are not unrelated—challenge can be met by fear and anxiety, or it can be met by a willingness to grapple with difficult issues with the aim of identifying common solutions. With each difficulty comes a chance to make things better, and the Kennedy model of citizenship instructs that this is not merely a right or a privilege, but an obligation to use our best efforts and jointly determine the best course forward. This is the idea behind the New Frontier. This is the approach Kennedy adopted, and it is one that we need today.

PART II

THE NEW FRONTIER

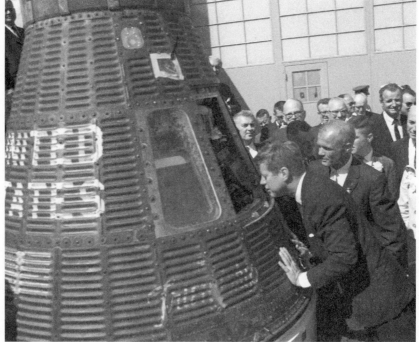

Photograph by Cecil Stoughton, White House Photographs/John F. Kennedy Presidential Library and Museum, Boston.

JFK and astronaut John Glenn peer inside the space capsule that transported Glenn in his orbit around Earth. The space race became a key element of the New Frontier.

Photograph by Abbie Rowe, White House Photographs/John F. Kennedy Presidential Library and Museum, Boston.

JFK speaks to a diplomatic corps of Latin American leaders and proposes the Alliance for Progress, an initiative to promote cooperation, development, and stronger economic ties among nations in the Western Hemisphere.

CHAPTER 4

An Appeal to Our Pride

"We choose to go to the moon in this decade and do the other things, not because they are easy, but because they are hard."

—JOHN F. KENNEDY,
speech at Rice University, September 12, 1962

ON THE CAMPAIGN trail and in his inaugural address, John Kennedy eloquently expressed the mission underlying the New Frontier. When he assumed office, it became time to convert his imagery to reality.

At the core of this transformation was the idea that new action would be required to fulfill the vision of citizenship Kennedy had conveyed. In some contexts, this vision meant individuals would be called upon to serve an important public interest. In other instances, it signified that there would be new national initiatives that catered to the spirit of progress and adventure he coveted.

Such efforts would cost money and other resources, including the efforts and personal sacrifice of the country's best and brightest citizens. But the cost would be little relative to the scope of the outsized goals he set, which were intended to appeal to Americans' pride and their sense of civic obligation and public service.

The Race to the Moon

The exploration of space was one such exciting endeavor. In his inaugural address, Kennedy alluded to this initiative by imploring the Soviets and an expectant world "to invoke the wonders of science instead of its terrors. Together," he said, "let us explore the stars."[1]

This effort would become an issue of tangible importance to the president's agenda, offering strategic value in the Cold War and advancing other aims at home as well. It had goals that personified what it meant to be exploring a New Frontier: the search for knowledge, the achievement of progress, and the idea of venturing into the unknown. All were connected to the underlying themes of citizenship and working for the common good. All increased the depth of pride citizens felt, which in turn boosted their devotion to the qualities Kennedy summoned.

Cold War Significance

The Cold War implications of the space race were clear. In 1960, Kennedy had repeatedly criticized the outgoing Eisenhower administration, including Vice President Richard Nixon, for what Kennedy perceived to be American defeats by the Soviet Union in the quest to explore outer space. He spoke of an alleged "missile gap," hinting that Soviet advances in science and technology were rapidly outpacing similar American efforts. This gap led to security concerns and emotional worries. Indeed, Soviet innovation in this area progressed concurrently with Soviet military prowess, as the rocket engines used in space technology could be used for other, more aggressive military purposes. This progress not only wounded the competitive American spirit, but also instilled fear in American citizens. If the Soviets could beat us in space, people wondered, where else could they beat us? How could we defend ourselves?

The concerns had lingered for some time. In contrast with the Soviet Union, which emphasized initiatives to explore space in the postwar years, the United States did not attach a high priority to such efforts. Harry Truman had cut the budget of the nation's space program drastically, and Dwight Eisenhower had not restored the cuts.

But everything changed in 1957 with the Soviet launch of *Sputnik*— the world's first man-made satellite—into space. Soon thereafter, the Soviets successfully put living animals into orbit and brought them home safely. These events contributed significantly to a growing concern that the United States was in fact losing the Cold War, a premise that candidate Kennedy and others in 1960 found intolerable. To Kennedy, falling behind in this arena did not merely symbolize Republican failures in the 1950s; it also legitimized his claim that the country needed to get moving again, that it was time to be bold and courageous.

He was convinced, moreover, that Americans did not fully grasp the long-term ramifications of lagging behind in such a race toward supremacy in this new and larger universe.[2] Soviet supremacy in space would mitigate attempts by the United States to influence global life on Earth, and the superior development of the Soviet program could increase America's vulnerability to an attack on her soil. It might also diminish Americans' national pride, a vital dynamic in the individual citizen's motivation to realize the civic responsibilities Kennedy had been outlining.

In other words, defeats in space could compromise some of the more personal goals associated with the promotion of citizenship, and the prestige factors counted heavily. "Kennedy had no doubts about the wisdom of landing a man on the moon by the end of the decade," Robert Dallek noted. "Budget deficits and demands for greater spending on domestic programs could not deter him from a commitment he believed essential to America's international prestige."[3] And prestige was critical because it generated enhanced pride in being American, in living in a free society—and therefore had a tangible impact on individuals' inclinations to be good citizens.

Fulfilling a National Duty

Upon entering office, Kennedy was informed by military advisers that the United States had no chance of beating the Soviets in the quest to launch a human into space—a prediction that proved true when Yuri Gagarin, a Soviet cosmonaut, completed a full orbit around the planet in less than two hours on April 12, 1961—just a few days before the Bay of Pigs invasion in Cuba would commence. The Cold War was getting cooler by the day.

But Kennedy was undeterred. The exploration of space was not merely a battlefield on which to wage the Cold War. It fulfilled the very essence of the national movement of which he spoke during the campaign. There was an emotional and psychological undercurrent to this idea. In Kennedy's America, regardless of the context, individuals and the nation were challenged to fulfill their potential and seek greatness.

If the potential to do something worthy existed, the thinking went, it needed to be tried; it needed to be done. It represented an obligation of citizenship, and it was a responsibility to be borne by all who could make a difference. American greatness required the exploration of this new and exciting endeavor.

The sheer romance of space exploration and the lure of the distant and forward-looking perspective also invited new appraisals of life on Earth. From space, the world seemed small, and from outer space, national borders and the sources of man-made strife were not obvious or even visible. The panorama of space therefore provided a sustained glimpse into the eternal and hinted at a better world in which Kennedy could put his rhetorical theme of progress into action. The effort, therefore, not only met the scientific goals of the United States but also served Kennedy's interest in reigniting a national progressive temperament the way Woodrow Wilson and Franklin Roosevelt had done.

At the core of the study of space rests the perpetual desire to improve and advance. The idea of conquering space was therefore both rhetorically and spiritually appealing to Kennedy. To him, scientific advances were a key dimension of progress and the techniques needed to bring progress about. Such advances demonstrated the possibilities of rational management of both man-made and natural problems and offered a new canvas for individual and collective mastery.

Again, Kennedy was responding to an international imperative. Soviet Premier Nikita Khrushchev simultaneously trumpeted many of the same goals for the U.S.S.R., and as science and technology permitted, each side grew increasingly intent on capturing the world of outer space. These decisions made by Kennedy were consistent with the character of his energizing notion of exploring a New Frontier—and in this instance, there was no substitute for victory. As his trusted aide and speechwriter Ted Sorensen noted, "The president was more convinced than any of his advisers that a second-rate, second-place space effort was inconsistent... with the New Frontier spirit of discovery."[4]

And so Kennedy felt forced to take immediate action in order to ensure that the U.S. space program—and the American spirit—could be restored. While struggling to pass legislation in a recalcitrant Congress, dealing with an economy steeped in recession, and the debacle of the Bay of Pigs, Kennedy sought to effectively restart his presidency by calling for a joint session of Congress so he could address certain urgent national needs, which included efforts in space.

"These are extraordinary times," Kennedy began the address on May 25, 1961. "And we face an extraordinary challenge. Our strength as well as our convictions have imposed upon this nation the role of leader in freedom's cause."[5] The stakes were clear: in the battle between freedom and tyranny, Gagarin's flight "should have made clear to us all... the impact of this adventure on the minds of men everywhere who are attempting to make a determination of which road they should take."

To the president, space lay at the core of what it meant to live in the New Frontier—an adventurous time, a time of advances in science and technology that would correlate with American supremacy, not just over the Soviets, but over the entire world. At the height of the Cold

War, Kennedy recognized that space also had a spiritual dimension that transcended Cold War rivalries. He understood that space was a bridge to New Frontiersmen in other nations—a necessary one since the world was watching and evaluating the examples of enterprise and daring being offered by the superpowers.

Kennedy announced that Vice President Johnson would be placed in charge of reviewing the American space effort in order to canvass its strengths and weaknesses. The review—and action—were immediately necessary and could not be delayed, for the new frontier of space held the "key to our future on Earth."

The Soviets had a head start over the United States, Kennedy said; large Soviet rocket engines, he explained, were superior to those of America. "While we cannot guarantee that we shall one day be first," he stated, "we can guarantee that any failure to make this effort will make us last."

Kennedy identified several goals for the space program, most notably landing a man on the moon by the end of the decade. "No single space project in this period will be more impressive to mankind, or more important for the long-range exploration of space," Kennedy declared. "And none will be so difficult or expensive to accomplish." The goal of landing a man on the moon subsumed the particulars—the acceleration of the growth of the proper lunar spacecraft necessary to permit an astronaut to walk on the moon; efforts to improve the different kinds of fuel boosters and attempts at unmanned exploration; the need for government funding and popular support. "It will not be one man going to the moon—if we make this judgment affirmatively, it will be an entire nation. For all of us must work to put him there."

Kennedy called for developing the Rover nuclear rocket, an effort that would give "promise of some day providing a means for even more exciting and ambitious exploration of space, perhaps beyond the moon, perhaps to the very end of the solar system itself." Consider what this sounded like to Americans at the time. The United States had not yet sent a man into space, and the president was talking about exploring the end of the universe! There was infinite possibility, he suggested. We have the potential to do this, he implied. We can, therefore we must. Our citizenship demands these efforts.

Such notions of limitless progress had other unspoken connotations—if such grand goals could be achieved by mutual cooperation and ingenuity, were the problems at home truly intractable? Was space itself, therefore, not a transformative symbol of the progress that could be made in America and elsewhere when the fundamental notions of civic responsibility and public betterment could be harnessed? Any effort, Kennedy stated, required total commitment. "If we are to go only halfway, or reduce our sights in the face of difficulty, in my judgment it would be better not to go at all."

Kennedy's objective here was to bring the nation on board with him as pioneers in the new journey he had promised them. Exploration of space was the quintessential means by which the New Frontier could exist, thrive, and be waged. This was not a choice. Americans *needed* to be pioneers.

Kennedy paused over the wonders of outer space exploration. "No one can predict with certainty what the ultimate meaning will be of mastery of space," he noted. But the effort was necessary, and indeed it would not be worth doing if the end were already in sight.

Defining the Spirit

In time, the competitive goal of beating the Soviets into space would disappear almost entirely, and the space program would become synecdoche for the New Frontier as a whole. On September 12, 1962, in an address at Rice University in Houston, Texas—a city whose space center rests at the heart of the nation's space efforts—Kennedy focused an entire speech on the philosophy of the space program, giving voice to the transcendent and romantic notions afoot beneath it.

At Rice, Kennedy said he was delighted to speak at a school "noted for knowledge, in a city noted for progress, in a state noted for strength;

and we stand in need of all three; for we meet in an hour of change and challenge, in a decade of hope and fear, in an age of knowledge and ignorance. The greater our knowledge increases," he continued, "the greater our ignorance unfolds."[6] Kennedy laid out the themes of knowledge, progress, and strength as integral components of the space effort. All enhanced American chances of success; all would be needed to advance American goals.

Despite the feverish pace at which scientific and technological advances were occurring, Kennedy noted, it was unfathomable to assess "how far and how fast we have come." Indeed, to underscore the speed of modern advances, Kennedy asked the audience to consider, for a moment, reshaping the dimensions of time and space by metaphorically condensing the previous 50,000 years into the span of half a century.

In these terms, it had taken forty years for man to learn that he could clothe himself with animal skin. It was around this time that man emerged from caves and built his own shelter. Just in the previous five years, humans had learned to write; Christianity was but two years old; and only in the last two months, steam power had been invented. Just in the previous week did mankind discover the medicinal uses of penicillin and create the television. And just in the past minutes did it wander into space. The Kennedy calendar emphasized the momentum of innovation, evoking wonders and unease: How far had we come? How far could we go?

Kennedy's purpose was to demonstrate the extraordinary pace at which mankind developed. It was a pace that would lead to new problems as quickly as it dismissed old ones. But the high costs and suffering associated with sacrifice were outweighed by the rewards that were necessarily of greater value. Unstated were the penalties of not venturing the effort.

Going to space was a quintessentially American initiative. For "this city of Houston, this state of Texas, this country of the United States was not built by those who waited and rested and wished to look behind them. This country was conquered by those who moved forward—and so will space." Here Kennedy translated the uniquely American aura of confidence into the quest for dominance in space. The same zeal that secured independence, the very enthusiasm that rallied the nation to countless military and political victories, would be the identical passion necessary for this next endeavor.

Kennedy stated that all great achievements are accompanied by equally great difficulties. But the space effort, Kennedy maintained, would go on whether the United States decided to take part in it or not, and missing out on "one of the great adventures of all time" would strip America of its role as world leader. For "no nation which expects to be the leader of other nations can expect to stay behind in the race for space." And to be American—which was to be synonymous with being a good citizen—meant possessing a devotion to the can-do spirit that defines this country and its efforts toward achieving collective progress. It became part of the national purpose.

In his speech at Rice, Kennedy reinjected the generational theme that had dominated his campaign rhetoric and his inaugural address: "Those who came before us made certain that this country rode the first waves of the industrial revolutions, the first waves of modern invention, and the first wave of nuclear power, and this generation does not intend to founder in the backwash of the coming age of space." In this and other statements, Kennedy redefined the nation's nascent space effort, casting it as the best and only respectable course for a generation and country seeking to prove itself worthy of its global leadership and of its forebears, too.

Space was a new imperative and a new national duty. This new adventure, this New Frontier, was the vehicle that his generation needed to ride. The generation of his day, he suggested in his inaugural speech, had two responsibilities: to the past and to the future. To its predecessors, it was to be worthy of their mythical achievements. To the generations yet to come, it was obliged to perform deeds that would enhance the world they would inherit, which in this context meant riding the first wave of space exploration.

Again, there was the matter of national prestige and the fame that came to all who valued honor over comfort. In a memo supporting the space effort, Lyndon Johnson voiced a central reason for funding and winning the space race, which read in part: "This country should be realistic and recognize that other nations, regardless of their appreciation of our idealistic values, will tend to align themselves with the country which they believe will be the world leader—the winner in the long run. Dramatic accomplishments in space are being increasingly identified as a major indicator of world leadership."[7]

In the midst of the Cold War, America could not risk losing the space competition to the Soviets; such a loss would cast aspersions on the cause of freedom. There was no way but forward, Kennedy emphasized at Rice; "For the eyes of the world now look into space, to the moon and to the planets beyond, and we have vowed that we shall not see it governed by a hostile flag of conquest, but by a banner of freedom and peace."[8]

The quest for progress was urgent, he noted:

We set sail on this new sea because there is new knowledge to be gained, and new rights to be won, and they must be won and used for the progress of all people. For space science, like nuclear science and all technology, has no conscience of its own. Whether it will become a force for good or ill depends on man, and only if the United States occupies a position of preeminence can we help decide whether this new ocean will be a sea of peace or a new terrifying theater of war.

Why was the president so intent upon placing a man on the moon before the end of the decade? "We choose to go to the moon in this decade and do the other things, not because they are easy, but because they are hard," Kennedy declared to the Rice students. Accomplishing such a feat would "serve to organize and measure the best of our energies and skills, because that challenge is one that we are willing to accept, one we are unwilling to postpone, and one which we intend to win, and the others, too." Such a feat would be a tangible and un-deniable symbol of progress that would accentuate the very need for increased loyalty to the tenets of civic obligation that make such ad-vances possible.

Amidst heavy applause, Kennedy concluded by recalling the story of the British explorer George Mallory, who died in his attempt to climb Mount Everest. When asked why he had chosen to climb the world's highest mountain, Mallory had replied, "Because it is there." Kennedy continued: well, "space is there, and we're going to climb it, and the moon and the planets are there, and new hopes for knowledge and peace are there." We can, therefore we must.

This message—this unwillingness to permit the tide of history to pass his generation by—encapsulated his message of citizenship. One must have the virtue and courage to live up to his potential. Citizens needed to act in certain ways that reflected their country's goals and values.

A victory in space would not be solely an American triumph. American success in space would signify progress on behalf of all, Kennedy believed, for the achievements of free people are to be shared with other free people—individuals in any nation are part of the wider community of the human race. Therefore, such efforts on the part of Americans underscored Kennedy's desire to promote the theme of citizenship to all citizens of the world who chose to celebrate freedom.

Regenerating This Spirit

Kennedy did not live to see the historic flight of Apollo 11 that landed on the moon in 1969, which fulfilled his pledge to achieve that feat by the end of the decade. But his legacy in this arena remains important, serving as the foundation in spirit upon which modern space efforts and other advances can be based.

Though the challenges have changed and new goals have been iden-tified, such efforts in the twenty-first century continue to reveal the

critical importance of that first goal Kennedy set. Without his acceleration of the space program, our modern understanding of our planet
would be different and the knowledge we have about the solar system
would be considerably less.

We are much more advanced today than perhaps even Kennedy
could have envisioned. NASA has launched rovers to explore Mars; an
international space station, based on a level of mutual cooperation that
Kennedy sought but which was impossible half a century ago, explores
space; new gadgets such as the Hubble telescope have expanded our
understanding of the universe. Kennedy recognized the potential for
these innovations and discoveries.

Though improvements in science and technology have opened our
eyes to possibilities too distant in Kennedy's time, the spirit he aimed
to foster is still relevant and, in fact, timeless. From space, the problems
of our world are not apparent; boundaries remain indistinguishable;
we are one civilization, not a group of countries or peoples.

This perspective, which Kennedy envisioned, makes our political
squabbles and other challenges seem trivial. It magnifies the interrelatedness and fragility of our condition while diminishing the importance of our differences.

The Kennedy ethos can still guide us in these endeavors. The exploration of our universe is important and worthy of our efforts.
Advances in science, technology, and understanding are meaningful
to the human cause. They signify improvement, our ability to build on
past innovations, and the idea that we are living up to our potential as
individuals and as a country. These are critical elements of national
pride, which Kennedy knew was a key component of embracing the
rights and responsibilities of citizenship.

Whether we are sending humans to Mars, tapping the ocean depths,
increasing our understanding of this planet, or engaging in other efforts, we are by nature a civilization that aims to explore. We seek
knowledge and truth. We crave excitement. Thus, we must identify
large goals as the rational objectives of a people that values progress. To

do so, we should embrace Kennedy's affinity for adventure and make it part of our public discourse.

What does this mean in an individual context? Surely, most of us will not be involved in the space program, though some of us might. But either way, we can do things to support it. We can tell our elected officials that such endeavors are important and worthy of government support. We can visit NASA facilities, tour museums, and gain a better understanding of the work that is being done. We can read articles about advances in space exploration and take pride in knowing that our nation remains at the forefront of these endeavors. We can appreciate that many products used on a regular basis stemmed from NASA innovations, such as water filters, cordless tools, adjustable smoke detectors, shoe insoles, ear thermometers, scratch-resistant lenses, invisible braces, and the technology necessary for long-distance telecommunications.[9] We can be better-informed citizens and use this knowledge to shape our public discourse in ways that invite new adventure and renewed commitment to large, collective goals—to demonstrate that we are still pioneers in the search for new frontiers.

The Peace Corps

While soaring to new heights, literally, was one initiative that fulfilled the vision of the New Frontier, another was the establishment of a program that would send Americans abroad to help create goodwill, better understanding, and mutual appreciation between America and other countries. The program's aim, Kennedy explained in his inaugural address, would be to help struggling individuals around the world who sought freedom and progress to "break the bonds of mass misery."[10]

Kennedy had been considering the idea of a program like this for some time. As early as 1951, he spoke about how rewarding it would be for young college graduates to lend their technical skills to nations around the globe in dire need of assistance. In his foreign tours as a congressman, Kennedy had witnessed the limited nature of life in Third World nations, and it would be a fulfillment of his views on citizenship for young Americans to answer the global call to service. With the imprimatur of American sophistication and privilege, he believed, came an obligation to assist others' efforts to lift themselves out of their relative poverty.

Such a program would indeed help struggling individuals around the world, but it would also provide critical international experience to a rising generation of citizens who would need familiarity with foreign affairs if they hoped to participate in government at the national level. And it would have greater consequences still: it would increase global connectivity. It would offer a validation of democratic values and advance democratic initiatives in nations under the threat of communist influence. It would serve to advance the esteem in which Americans were held abroad. It would also bolster economic ties between nations that might enable new cross-border cooperation and perhaps lead to new innovations in business, science, and education, among other fields. And, of course, it would promote citizenship. Each of these facets reinforced the others and served the general goal of promoting American interests abroad while providing a platform for young individuals to answer the call to service—to be pioneers in the New Frontier.

Launching the Program

It came as no surprise that Kennedy established the Peace Corps within his first 100 days in office. Even before speaking about it in his inaugural address, he had endorsed the idea on the campaign trail. Though his remarks did not contain the term "Peace Corps," Kennedy sketched out the basic concept of the program on October 14, 1960, before a throng of University of Michigan students, whom he addressed at 2:00 A.M. after an exhaustive day of campaigning. As he often did when presenting a new idea, Kennedy posed questions to his audience intended to prompt thinking about their lives and what kinds of efforts each might consider making in order to make their life count. "How many of you who are going to be doctors are willing to spend your days in Ghana?" he asked. "Technicians or engineers, how many of you are willing to work in the Foreign Service and spend your lives traveling around the world?"[11]

It would be their willingness to do such deeds, Kennedy said, that would determine if a democratic society could survive in the wake of increased international struggle. He believed that Americans were willing to contribute but that the new efforts he sought to elicit would have to be greater in scope than previous efforts. "Unless we have those resources in this school, unless you comprehend the nature of what is being asked of you," he implored, "this country can't possibly move through the next ten years in a period of relative strength."[12] He reminded his listeners that the university where they were enrolled surely was not maintained merely for the private enrichment of its students, but for a greater public purpose. Privilege entailed responsibility, and Americans, especially young Americans, must commit themselves to a calling higher and more profound than that of individual interest.

The response was strong and immediate. While campaigning in Ohio shortly thereafter, Kennedy was unexpectedly greeted by a delegation of Michigan students who presented the senator with a lengthy list naming hundreds of people who expressed their willingness to serve abroad. The initial outpouring of support was indicative of the effect that his call for service commanded, offering an early confirmation that Kennedy's brand of citizenship—based on sacrifice and civic devotion—was appealing.

Once in office, Kennedy enlisted his brother-in-law, R. Sargent Shriver, to lead a task force to determine what kind of program might take shape out of this rhetoric. Shriver submitted to the president a report detailing the findings of the task force, highlighting three central purposes of a proposed program: the development of important countries and regions, the promotion of global cooperation and goodwill toward America, and more intelligent American participation in the world.[13]

All of these represented key aims of the New Frontier relating to service and action, and all would become basic tenets of the program. In March 1961, Kennedy issued an executive order to establish the program, in which volunteers would export useful technical skills while serving as a small army of ambassadors, sacrificing two years to serve in perhaps the most unique and challenging job they would ever experience. That Shriver, a family member, became the program's first director reinforced the importance Kennedy attached to the program.

Kennedy requested funds from Congress, and within days, recruitment of volunteers was underway and training camps were installed across the country. Kennedy called for an initial force of between 500 and 1,000 volunteers, but the response was so electric that within two years of its creation, the Peace Corps had several thousand volunteers. By the time Kennedy died, the program had 10,000 participants, a number that climbed to 15,000 by 1966—the highest number of volunteers serving at one time in the program's history. Most volunteers have been young Americans in their twenties and thirties, but there have also been older Peace Corps volunteers, including Jimmy Carter's mother, Lillian, who joined the program in 1966 as a public health volunteer in India at age sixty-eight.[14]

In his March 1, 1961, speech announcing the program's establishment, Kennedy declared: "The initial reactions to the Peace Corps proposal are convincing proof that we have...an immense reservoir of such men and women—anxious to sacrifice their energies and time and toil to the cause of world peace and human progress."[15] In other words, Kennedy was not the only one who saw the New Frontier as a set of challenges that required sacrifice; young American pioneers, as their forebears had, were responding to the trumpet's call to service. In creating the program, Kennedy continued, the country would look to its major institutions—universities, government and private agencies, and the business world—to "share in this effort—contributing diverse

Photograph by Rowland Scherman, Peace Corps/John F. Kennedy Presidential Library and Museum, Boston.

JFK greets more than 600 Peace Corps volunteers training for their overseas assignments.

sources of energy and imagination, making it clear that the responsibility for peace is the responsibility of our entire society."

Weeks earlier in the inaugural address, Kennedy had asked his fellow citizens to "join in that historic effort" of creating "a grand and global alliance" that could "assure a more fruitful life for all mankind"—the Peace Corps was a means of such engagement. Then in his March Peace Corps speech, Kennedy again asked for shared effort to tackle the problems of poverty and despair, indicating that contributions from all citizens in all walks of life would be expected. In the global context, the United States was among the most privileged nations in the world, and therefore its citizens had a responsibility to act—regardless of their background or station in life. Hence, Kennedy sought the support of all individuals who were willing to contribute, especially young people, and he appealed to their sense of adventure as well as their sense of duty. Corps involvement demonstrated how sacrifice is about personal struggle, about courage, and about accepting responsibility.

Kennedy determined to organize the Peace Corps as an undiluted symbol of American idealism and a collective commitment to public service. This goal was evident in his decision to keep the program independent of the Agency for International Development and the State Department, which saved the program from the centralizing bureaucracy of the foreign affairs hierarchy and armed Shriver with far greater latitude to run the organization without intervening authorities. More basically, the decision underscored the elite status of the Peace Corps and the Peace Corps volunteer.

The program, Kennedy suggested, was not "an instrument of diplomacy or propaganda or ideological conflict," but was designed to enable people "to exercise more fully their responsibilities in the great common cause of world development."[16] The president, in effect, was universalizing the notion of the "free society" that he developed in his inaugural address, asserting that the gap between the privileged and those less fortunate was not a partisan question but an imperative;

a question concerning American interests overseas and, by exten-sion, American survival at home. Kennedy's suggestion—that things are worth doing if they require great effort, and that individuals can, in fact, make a difference in the wider communities to which they belong—caught on. In late 1962, Gallup poll results suggested that the Peace Corps was already a success. Seventy-one percent of Americans approved of the program and what it represented.[17] On the basis of the overall trend of events under Kennedy's leadership, 62 percent of respondents indicated that if the presidential election of 1960 were to be held again, they would cast their votes for Kennedy.[18]

While sweeping in scope and ambitious in its aims, the Peace Corps is actually not a very expensive program when compared with many other programs and costs in the federal budget. Therefore the program underscores a basic Kennedy point: sacrifice does not necessarily mean economic sacrifice in the form of higher taxes or spending great sums of money. It goes much deeper.

Extracting Meaning

Kennedy's approach to this endeavor is particularly instructive in terms of what we can learn from it, both politically and as a society. At the core of the program was a sense of community and interdepen-dence that spoke not to partisan predispositions, but to national pride and the feeling that individuals could—and were obliged to—help one another.

The way he framed his rhetoric is also informative. Rather than begin with his conclusion—that he wanted citizens to use their tal-ents overseas in the global struggle for progress—he initiated his pro-posal by asking questions intended to condition his audience for the responses he sought. In doing so, he crafted a message that spoke to individuals' feeling that they had the potential to partake in and even improve the quest for progress. Once they subscribed to this notion, he then flipped his message to become one of challenge; if citizens had this potential, the reasoning went, would they not use it? Would they not accept the challenges of their generation and join in the collective adventures he outlined?

There was a Socratic element to it all that is readily discernible to anyone who has sat in a law school class. It was an effective means of joining the leader and those being led, uniting them to make a rhetorical journey together. It was a tool mastered by ancient orators that Kennedy knew well from his reading and that he would use again in other settings to influence the perspectives of his audience.

The Peace Corps Today

Since its inception, more than 210,000 individuals have served with the Peace Corps in 139 countries, and the program continues to thrive in the twenty-first century. With an annual budget exceeding $375 million today, there are presently more than 8,000 active volunteers and trainees in the program working in more than seventy-five countries.[19]

Peace Corps volunteers work in a variety of different fields and geographic destinations, and the scene today reveals much about what the United States perceives to be the most important global needs in struggling communities—and where this help is most needed. The majority of volunteers are sent to Africa (43 percent) and Latin America (21 percent). Nearly half (43 percent) work in education, seeking to arm individuals with the intellectual and technological tools needed to bring them out of poverty; 21 percent work in health care; 12 percent each work in community economic development and protection of the environment; and the remainder generally work in youth development and agriculture.[20]

The program has also evolved considerably in its half century of existence. Whereas when Kennedy first instituted the program most volunteers were men, today nearly two-thirds of volunteers are women. The scope of services provided has expanded dramatically to include new forms of aid not envisioned in Kennedy's time, such as teaching people in local villages the value of using advanced technology or offering innovative solutions to medical problems.[21]

Service in the Peace Corps has been very rewarding to many of its volunteers. Many alumni have gone on to successful careers in government, the arts, education, business and industry, and nonprofit development work, and some credit their success to the unique experience they had in the Peace Corps. "You learn how to do a lot of things on your own," noted Peace Corps alumna Donna Shalala, the health and human services secretary under President Bill Clinton. "Of all the preparation in my life, [the Peace Corps] was the best. You can drop me any place on Earth, and I could figure out a way to organize anybody."[22]

The ways in which the Peace Corps has advertised the program to recruit volunteers is also revealing of its underlying purpose and the mission Kennedy envisioned. In its televised public service announcements, the Peace Corps' 1968 marketing campaign depicted the palm of an individual's hand with a caption that read: "This is your life line. If you're not doing something with your life, it doesn't matter how long it is."[23] In 2003, the organization launched a marketing initiative to engage a new generation of volunteers with the campaign slogan: "Life is calling. How far will you go?"[24] Some advertisements had the tagline: "The difference between a career and a purpose is about 8,000 miles." These ads underscored another pivotal aim of the New Frontier: to create an outlook of service that went beyond the specifics of where someone served or what work he or she did—to foster a mentality that guided personal decisions.

The idea that individuals must choose a purpose to fulfill reflects the way in which Kennedy envisaged life in the Peace Corps and the promotion of good citizenship generally. America has great national purposes, and its citizens are summoned to play individual roles to help bring these purposes to fruition. Each individual is challenged to identify the purpose that he or she aims to fulfill.

Of course, not everyone will join the Peace Corps. But the organization highlights ways in which citizens can contribute in their own neighborhoods. One does not need to go thousands of miles away to bring about change and to volunteer one's time to improve the lives of those who need help. Just as there are global communities struggling to make progress and improve their lives, there are communities in America that have the same needs and goals. There are places in America that need access to better health care, training in how to use information technology, better educational systems, more support of the environment, local economic development, agricultural aid, and the mentoring of youth—all attributes of life in the Peace Corps. Here at home, AmeriCorps, created by Bill Clinton in 1993, promotes the same dedication of service to those in underserved communities in the United States as the Peace Corps does abroad. It is a way to be an engaged citizen without traveling far. This, therefore, is the tangible significance of Kennedy's establishment of the Peace Corps: it stresses the breadth of our ability to make a difference and be good citizens.

The Alliance for Progress

Latin America was to be the testing ground for an idea different from but related to the implementation of the Peace Corps: that a mutual respect and regard for the independence and self-sufficiency of other states is the glue of international order and development. More basically, this meant that the United States needed to be a good neighbor in order to promote the global aims it desired, reiterating that the spirit of sacrifice and cooperation Kennedy demanded at home was a critical element to successful diplomatic relations abroad. And in fact, they reinforced one another: the promotion of global citizenship would also advance calls for shared progress in the United States.

Kennedy's goal was to achieve a better hemisphere, not merely a safer one, and so he launched the Alliance for Progress to buttress

Latin American chances for success. This effort universalized the concept of citizenship, propagating both personal responsibility and mutual accountability. Irrespective of national borders, Kennedy reasoned, we all belong to the same global community that requires collaboration and interdependence—notions that still require emphasis. In enhancing the prestige of citizenship in the American states, Kennedy simultaneously advanced a theme of human rights that helped lay the framework for some of his longer-term domestic objectives lurking in the distance. At the same time, helping neighbors in the world arena was something that could be replicated on local levels by ordinary Americans. It was a mindset—a perspective Kennedy emphasized. Helping others abroad also increased the pride and prestige factors at home. Yes, we *have* the power to help others; yes, we *are* fortunate to have the society that we do. It all reinforced the spirit of citizenship.

An Unstable Region

The 1950s were marked by significant political, social, and economic instability in Latin America. Rising levels of widespread poverty were accompanied by ephemeral military dictatorships that contributed mightily to the volatility of the region. By 1961, nearly half of the 200 million people living in Latin America were illiterate; almost a third of the people were not expected to live past forty; a mere fraction of the population owned half of the region's riches; and in the thirty years before Kennedy's election, there were no less than "ninety-three illegal changes of regime."[25] Moreover, since 1945, the area had fallen into neglect because of America's steep involvement in Europe, in the Korean War, and in Southeast Asia. We had been too busy to focus on helping our neighbors. But now, we could aim to turn our attention to the plight of such countries as Honduras, Chile, Peru, and Brazil. Doing so was not only a duty of citizenship, but it was also necessary for purposes of strengthening our national security.

Throughout the presidential campaign of 1960, Kennedy had focused a significant amount of attention on the problems facing Latin America—in response to Fidel Castro, in particular, but out of a concern with the hemisphere in general. These problems, he asserted, were American problems, suggesting in speech after speech that instability south of the American border could lead to a potential infiltration by the communists there. And the success of Latin American societies was, in turn, "inescapably linked to the actions and attitudes of the United States."[26]

"Hate us or like us," Kennedy speechwriter Dick Goodwin noted, "they could not leave us. Nor could we afford to ignore the reality of newly liberated desires and energies which were beginning to shatter the ruling structures of long-settled societies."[27] In other words, while the welfare of Latin American nations was tied to prevailing American attitudes, American security interests were likewise bound up with these fledgling democracies. A threat to one nation was by nature a threat to its neighbors, signaling yet again the need for a more universalized sense of interdependence.

Crafting an Alliance

Improving political and economic stability in Latin America, while also increasing the prospect of social mobility for underserved communities in the region, became a top early priority—less because of the immediacy of the problems there than because of the need to begin shifting America's focus and because of the alliance's wider symbolic importance.

In his inaugural address, Kennedy had spoken of the need for an alliance in the region. He had pledged American aid in mutual defense and support for providing the means by which the region's endemic problems could be resolved. The Alliance for Progress, "*Alianza para el Progreso*" in Spanish, was to spearhead the effort. Kennedy plainly intended Latin America to serve as a proving ground for the progressive alternatives to communism he advanced, to train the spotlight on the problem of poverty, to identify the key problems of the American neighborhood as well as the problems faced at home, and to convince others that citizens of these sister republics were in fact citizens of the same larger community who should not be "barred the way to a better life."[28]

The idea of the alliance developed on the 1960 campaign trail, and Kennedy asked Ted Sorensen to identify a potential policy phrase that could be used as effectively for the coming decade as Franklin Roosevelt's "Good Neighbor Policy" had been used years before.[29]

The choice of the phrase "Alliance for Progress," like "Peace Corps," fused military and nonmilitary imagery, thereby reinforcing Kennedy's broader suggestion that the Cold War, as understood and waged in the late fifties, had run its course and that the time had come to change direction. By conflating civilian, diplomatic, and military terminologies, Kennedy would also infuse the new political priorities with urgency, and clothe softer and more sentimental ideas in rhetorical armor. Progress was the idea of thinkers; to achieve it, America would form an alliance. Peace was the dream of poets; to achieve it, Americans would assemble into divisions and corps.

During the presidential campaign, Goodwin recalled, the theme had served a partisan purpose. "Kennedy had approved and delivered the call for a new Alliance for Progress. But that was politics, a rebuke to Republican failures in Latin America. Now we would transform the polemics of domestic combat into the official policy of the United States."[30]

At the same time, the economic and social problems in Latin America were linked to the ever-present communist dilemma. If the United States were to maintain a blind eye to communist involvement in the republics south of its border, the area could pass to the Eastern bloc by default. The aspiring countries of the Americas could not achieve self-sufficiency and confidence in isolation, and the concerns of one were the concerns of all.

The health of democratic reform in the American neighborhood would influence the spread of democracy everywhere—including the spread of democracy at home. By depersonalizing many of the issues that divided the United States and by placing them in the context of other nations' agendas, Kennedy could put forward versions of his domestic plans in other countries—in concept, Americans espoused civil rights in foreign lands, for instance; should it be different at home? Did Americans have different standards of citizenship at home than they promoted abroad? By taking issues that he saw as pertinent to the progress of the United States and projecting them outward beyond the nation's borders, Kennedy built intuitive understanding of the agenda he was advancing at home.

The Benefits of an Alliance

In practical terms, the young Kennedy presidency benefited from the alliance in meaningful ways. Early in his term, there would be new directions in U.S. foreign policy despite the ever-present Soviet threat. Visible progress would build support for the key ideas underlying such advances. Discernible success and acceptance of his ideas would tend to cement the verities at home and serve as a continual reminder of conditions there through contextual and visual associations. In the final analysis, Kennedy was expressing empathy for the poor and voicing his concern about the hazards of inaction in the face of poverty, however much the alliance was associated with a hard-line stance toward Cuba and mixed up in the politics of the Cold War.

In a memorandum "on the dilemmas of modernization" in the region, Kennedy aide Arthur Schlesinger Jr. wrote to the president, "Latin America is waiting expectantly for new initiatives in Washington.... The Inaugural Address evoked particular admiration. People are looking on [Kennedy] as a reincarnation of [Franklin Roosevelt]. To a surprising degree, the slate has been wiped clean of past neglect and error."[31] The stage was set.

Turning Rhetoric to Reality

The Alliance for Progress was formally introduced on March 13, 1961. In a White House ceremony with Latin American heads of state, Kennedy delivered a speech intended to demonstrate his commitment to democratic modernization in their countries while stimulating Congress to begin appropriating funds for his proposed program.

As in his inaugural address, Kennedy emphasized empowerment in the face of the twin struggles for peace and democracy:

> The genius of our scientists has given us the tools to bring abundance to our land, strength to our industry, and knowledge to our people. For the first time we have the capacity to strike off the remaining bonds of poverty and ignorance—to free our people for the spiritual and intellectual fulfillment which has always been the goal of our civilization.[32]

Here, Kennedy reiterated his idea of what it means to be part of a community. Societal advances are to be shared—we have obligations to one another. When we share our success, people are freed to reach their maximum potential. Civilization moves forward. Kennedy continued:

> I have called on all people of the hemisphere to join in a new Alliance for Progress—*Alianza para Progreso*—a vast cooperative effort, unparalleled in magnitude and nobility of purpose, to satisfy the basic needs of the American people for homes, work and land, health and schools—*techo, trabajo y tierra, salud y escuela.*

The alliance was intended to be a ten-year program emphasizing democratic progress. If successful, the program would bring forth a new global era, marked by the improvement of living standards, access to education, eradication of hunger, and self-sufficiency. Every nation in the Americas, therefore, could "be the master of its own revolution and its own hope and progress." The success of the program would hinge upon the efforts of the American nations themselves to "modify their social patterns so that all, and not just a privileged few, share in the fruits of the growth."

To begin these efforts, Kennedy called for the appropriation of $500 million by Congress to combat the high rates of illiteracy, to help cure the widespread diseases in many of the Latin American nations, to get rid of land taxes that kept the class system intact, and to provide new educational initiatives to assist in making new benefits available to all.

The idea of an alliance proved to be very popular. Chief Kennedy pollster Lou Harris did polling after the speech and wired Kennedy: "Public popularity has risen to perhaps record heights"; the president had higher approval ratings than Franklin Roosevelt and Dwight Eisenhower had experienced in their early days in office.[33]

It is worth noting that, as with the Peace Corps, the relative cost of the Alliance was minor: $500 million, even in 1961, did not represent a sizable portion of the national budget. More important was the basic purpose of the program and the underlying goals the president identified. Kennedy's aim was to transform attitudes, to prime people and nations for the change he sought. Mutual cooperation did not necessarily require tangible economic sacrifice. It meant recognizing that to realize one's citizenship required a certain philosophy about individual contribution; it placed emphasis on the idea that personal gain without societal growth does not advance the goals of any civilization.

Embracing This Legacy

Despite making some improvements in access to education and housing, and some attempted reforms aimed at improving corrupt tax systems in Latin America during the 1960s, the Alliance for Progress no longer exists. In the years after Kennedy died, the program received reduced funding and ultimately lost the emphasis that Kennedy had placed on it. Yet the Kennedy legacy in Latin America remains important as a symbol of the kind of mutual cooperation and common aspirations that Kennedy expressed. Individuals and nations do have areas of shared interest and concern, and therefore we should conduct ourselves in ways that invite collective effort. In the global context, this conduct should be meaningful to a new generation of leaders who have come of age in the era of globalization—when the interconnectivity among nations is immediate and self-evident.

These efforts are related to those made in connection with the Peace Corps. With the privilege of American wealth and prestige come certain responsibilities; we can use our resources to help others in ways we would want to be helped if situations were reversed. The concept on the global level is the same as on the local level: our citizenship requires us to accept a role of accountability. We must embrace the pride we feel as citizens of a great country and convert this sentiment to action.

Most people will never consider a career in the Foreign Service or other diplomatic endeavors, but those who do play an integral role in maintaining world order and increasing the contributions that America makes to achieve a safer and more hopeful world. This vital function should invite our respect, gratitude, and admiration—highlighting once again the need for each of us to consider how we are contributing to improving our society, whether in volunteering our time, choosing a certain career, supporting others who do important work, being informed about relevant issues so we can appreciate the kinds of efforts being made, or in other ways. This is how citizens support one another and embrace the ideals underpinning citizenship in Kennedy's time and today.

Photograph by Abbie Rowe, White House Photographs/John F. Kennedy Presidential Library and Museum, Boston.

During the Cuban Missile Crisis, JFK signs a quarantine order on October 23, 1962, to blockade the island and prevent Soviet ships from entering its waters. It would prove to be one of the best policy decisions JFK made.

Photograph by Cecil Stoughton, White House Photographs/John F. Kennedy Presidential Library and Museum, Boston.

JFK gives famous commencement speech at American University about peace and highlights the areas of common concern shared by Americans and Soviets alike. The speech was well received in Moscow and led to a Limited Nuclear Test Ban Treaty in August 1963.

CHAPTER 5

Challenges Abroad

"In the final analysis, our most basic common link is that we all inhabit this small planet. We all breathe the same air. We all cherish our children's futures. And we are all mortal."

—JOHN F. KENNEDY,
commencement address at American University,
June 10, 1963

AS PRESIDENT, JOHN Kennedy was responsible for managing foreign affairs, and as the most powerful citizen in the country, he needed to act in certain ways that underscored his conceptions of citizenship. In some instances, this meant advancing the idea of global citizenship in manners similar to the mission he sought at home. In other cases, it meant demanding a level of personal devotion to the ideals he promoted in ways that justified his leadership.

Certain historical episodes vividly reveal Kennedy's mission of fostering these traits and accepting responsibility as a leader. While different situations invited different responses, the paradigm of accountability Kennedy constructed was a pivotal force in approaching all of them—and it is one that still resonates today.

Early Setbacks

In his first eight months in office, Kennedy faced large-scale hurdles that frustrated many of his good intentions. These events dealt principally with the Cold War, and they tested his pragmatism and resolve considerably. They also clarified and deepened Kennedy's commitment to the ideals he had been emphasizing for some time, which over time became increasingly pronounced.

An Inherited Plan

The first and most visible failure in the early part of Kennedy's presidency was the botched Bay of Pigs invasion in April 1961. Shortly before his inauguration, Kennedy had been briefed by Dwight Eisenhower on a planned military operation that had been afoot for some time: CIA-trained Cuban exiles would assault Fidel Castro's communist Cuba, seeking to overthrow the government and spur a revolution. By the time JFK became president, the training of Cuban émigrés had been well underway, and pressure from the CIA and military leaders mounted on Kennedy to authorize the invasion. "The momentum behind the effort seemed almost unstoppable," the historian Alan Brinkley noted. "Kennedy remained uncertain about the likelihood of success, but he tentatively agreed to move forward because [CIA chief] Allen Dulles, his deputy Richard Bissell, and other CIA officers seemed so confident."[1]

Much was at stake, and Kennedy was well aware of the risks. A failed invasion so early in his presidency would seriously jeopardize efforts at waging the Cold War; similarly, he would look ineffectual at home, justifying campaign criticisms leveled by Richard Nixon relating to Kennedy's inexperience. The pressure continued to build.

CIA memos described precise plans that the exiles would follow in order to succeed. The battle would begin in the air, the plan went, with planes flying over the island and bombing Castro's defenses, immediately followed by an amphibious attack on Cuban shores at the Bay of Pigs. The surprise assault would ignite a groundswell of support among locals sympathetic to the exiles, dramatically increasing the size of the attacking force and making Castro's defense of the island more tenuous. In addition, the United States would covertly supply the troops with sophisticated weaponry to conduct the operation. The planning seemed strong, and the CIA insisted that the prospects of success were good. Failure to remove Castro was a riskier threat to American security than taking a chance at the Bay of Pigs, or so the thinking went.

Yet the plan had opponents. Adlai Stevenson, now ambassador to the United Nations, and Secretary of State Dean Rusk were skeptical. The Joint Chiefs of Staff questioned the efficacy of the plan. William Fulbright, the powerful chairman of the Senate Foreign Relations Committee, opposed it—isn't this the same kind of covert activity for which the United States regularly criticized its Cold War adversary? he wondered.[2]

Kennedy was hesitant. He trusted his military advisers; after all, weren't these the smartest military minds in the world? On the other hand, the plan never truly sat well with him—it had been hatched while Eisenhower was in office, and he had not had a hand in planning the attack or supervising the training.

After lengthy deliberations, Kennedy provided the authorization that the CIA sought—but he made clear that no American troops could be used to reinforce the attack or save the exiles if things went poorly: it was not to be seen as sponsored by the United States.

On April 17, 1961, approximately 1,300 of the American-trained exiles stormed the island. But at the outset, there were problems. Weather conditions were unfavorable, causing delays in the landing of the troops and delays in transporting the munitions. Worse, there were intelligence leaks—Castro's troops learned that an invasion was in motion, and the highly strategic element of surprise was lost. Worse still, the popular uprising predicted by the CIA never occurred. Without the authority to provide American military support, the CIA—thinking Kennedy would change his mind about using American troops once the battle was underway—watched the operation fail before its eyes. The debacle included the fatalities of four American pilots and the imprisonment of some CIA operatives clandestinely positioned on the island, in contravention of the president's orders. The surviving exiles were imprisoned, and some were tortured.

As if matters could not worsen, it quickly became apparent to Cuba and the rest of the world that America had aided in the failed attempt. Kennedy's reputation in the international arena diminished significantly, especially given his recent inaugural call to let both sides "begin anew." After promising negotiation and compromise, Kennedy had broken his word. It was an unmitigated disaster.

Lessons Learned

The fiasco upset Kennedy deeply, spurring a permanent distaste in him not only toward the small island ninety miles off the coast of Florida, but also toward the CIA and the military apparatus generally. Though he could have blamed the defeat on his advisers or Eisenhower or the ineffectual Cuban exiles, Kennedy endeavored to do two things: he would accept responsibility for his actions—an obligation he believed all citizens had—and he would try to learn from the experience—another element of the quest for self-improvement that defined his mission.

On April 21, Kennedy held a news conference and offered what in reality was a rare presidential concession, in which he accepted personal responsibility for the failure: "There's an old saying that victory has 100 fathers and defeat is an orphan.... I'm the responsible officer of the government," Kennedy maintained.[3]

In addition to embracing his responsibilities, he learned a vital lesson in self-confidence. While Kennedy valued the insights of his advisers, he understood the need to trust his instincts and rely on his own judgment. On a certain level, this realization highlights an important extract of Kennedy's conception of citizenship: each individual is expected to take ownership of his or her own life and not let others make decisions on their behalf. As citizens, we have this duty.

Remarkably, in the wake of his admission of culpability, Kennedy's approval rating skyrocketed to 83 percent.[4] This dramatic increase is revealing of the prism through which the American public viewed the events. Despite the catastrophe that had transpired on Kennedy's orders, citizens seemed more drawn to his apparent apology for making a mistake than they were upset with the mistake itself. This reaction reveals the public's craving for honest dialogue with its leaders. How rare, it seemed to Americans, that a public official—let alone the president they had elected just months earlier—did not put a political "spin" on an event that reflected poorly on his leadership. It was actually endearing. People empathized with Kennedy; he was human, like everyone else; he made mistakes, and people could relate to him.

Public officials who make mistakes today could learn from this refreshing dose of humility. And if the public response to Kennedy's candor illustrates what can happen, then in some cases it might not actually be bad politics either. A key highlight here is that regular and honest discourse with elected officials is an expectation voters rightfully have. People want to hear about the issues confronting the nation. They also want to learn how their elected leaders envision meeting these issues so they can understand what the path forward will look like—they want to see how politics will shape policy. This expectation is an obligation of citizenship to which all leaders accede.

More recently, President Obama apparently learned a similar lesson. In looking back at his first term during a July 2012 interview with CBS *This Morning* anchor Charlie Rose, Obama noted that "[t]he mistake of my first term . . . was thinking that this job was just about getting the policy right. And that's important. But the nature of this office is also to tell a story to the American people that gives them a sense of unity and purpose and optimism, especially during tough times."[5] In other words, the implementation of policy goes hand in hand with the ability to effectively communicate a vision to move the nation forward.

Another message here is that to admit a mistake does not equate to showing weakness. Rather, the opposite is often true: conceding an error demonstrates one's confidence in his ability to continue leading while moving forward. And in demonstrating to the public that a leader is willing to acknowledge his mistakes, the leader may find the public more willing to place trust in him or her in the future.

Each of these lessons is not unrelated to the wider themes of civic obligation and public betterment. An open and cohesive discourse based upon mutual trust invites a more productive general dialogue to advance collective goals.

A Summit in Vienna

In his special message to Congress in May 1961, Kennedy noted that he would soon be meeting with Nikita Khrushchev for "a personal exchange of views."[6] The anticipated summit would take place in Vienna, Austria, in early June. Hampered by the failed Bay of Pigs invasion, Kennedy sought new understandings about the Cold War, understandings about potential points of tension, and, hopefully, understandings about potential areas of cooperation.

The summit would cover a wide range of issues; the most important was the future of Germany—in particular the future of Berlin.

In the wake of World War II, Germany and Berlin were each carved into four regions and occupied by the United States, Great Britain, France, and the Soviet Union. New geopolitical questions arose: How long would this de facto partition last? Would it become formalized, and would German aspirations for a reunified state be formally forbidden as the keystone of international stability and accord? In the decades to come, the Soviet drive for recognition of a formal partition of Germany became the point at which East and West clashed most vividly.

The nature of the split country warranted discussion in Vienna. Both sides wanted to avoid war, but both sides also insisted that they were unafraid to deploy the might of their militaries in order to achieve their objectives: America wanted to defend the Berlin status quo; the Soviets wanted a permanent partition.

Berlin was indeed a flashpoint in the rivalry, but to Kennedy it also had symbolic importance. It was the city where his philosophical vision of global citizenship was most hotly contested—where one side shared his belief that individuals in any state were part of the larger global community with certain shared aims, obligations, and concerns, and the other rejected it. It would be the place where his vision was realized or ignored, which in turn could affect American pride at home and complicate the thrust of his goals there. Thus, victory on issues relating to Berlin was important, and so Kennedy would have to convince Khrushchev that the ideals he espoused could offer workable solutions to the challenges posed by the divided city—including Western access to it and the need to avoid armed conflict—amidst the growing ideological struggle.

The leaders met in the American Embassy in Vienna, and the discussion quickly became heated. Khrushchev admonished Kennedy for what he perceived to be a series of American actions that caused the tension between the superpowers. Kennedy made clear that his objective was to find ways to consolidate a peace between the two nations, stating that he believed it was the Soviets who were threatening the peace.

Near the end of the first day of meetings, Khrushchev noted the need to discuss Berlin. The Soviets wanted to sign a peace treaty with the German Democratic Republic (GDR), or East Germany, formally recognizing this state, thereby cementing the geographic and metaphorical partition. Western access to the western portions of Berlin, Khrushchev maintained, would be a matter the Allies would have to work out with the GDR, hence the required diplomatic recognition of the GDR. Therein lay the rub.

Khrushchev asserted that America could not prevent the Soviet Union from staging a ceremony to sign a peace treaty with the GDR.

Subsequent violations of such sovereignty would be interpreted as acts of aggression and treated accordingly. This Soviet policy, the premier warned, was "firm" and "irrevocable."[7] Khrushchev viewed this segment of the negotiations as a victory; he had laid the foundations for the Berlin Wall, and he detected in Kennedy a disinclination to interfere with anything the Soviets might attempt to do that did not involve Western rights. Khrushchev was perpetuating the climate of tensions that was certain to push the GDR further into the Soviets' corner.

By the end of the first day, the two leaders had tested each other's positions. Their discussions showed Khrushchev strongly committed to a course that would strengthen the Soviet position on Germany and Berlin, around which everything else centered. And as long as the Soviet fixation with Germany lasted, Kennedy had reason to despair about his ability to find a way out of the Cold War impasse. Kennedy had called for a fresh understanding of the concept of freedom, but he would not compromise on maintaining American support for countries threatened in Asia or Latin America, nor could he risk any questioning among America's allies of its commitment to global democracy.

To temporarily settle the issue of Germany's future, the two leaders agreed to a six-month period in which the Germans themselves could debate what course they desired. Nevertheless, Khrushchev remained staunchly determined to sign a separate peace treaty with the GDR.

That night, Kennedy carefully considered the approach to be taken the next day. Should he continue to oppose the Soviet Union in Germany and risk inducing Khrushchev's wrath? Or should he qualify his positions in the hope that Khrushchev would act prudently and seek understandings in other areas? Which approach would promote the harmony and cooperation he envisioned for a new era of collaboration centered on the themes he had been emphasizing elsewhere?

These concerns were not merely international in scope. Perceived defeats abroad could weaken Kennedy's ability to elicit the service and sacrifice he was commanding at home. His emphasis on citizenship was itself predicated on a foundation of national pride, and such pride in one's country was intricately linked to strength overseas and national prestige. Along these lines, procuring peace abroad would in fact provide a more robust platform for Kennedy to promote his values at home. With these interests in mind, Kennedy would stand strong against Khrushchev, and the next day, Kennedy made clear that America would do whatever necessary to preserve Western influence and rights in West Berlin.

Khrushchev, however, was unmoved, so Kennedy tried to steer the discussions toward larger questions relating to the international balance of power and the appropriate arena of U.S.-Soviet cooperation. Why clash over Europe? The United States would not give the Soviets formal recognition of the GDR, but the United States proposed nothing more than extending the status quo. Kennedy offered Khrushchev a proposed course along these lines: both sides would treat the balance of power in Europe as settled, an agreement the two sides might reinforce by signing a Test Ban Treaty aimed at prohibiting the testing of nuclear weapons (which would restrict other nations' efforts to develop such weapons). Elsewhere, the balance of power in the postwar world was something to be contested—through peaceful competition. The United States and the Soviet Union could fruitfully cooperate on key developmental issues—for instance, nuclear proliferation. Could the superpowers agree to disagree on certain issues, Kennedy wondered, but nonetheless recognize the critical importance in this area of common concern? Was this not an obligation of global citizenship, to seek the peaceful collaboration of rivals? Wouldn't a more dangerous planet threaten their mutual desire to improve the lives of fellow citizens of the world who were peacefully seeking help? These questions could be asked today, as well.

Thus, Kennedy supported preservation of the existing balance of power, though imperfect, as a means of adhering to the central belief with which he approached geopolitical issues: peace was possible, and he would take actions for the sake of the larger goals he pursued. While he would not give up on areas of discord, he would seek out the issues upon which consensus could be built. Such was the responsibility of the leader of a republic who was demanding sacrifice and action in other areas.

Publicly, Khrushchev called his meetings with Kennedy "a very good beginning."[8] In reality, this reflected his belief that he could manipulate Kennedy and get what he wanted in Berlin and perhaps elsewhere, notwithstanding Kennedy's push for new understandings. Yet Kennedy recognized that the détente he sought required patience and resolve, and he was determined to continue to work toward his goal—even if this meant running the risk of escalation to military action in certain contexts.

Kennedy's legacy here remains instructive in teaching that we must recognize that sometimes—often—our diplomacy is in fact imperfect, because foreign affairs itself is imperfect. Therefore the choices we make as a nation, and the priorities we identify, should reflect this reality. There is still value in seeking to focus our efforts on points of common concern as the best means of achieving peace and collective progress.

Formulating a Response

Once back in Washington, Kennedy consulted with veterans of past confrontations to assess an appropriate course to combat Khrushchev's aggression. Dean Acheson, the secretary of state under Harry Truman, was militant, advising Kennedy to meet Soviet aggression with retaliatory force. Kennedy concurred with Acheson's reasoning but sought advice from others who opposed the arms build-up, such as Adlai Stevenson, a consistent voice of restraint. Stevenson took the view that Acheson's response might be right, "but his position should be the conclusion of a process of investigation, not the beginning. He starts at a point which we should not reach until we have explored and exhausted all the alternatives."[9] At the core of Acheson's argument was the notion that "West Berlin was not a problem but a pretext."[10]

Kennedy's parallel conversations with advisers of opposing views reflect an element of his leadership style worth noting. He recognized the importance of understanding each side of an issue and wanted to ensure that, in each case, he considered the merits and deficiencies of different approaches. This enabled him to make more informed decisions that underscored a central assumption of his approach to civil discourse more generally: there is usually merit to each side of a genuine argument; therefore, it serves the collective purpose of all involved to be open-minded and listen to one another. This open-mindedness was a means of being worthy of his power. It also highlights a glaring paucity in contemporary public discourse: the need to listen to people with opposing views and acknowledge the merits of their opinions when reasonable. If our leaders—as well as each of us—did this more often, the tone of our rhetoric could gradually become less divisive, reinforcing the sense that we in fact belong to the same community.

In the case at hand, Kennedy sided with Acheson. On July 25, 1961, he delivered a televised address that presented his intention to raise the number of American security forces in Germany. Khrushchev was furious, even scolding an American diplomat for what he perceived to be a preliminary declaration of war on the U.S.S.R.[11] Was Kennedy's strategy of showing force as a means of seeking peace working? Could he create a world that was peaceful enough for its citizens to fix its many problems?

Kennedy here reinforced several key themes of his presidency: the defiance of threats was the price that free individuals paid for enjoyment of their freedoms; he would defy Khrushchev's efforts to collapse the Western position on Berlin. Yet America would not initiate hostilities, and the door to greater reasonableness would always be held open. Kennedy staked out a strong—even risky—position, but in doing so, he never closed the door to greater understanding and empathy. The courage called for in the current situation also required the intelligence to look beyond the conflict, to leave room to maneuver, to enable the Soviet leadership to reconsider its course and in time to embrace the new status quo that Kennedy was offering—one based on recognition of the vital security interests of all sides, coupled with a shift of focus away from points of confrontation and toward areas of peaceful and perhaps mutually rewarding competition.

There would be "no quick and easy solution," Kennedy noted, but if met with courage and resilience, the present crisis could be averted.[12] As it was in the individual context, courage was also a key ingredient of global citizenship. It required leaders and nations to act not out of self-interest but out of mutual—even worldwide—interest.

Roughly two weeks later, Khrushchev announced the planned construction of the most searing figurative reminder of the growing dissension between East and West: the Berlin Wall. In response, Kennedy ordered 1,500 American troops to be sent into the western city to remind West Berliners of America's commitment to the region. This decision was thus far the "most anxious moment" Kennedy faced in his handling of the Cold War, for it entailed inaction in the face of Khrushchev's actions—curtailing Western access to the eastern portions of the city.[13] Kennedy decided that no specific action should be taken to destroy the wall since it was technically legal. Yet it revealed a Soviet failure of the brand of citizenship Kennedy had been building: legality does not equate to morality, and in the international context, this idea means that leaders should strive to do not only what is legal but also what is "right." Khrushchev clearly was not.

Moving Forward

Here was Kennedy, just several months into office—despite the enthusiasm associated with his inaugural address, the new goal of landing a man on the moon, and the establishment of the Peace Corps and the Alliance for Progress—facing real setbacks indeed. The Bay of Pigs was in the past, but Khrushchev's rebuke in Vienna was still stinging, and the construction of the Berlin Wall went against everything for which Kennedy had been working.

Yet, Kennedy embraced his responsibilities by deepening his resolve and committing himself to learn from these experiences and move forward with the same aims in mind. Fortitude and grit are key components of courage, and courage would be needed to bring events back on track. Similarly, individuals needed to exhibit these traits in their personal lives by rising above challenge and adversity to be good citizens—this is why Kennedy emphasized the theme of sacrifice.

A Chance for Victory

An opportunity for redemption came the following year, when it became apparent that Soviet missiles were under construction in Cuba and would soon become operational. At the Bay of Pigs and again when he decided to pursue an arms build-up in the wake of Vienna, Kennedy had received hawkish advice from his military advisers. He was never quite comfortable with the counsel in either instance, and he would find himself in similar territory this time again. Had he learned from previous missteps? If he could achieve some sort of victory, could he muster the strength and ingenuity to build upon it? All these related to the symbolic questions he was concurrently asking the American people: Were they imprisoned by their past? Could they gather the energy and courage to face difficult questions? The world would find out Kennedy's answers soon enough.

Heading Toward Another Crisis

In the wake of the Bay of Pigs invasion, Khrushchev sought to establish both a defensive military position in Cuba and a potential base of attack against the United States. To this end, he sent medium-range missiles to the island, where they could be installed within range of major U.S. cities. Such a maneuver "represented the supreme Soviet probe of American intentions. No doubt a 'total victory' faction in Moscow had long been denouncing the government's 'no-win' policy," all this "because the Americans were too rich or soft or liberal to fight."[14]

Shipments of Soviet supplies, including missiles and fighter planes, reached Cuba by midsummer 1962. By September 2, the Soviets had "publicly acknowledged for the first time that they were sending 'armaments' and technical advisers to Cuba."[15] Meanwhile, Anatoly Dobrynin, the Soviet ambassador to the United States, assured the administration that Khrushchev had no intention of installing offensive weapons in Cuba. Rather, they were a means of defense for a political ally that happened to be off the coast of the United States. Four days later, Dobrynin read Kennedy aide Ted Sorensen a message from Khrushchev, reiterating that the armaments to be constructed in Cuba were purely defensive in nature.[16]

Though the Cold War existed on many fronts, none was closer in proximity than—and none threatened American security as much as—Soviet missiles stationed in Cuba. The development of the missiles and powerful aircraft in Cuba would enable the Soviets to wage an all-out nuclear war with America in any region of the world.

In early October 1962, photographs taken by American military aircraft detected the construction of the missile sites in Cuba. Immediate action was required, and time was of the essence. Failure to prevent the construction sites from becoming operational would compromise American security interests at home and abroad. Preventing their development, however, could result in nuclear war. To complicate matters further, Soviet ships were en route to Cuba to aid in the construction of the missile sites.

McGeorge Bundy, Kennedy's national security adviser, alerted the president to the missile construction on the morning of October 15, 1962. As Arthur Schlesinger Jr. noted, Kennedy was "furious." After all, "[I]f Khrushchev could pull this after all his protestations and denials, how could he ever be trusted on anything?"[17]

Kennedy asked Bundy to convene a meeting with all of his chief advisers in the Cabinet Room. This request demonstrated Kennedy's commitment to certain principles of leadership: that to solve a crisis, a leader should utilize all available resources and surround himself with individuals who possess different kinds of expertise so he can consider diverse perspectives and make the most informed decision possible. Those present, some fifteen men, became part of what would be dubbed the Executive Committee of the National Security Council, or "ExCom."

Weighing His Options

A wide range of alternatives was considered. At first, debate centered on whether the president should simply wait, see how events developed, and assess in real time what action might be needed or whether an air strike would be appropriate to destroy the missile sites.

Inaction, Kennedy soon decided, was not an option. The United States could not permit the missile sites to become operational. But an air strike? Such a move would be definitive and immediate, sending a strong message to the Kremlin. Yet it would also be an unambiguous act of war, and there was ample reason not to take this course: first, faced with similar pressure, Khrushchev could not permit such an attack to go unpunished, meaning that the escalation to full-scale war would occur rapidly. In addition, Khrushchev would gain political ground. If the Americans attacked Cuba, he could legitimately claim a defensive position on behalf of his ally. This claim would open the door to further Soviet aggression. No, a preemptive American attack could not be waged.

In observing the debate, Robert Kennedy passed a note to the president that reflected the immense pressure they felt: "I now know how Tojo [a World War II Japanese general] felt when he was planning Pearl Harbor." The pressure was immeasurable. "This sort of first strike on a small neighbor," Thomas Reeves observed, "could blacken the reputation of the United States permanently, especially in Latin America," where there had been a burgeoning spirit of cooperation.[18] The interconnectedness of these issues, in other words, was especially ripe.

With the prospects of an air strike or a land invasion ruled out, ExCom was forced to consider other options. Organizing diplomatic pressures was considered, but such measures were soon ruled out, too, in fear that they were not significant enough to dissuade Khrushchev from taking further action. Nor would such maneuvers have any effect on the soon-to-be-operational missile sites already on the island. Yet there remained another alternative: a naval blockade.

In this plan, American battleships would surround the island, preventing the Soviets from providing military assistance to Cuba. Though it would heighten the risk of confrontation, the Soviets would be forced to choose between engaging the American ships and re-treating. Kennedy liked the idea of putting the pressure on the Soviets, but a quarantine was still risky—however peaceful, the decision to deploy American ships would nonetheless be the first public military action taken by either side since news of the missiles had been learned. Hence, Kennedy remained cautious and hesitant.

There were other drawbacks to consider concerning the blockade. In addition to the dilemma of how the Soviets would react to the deci-sion, there was fear of how the rest of the world would interpret the surrounding of Cuba by American ships without going through the proper diplomatic channels. There were also fears about the strategic value of the action itself, given the tightening time period and the un-certainty associated with what Khrushchev's countermoves might be. Ted Sorensen recalled the quandary of moving ahead:

> [I]t offered a prolonged and agonizing approach, uncertain in its effect, indefinite in its duration, enabling the missiles to become op-erational, subjecting us to counterthreats from Khrushchev, giving him a propaganda advantage, stirring fears and protests and pickets all over the world, causing Latin-American governments to fall, permitting Castro to announce that he would execute two Bay of Pigs prisoners for each day it continued, encouraging...our allies to bring pressure for talks, and in all these ways making more difficult a subsequent air strike if the missiles remained.[19]

Yet despite all the ramifications of this scenario, Moscow faced a similar predicament. If the Soviet ships did not heed the warning of the blockade, then their continued movement toward the American ships could be interpreted as an act of Soviet aggression.

In spite of the potential drawback of having to fire the first shot, ExCom advised Kennedy that the blockade would force Khrushchev to take *some* action. Either he would ignore the blockade and order his ships to continue on their intended course, or he would order his ships to abort their mission. It would be the Soviets who would begin a war.

Briefing the Nation

On October 22, 1962, in the second week of the crisis, Kennedy briefed the nation in a televised address. "This government, as promised," he declared, "has maintained the closest surveillance of the Soviet military buildup on the island of Cuba."[20] Irrefutable evidence had confirmed the fact that there were offensive missile sites in Cuba, he said, and he had instructed American intelligence to step up the level of surveillance there to learn the capabilities of the weapons.

He then alerted the American people to the dangers that had plagued him for a full week. America and the world could not tolerate "deliberate deception and offensive threats on the part of any nation, large or small. We no longer live in a world where only the actual firing of weapons represents a sufficient challenge to a nation's security to constitute maximum peril," he stated. Weapons were so advanced that any "substantially increased possibility of their use" was a serious threat to peace.

Kennedy propounded a theme learned the hard way decades earlier: "The 1930s taught us a clear lesson: aggressive conduct, if allowed to go unchecked and unchallenged, ultimately leads to war....Our unswerving objective, therefore, must be to prevent the use of these missiles against this or any other country, and to secure their withdrawal or elimination from the Western Hemisphere." In the modern context, similar concerns abound regarding Iran and North Korea and what preemptive actions may be appropriate.

Almost at War

Though some advisers still pushed for a military strike, Kennedy determined that the naval blockade was the best course of action. In the meantime, many of the missiles in Cuba became operational. And to make matters worse, a U.S. spy plane was shot down over Cuba, killing the pilot and prompting renewed debate as to what retaliation might be appropriate, if any. Kennedy considered his options. Some advisers insisted on an immediate military response; others counseled more caution. Evidence indicates that he remained resolute and collected. Avoiding war continued to be his objective, and he decided that he had to look past the first death of the crisis and consider the larger implications of a military strike.

This critical preliminary decision is often overlooked in historical accounts. The Soviets were aware that the spy plane had been shot down. Kennedy's decision not to pursue immediate retaliatory action could have been interpreted as weakness by an adversary that seemed determined to push the conflict forward at any cost. Moreover, he had pugnacious military advisers seeking to convince him that he had no choice but to retaliate, to do *something* to show that he was ready for armed confrontation if necessary. After all, an American had been killed. But Kennedy had learned to trust his instincts and put aside the potential political consequences—as had the individuals he featured in *Profiles in Courage*—and in this case, the risk of escalating the conflict at this point was too great. He would proceed with the blockade as planned.

The blockade went into effect on the morning of October 24. Armed with nuclear weapons, bombers and submarines positioned themselves for the order to fire on the approaching Soviet ships. It was time to wait. The following day, the Soviet ships neared the blockade, and the point of confrontation grew imminent. With each passing moment, tensions rapidly increased to nearly intolerable levels. Robert Kennedy later observed that those "few minutes were the time of greatest worry by the President. His hand went up to his face and covered his mouth and he closed his fist. His eyes were tense, almost gray, and we just stared at each other across the table."[21]

At last, a move was made. To Kennedy's and the world's great relief, Khrushchev ordered the ships to turn around and move away from Cuba. The immediate crisis had been averted, but concerns lingered: offensive missiles still remained in Cuba.

Through significant diplomatic maneuvering, Kennedy used back-channel negotiations to communicate confidentially with Khrushchev in a series of tense exchanges. Finally, a deal was reached. In exchange for America not invading Cuba, the Soviet Union would remove all of its missiles from the island. Khrushchev could claim a political victory at home in preventing an American invasion of the Soviets' ally, Cuba; Kennedy could do the same in avoiding nuclear war. Months later, amid less fanfare, and as part of the deal, the United States would also remove certain Jupiter missiles located in Turkey.

It was a major victory for Kennedy. Polls conducted just after the crisis revealed that the president's popularity had soared again. The Bay of Pigs was now a distant remembrance, and Kennedy had displayed the kind of presidential leadership Americans search for when they go to the polls.

Kennedy's actions in the wake of the missile crisis remain instructive. It is not enough merely to be satisfied with our victories—we need to build upon them and use them as a foundation for other advances and new good deeds. This is how the work of one generation adds to the work of previous ones, cumulatively creating a better and more prosperous nation. With his successful handling of the crisis behind him, Kennedy endeavored to do just this. He recognized that there was an opportunity to redefine the Cold War and redirect actions toward points of mutual concern. And if he could achieve this understanding with the Soviets, then surely similar goals could be achieved in America, too.

Twenty-one months into his presidency—after nearly two years of serious dangers and uncertainty, after Kennedy's steadfast efforts on many fronts to inculcate new approaches and thinking, and after all the risks taken that were now justified—the Soviets had finally accepted his offer of détente. This was the pinnacle of his statesmanship to date; it had been a long time coming.

The Quest for Peace

In the postwar period, Truman and Eisenhower had spent more time focused on Cold War and international policy issues than on domestic issues. Kennedy sought to flip the order of these two priorities without compromising international commitments and global diplomacy. The missile crisis had tested Kennedy's pragmatism and his ability to lead during a time of crisis. It also clarified and helped define his vision for establishing a post–Cold War world. This vision would be borne out in different ways, but what became clear to Kennedy after the Cuban crisis was that the opportunity to redefine U.S.-Soviet relations did in fact exist—he had bested the Soviets, so he was empowered to seek peace and a safer world. Such a new world required new strategies and rhetoric to meet the challenges of old problems, just as the New Frontier itself was built on efforts to reframe and reassess public life.

In the early months of 1963, Kennedy no doubt devoted much time and energy to formulating these new strategies. Up until this point, his rhetoric and actions had primed an expectant nation and world for changes that would reshape geopolitical understandings of conflict around points of mutual interest and interdependence. With the crisis in Cuba averted, the stage was set for Kennedy to make his move. By June 1963, the moment had arrived, and a speech at American University was the scene of its arrival. The address would center on support for world peace. In preparing the address, Kennedy asked his advisers to take inventory on U.S.-Soviet relations and other outstanding concerns on the international scene. The speech would contain the announcement—made simultaneously in Moscow and London—of final three-way talks to adopt a Test Ban Treaty later that summer, a major step toward mutual cooperation that had seemed impossible just months earlier amidst the missile crisis.

His speech to the students that summer day is particularly revealing of how Kennedy's notions of citizenship had evolved to date, including a dramatic intersection between the underlying ideals of his promotion of democracy at home and abroad. These conceptions offer a pivotal understanding of the aims Kennedy was seeking to foster as he shifted his agenda away from managing global ideological discord and toward rebuilding a nation of responsible and virtuous citizens. Of more universal import, they are the same themes that can guide a new generation in new quests for progress and collective action for the common good.

Seeking a New World Order

The commencement speech presented a series of workable agreements already achieved with the Soviets—thus constituting an end of the confrontational era of the Cold War in principle, setting up an immediate segue into a speech that he would deliver the following evening from the White House sketching the underlying provisions of an urgently needed bill to address the long-neglected question of civil rights. In its most basic sense, Kennedy's speech at American University presented the Cold War—subject to acceptance and understanding on the part of Americans—as "solved" and the civil rights question essentially as "unsolved." Hence, June 1963 would mark the first moment in decades that domestic issues would be at the forefront of an American president's agenda—and the precepts of citizenship would be crucial to the struggle for equality.

Early in the speech to the students, Kennedy reiterated his demand for good citizenship by connecting the university's mission to public service: "Every man sent out from a university should be a man of his nation as well as a man of his time, and I am confident that the men and women who carry the honor of graduating from this institution will continue to give from their lives, from their talents, a high measure of public service and public support."[22] Kennedy laid the foundation for his deeper messages by rehearsing America's responsibilities and again affirming that the dangers in the world required vigilance, arms, and steadfastness. His topic was peace:

> What kind of a peace do I mean? And what kind of a peace do we seek? Not a Pax Americana enforced on the world by American weapons of war. Not the peace of the grave or the security of the slave. I am talking about genuine peace, the kind of peace that makes life on Earth worth living, the kind that enables men and nations to grow and to hope and build a better life for their children—not merely peace for Americans, but peace for all men and women—not merely peace in our time but peace in all time.

The two questions in this passage alert the audience to their role in achieving the goals to which Kennedy's vision aspired, and they define the notion of peace in important ways. Like progress, peace describes a journey toward something better, and to achieve it requires inward qualities that enable individuals and nations to live in peace. Kennedy's interrogatory "What kind of a peace do we seek?" placed his audience in the same position as himself as leader—inviting them to consider the word, to invest it with meaning, to evaluate the concept as he was evaluating it. A speaker who gives his audience a similar stake in the battle fuses leadership within them, in this case defining peace as sharing the responsibility and mutual respect that the concept enjoins.

As he did in the inaugural address, Kennedy instructed his audience to think rationally and in new ways about the Soviet adversary, whom he knew would be listening:

I speak of peace because of the new face of war. Total war makes no sense in an age where great powers can maintain large and relatively invulnerable nuclear forces and refuse to surrender without resort to those forces. It makes no sense in an age where a single nuclear weapon contains almost ten times the explosive force delivered by all the Allied air forces in the Second World War. It makes no sense in an age when the deadly poisons produced by a nuclear exchange would be carried by wind and water and soil and seed to the far corners of the globe and to generations yet unborn.

Securing a better future, Kennedy suggested, entails a willingness to bear sacrifice and serve one's nation in the present. He continued his speech with a theme of eternal improvement. At the cornerstone of a successful society is recognition of the fact that there are always improvements to be made—that complacency is a recipe for demise. As heirs to a special legacy, people engaged in the service and sacrifice that he called forth connected the mythical past and a never-to-be-seen future, in which the work of the journey is its own reward.

Kennedy's themes now take on new immediacy. With the Cold War crisis of Cuba fresh in memory, the opportunity to build on the outcome of that event is a fleeting one. "I speak of peace, therefore, as the necessary rational end of rational men. I realize that the pursuit of peace is not as dramatic as the pursuit of war—and frequently the words of the pursuer fall on deaf ears," he declared. "But we have no more urgent task." Here, Kennedy readies the audience for a challenge that he will soon pose to the Soviet Union:

Some say that it is useless to speak of world peace or world law or world disarmament—and that it will be useless until the leaders of the Soviet Union adopt a more enlightened attitude. I hope they do. I believe we can help them do it. But I also believe that we must re-examine our own attitude—as individuals and as a nation—for our attitude is as essential as theirs. And every graduate of this school, every thoughtful citizen who despairs of war and wishes to bring peace, should begin by looking inward—by examining his own attitude toward the possibilities of peace, toward the Soviet Union, toward the course of the Cold War and toward freedom and peace here at home.

In this instant, the beam of light is turned inward. By seeking a reexamination of Americans' own views, Kennedy not only set forth a plea for peace with the Soviets, but his argument also took on the character of shared responsibility in the context of right thinking at home and improvement of ourselves.

This effort enabled him to call for what became known as the Kennedy détente—essentially the status quo of peaceful coexistence that Kennedy had offered at Vienna, rather than a victory of arms—the rational choice of rational men. The audience was being invited to consider the terms—and venue—of the tests everyone would meet and overcome in their lifetimes.

Kennedy delved into his plans for how to fashion the peace. "First: Let us examine our attitude toward peace itself. Too many of us think it is impossible. Too many think it unreal. But that is a dangerous, defeatist belief. It leads to the conclusion that war is inevitable—that mankind is doomed—that we are gripped by forces we cannot control." Here, Kennedy told his audience that, as citizens in a free world, they controlled their own destiny. The decisions they would make would have consequences—but making the right ones would build a safe and worthy bridge to the future.

"Our problems are man-made," he declared. "Therefore, they can be solved by man. And man can be as big as he wants. No problem of human destiny is beyond human beings. Man's reason and spirit have often solved the seemingly unsolvable—and we believe they can do it again." Further responsibility was placed in the hands of his fellow citizens, but it was the convincing confidence and the power of this man—and his devotion to the ideals he had been expressing for some time—that advanced his cause.

Embracing the Tenets of Citizenship

Kennedy challenged his audience to consider the views of the previous generation and to lift their sights higher. Embracing this challenge to build upon the deeds of past generations, he understood, was a key requirement for being a good citizen.

A basic component of this notion—borne out in his vision of détente—was the constant need to reappraise and question. To make progress, one—whether an individual or a nation—must continually assess the attitudes and actions that led to the current moment and then either continue along the same path or shift gears as needed to move forward. It is essential to the achievement of an improved national status.

In seeking peace, therefore, Kennedy did not reach for the unattainable, a revolution in human nature—he did not conjure magic formulas in the coming rounds of diplomacy—but rather he challenged his listeners to accept the prospect of change as a necessary step toward progress. This required a "dynamic peace—not static, [but] changing to meet the challenge of each new generation. For peace is a process—a way of solving problems."[23]

In his inaugural address, Kennedy placed himself outside and above the endemic conflicts of the day by employing the anaphora "Let both sides...." But in this speech two and a half years later, Kennedy—carrying his audience along with him—gazed down on the intractable conflicts of the day, moderating between two warring sides, prevailing in the conflict, and transcending its significance in meaning and application. Kennedy defined peace as a "process"—an indefinite projection of hope and progress into a vast unknown future.

Kennedy quoted a biblical prophecy that reflected the approach he brought to the Cold War: "The wicked flee when no man pursueth." In other words, the United States could alter the attitudes and approaches of the Soviets by not pursuing the "war" in traditional terms. By changing American attitudes toward the Cold War, Kennedy surmised, he could alter international discourse favorably, transforming the conflict in nuanced ways. Indeed, Soviet waging of the Cold War would change and help redefine a new world order with new emphasis on communal progress and interdependence—or at least peaceful competition. In his redefining of the Cold War as a quest for mutual cooperation and deeper understanding, the challenges could be re-shaped by those interests that brought the superpowers together. This reshaping, Kennedy asserted, could help erase the political boundaries man had created in favor of global appraisals of life in the twentieth century—not just in the United States or the Soviet Union, but any-where and in any age.

At its foundation, this notion laid the framework for the precepts of global citizenship in a new age marked by solidarity and shared prog-ress. "Let us not be blind to our differences," Kennedy implored, "but let us also direct attention to our common interests and to the means by which those differences can be resolved." Doing so would require new negotiations—without fear and without a fear of negotiation—with an eye toward the things that united the two sides, not a focus on belaboring those things that divided them.

"We are not here distributing blame or pointing the finger of judg-ment," he continued. To truly move forward, both sides would have to accept the past as it was—a part of history. The next chapter of world history was yet to be written—what was required was a new attitude that could shed the shields of suspicion that had marked international di-plomacy since 1945. We would do well to adopt this approach in our modern political discourse today at home and abroad. Past rivalries and past disagreements do not need to shape future ones. We can begin our public discourse anew and embrace these timeless traits of citizenship.

On Behalf of Civil Rights

In the final six paragraphs of the American University speech, Kennedy came to the key point of his address—implicit in 1961, now made ex-plicit. While the speech was predominantly about peace, Kennedy provided the audience with the appropriate context by which that harmony could be achieved. "Finally, my fellow Americans," he declared, "let us examine our attitude toward peace and freedom here at home." The question of freedom was nowhere more evident than at home, and since assuming office, the president had not yet fully and publicly dealt with the issue of civil rights.

Domestic freedom had been given a cursory mention in the inaugural address: "Americans... [are] unwilling to witness or permit the slow undoing of those human rights to which this nation has always been committed, and to which we are committed today *at home* and around the world." The words "at home" were hastily and belatedly added to send the black community a signal of the president's intentions. In this context, the words at American University were expanded to say, "The quality and spirit of our own society must justify and support our efforts abroad." This statement was crucial because it marked the first time that a U.S. president fully and unrepentantly advanced the idea that America's leadership in the world was at risk so long as her values were at risk "at home."

The struggle for an improved America with full equality must be brought into the lives of all American citizens, he said. "We must show it in the dedication of our own lives—as many of you who are graduating today will have a unique opportunity to do." He continued: "Wherever we are, we must all, in our daily lives, live up to the age-old faith that peace and freedom walk together. In too many of our cities today, the peace is not secure because the freedom is incomplete."

Suddenly "peace" was a holistic idea that embraced Americans and everyone in the same way. His choice of the word "incomplete" was noteworthy because it suggested that progress had been made toward its completion but that more work was needed. Hence, the fundamental theme of Kennedy's speech and his presidency is revealed: equality, based on the foundation of citizenship. Kennedy's characterization of peace as "the most important topic on Earth," and a lack of universal freedom as the reason why peace had not been achieved, alerted the audience that at the root of many problems is the vast inequality experienced within America. Therefore, it is the freedom of *American* citizens that represents "the most important topic on Earth," because it is *this* freedom—this equality—that makes peace possible.

Forecasting the civil rights speech to come the next night, Kennedy bluntly stated, "It is the responsibility of the executive branch at all levels of government—local, state, and national—to provide and protect that freedom for all of our citizens by all means within their authority...the responsibility of the legislative branch at all levels...where that authority is not now adequate, to make it adequate...the responsibility of all citizens in all sections of this country to respect the rights of all others and to respect the law of the land." As he emphatically defined equality as the concern of government, all present were encouraged to join in.

"All this is not unrelated to world peace," he concluded. "'When a man's ways please the Lord,' the scriptures tell us, 'he maketh even his enemies to be at peace with him.' And is not peace, in the last analysis, basically a matter of human rights—the right to live out our lives without fear of devastation—the right to breathe air as nature provided it—the right of future generations to a healthy existence?"

Kennedy's biblical reference lent moral weight to a message that encapsulated his entire argument. Were American ways not being judged? Was the key to peace not the "inner peace" that Americans might achieve when their ways became pleasing to the Lord who would then maketh even their enemies to be at peace? Through Kennedy's citation of scripture, and his eloquent peace-making oration, the central challenge became universal, reinforced by his immortal words: "For in the final analysis...we all inhabit this small planet. We all breathe the same air. We all cherish our children's futures. And we are all mortal."

Even the Soviets were moved by his address. Khrushchev's government broadcast a translated version of the entire speech, and the government-controlled press reprinted it in its newspapers. The Soviets had indeed accepted Kennedy's offer of peace.

Off to Berlin

On the heels of his détente speech and a landmark civil rights address— now that he had redefined certain global understandings—Kennedy traveled to Germany to hold up to the world the true meanings of the Berlin Wall and what it implied about the two sides of the Cold War. Kennedy's efforts were not necessarily intended to embarrass the Soviet Union; rather, they were directed at the more fundamental aim of drawing contrast between the superpowers so that the universal appeals Kennedy voiced could be assessed more favorably by open minds. In other words, Kennedy sought to present his brand of world citizenship to demonstrate American worthiness in the new détente of peaceful competition.

At his first stop in Bonn, Germany, he reaffirmed American commitment to the region. "Your liberty is our liberty," he declared, "and any attack on your soil is an attack upon our own.... The U.S. will risk its cities to defend yours because we need your freedom to protect ours."[24] He was suggesting that we are all citizens of the world.

After four hours of touring the divided city of West Berlin, including a visit to the wall, Kennedy spoke on a large platform to a massive crowd estimated to represent two-thirds of the city's entire population.[25] "Two thousand years ago," Kennedy proclaimed, "the proudest boast was *'civis Romanus sum'* [I am a Roman citizen]. Today, in the world of freedom, the proudest boast is *'Ich bin ein Berliner'* [I am a Berliner]."[26]

Kennedy then proceeded to place the battles of the Cold War in the context of the partitioned city of Berlin:

There are many people in the world who really don't understand, or say they don't, what is the great issue between the free world and the Communist world. Let them come to Berlin.

There are some who say that communism is the wave of the future. Let them come to Berlin.

And there are some who say in Europe and elsewhere we can work with the Communists. Let *them* come to Berlin.

And there are even a few who say that it's true that communism is an evil system, but it permits us to make economic progress. *Lass' sie nach Berlin kommen*. Let *them* come to Berlin.

The crowd roared its approval. With each repetition, Kennedy grew more emotional. "Freedom has many difficulties, and democracy is not perfect, but we have never had to put a wall up to keep our people in," he continued.

"While the wall is the most obvious and vivid demonstration of the failures of the communist system, for all the world to see, we take no satisfaction in it, for it is...an offense against humanity." Again, the juxtaposition of the two systems that the wall and the city so starkly provided is apparent—the contrast that had defined the two decades of his political life and the memories of most present.

"You live in a defended island of freedom, but your life is part of the main," Kennedy continued. "So let me ask you...to lift your eyes beyond the dangers of today, to the hopes of tomorrow, beyond the freedom merely of this city of Berlin...to the advance of freedom everywhere." We are all connected, Kennedy instructs.

Then came a hallmark of his political thought: "Freedom is indivisible, and when one man is enslaved, all are not free." This central facet of citizenship—what happens to one human being affects all others—served as a focal point of his civil rights rhetoric, which he would be expressing within hours. When the freedom of others is impinged, we must act for the dual purposes of freeing a fellow citizen and securing our own freedom. We belong to a wider community, he implies again. We share the fate of those in Berlin, Kennedy suggests, and therefore we are all the same—boundaries and differences are

JFK delivers his renowned "Ich bin ein Berliner" speech, capping a historic visit to Germany.

invisible in this regard. We are all citizens of the world; we are one civilization.

Kennedy's Berlin speech was an epitaph for an era and the beginning of a new one. Dying was the old era of superpower confrontations and brinkmanship over Germany; dawning was a détente in Europe and a new, if not better, Cold War, one marked less by international tension and war, and more by the competition between the major powers as models of future progress.

Berlin defined the attractive difference that favored the West; Berlin also held the key to understanding the dynamics of democracy. The West was more desirable because it offered protections and individual freedom, and in turn, these protections and freedoms made the West more prosperous. Liberty was critical, as were the courage and determination necessary to defend it for Germans and Americans alike.

Kennedy's Berlin speech would become a standard of sorts for other presidential rhetoric. Standing before the Brandenburg Gate, separating East and West Berlin, in 1987, President Ronald Reagan spoke of Kennedy's visit and adopted his use of German to underscore a basic point. "I join you...[in] this unalterable belief: *Es gibt nur ein Berlin* [there is only one Berlin]."[27] Later in the speech, he famously challenged General Secretary Mikhail Gorbachev: "Come here to this gate! Mr. Gorbachev, open this gate! Mr. Gorbachev, tear down this wall!"

In the aftermath of the Oklahoma City bombing, Bill Clinton said in his April 23, 1995, speech: "If anybody thinks that Americans are mostly mean and selfish, they ought to come to Oklahoma. If anybody thinks Americans have lost the capacity for love and caring and courage, they ought to come to Oklahoma."[28] The lines suggested that Clinton had looked to Kennedy's Berlin speech for inspiration. Similarly, on the 2008 campaign trail, Barack Obama visited the German capital, attracting enormous crowds and evoking Kennedy's visit in a speech in which he reminded his audience: "This city, of all cities, knows the dream of freedom."[29] Such was the power of Berlin.

The salient point in understanding these events is to observe the universality of the themes Kennedy was advancing as part of his doctrine of citizenship. No matter the specifics, certain truths remained: the pursuit of peace was worth almost any price and could not be sacrificed; only in working together to identify solutions to common challenges could men and nations maximize their potential in the quest for a more enlightened future. In short, Kennedy suggested, man has the ability to solve man-made problems, and nothing is intractable when individuals and nations focus on what unites them rather than on what divides them.

This reasoning could be applied in other contexts at home, as well. It was time to look inward.

The Kennedys transformed Washington into a hub not only of political preeminence, but also of cultural appreciation. At JFK's invitation, famed cellist Pablo Casals performs at the White House on November 13, 1961. *Photograph by Robert Knudsen, White House Photographs/John F. Kennedy Presidential Library and Museum, Boston.*

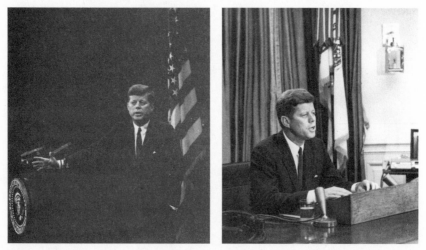

ABOVE LEFT: JFK holds a press conference in which he lambasts steel executives for ignoring the spirit of citizenship he aimed to foster. In return for enjoying the fruits of private enterprise, Kennedy said, citizens must also accept certain public responsibilities. *Photograph by Abbie Rowe, White House Photographs/John F. Kennedy Presidential Library and Museum, Boston.* ABOVE RIGHT: JFK gives a landmark televised address to the nation, declaring that civil rights is "a moral issue. It is as old as the scriptures and is as clear as the American Constitution." *Photograph by Abbie Rowe, White House Photographs/John F. Kennedy Presidential Library and Museum, Boston.*

CHAPTER 6

On the Homefront

"We face, therefore, a moral crisis as a country and as a people. It cannot be met by repressive police action. It cannot be left to increased demonstrations in the streets. It cannot be quieted by token moves or talk. It is time to act in the Congress, in your state and local legislative body and, above all, in all of our daily lives."

—JOHN F. KENNEDY,
civil rights address, June 11, 1963

WITH CUBA BEHIND him and Cold War reappraisals in motion, John Kennedy could direct his efforts elsewhere. The civil rights movement was on the horizon, and the impetus for real change had been brewing; the speech at American University had signaled the direction in which he would move. Meanwhile, Kennedy had been advancing the tenets of citizenship in the public at large, methodically injecting his views on the subject into his speeches and actions. The quest for civil rights required an understanding of each individual's role in society, just as reaching accords with the Soviets required introspection and critical thought. Similarly, what kind of society America could have was dependent upon the values it cherished and the kind of traits it promoted. To these ends, Kennedy needed not only to define what it meant to be a good citizen—a pioneer in the New Frontier—but also to teach how the good citizen's actions could benefit all.

Certain events of his presidency afforded Kennedy the chance to expound upon these themes. The so-called steel crisis highlighted in sharp contrast the president's vision for a better America with that perceived to be held by certain others. His unique promotion of the arts raised the profile of an underappreciated field that served to reinforce his conceptions of citizenship and his image of what America would look like when it lived up to its potential. The coming sequence of events in Mississippi and Alabama would require immediate and decisive presidential action, bringing forth in Kennedy a rare emotion that guided arguably his best moments as president. All these were not unrelated. Advances in one area could be used to push forward movement in others; they were all part of the same vision of a better and more just world.

The Steel Crisis

JFK's conception of the citizen is apparent and well-defined in many of his speeches. Yet for every example of citizenship that he extolled, there were counterexamples of citizenship responsibilities declined. For these situations, Kennedy reserved a special wrath, as the steel crisis of 1962 attests—an episode that vividly highlights the contrast between the ideals Kennedy fostered and the perspectives he sought to change.

Fighting Inflation

Kennedy became president amidst an economic recession, but by his second year in office, the economic tides had turned and the country was on its way to recovery. In January 1962, the Council of Economic Advisers announced a growing concern about inflation and suggested that, in order to serve the public interest, industry should grant workers only small wage increases, if any. Anti-inflationary measures, such as controlling prices, preventing monopolies from dominating industries, and preventing labor disputes were all among the efforts of the Kennedy administration's plan for economic recovery. As the historian Thomas Reeves noted, tantamount to this plan was the role played by the steel industry, for "an accurate epigram" was this: "as goes steel, so goes inflation."[1]

In the ensuing months, steel industry leaders met with representatives of the steel workers under the auspices of Kennedy and the secretary of labor, Arthur Goldberg. The president faced the difficult task of seeking to restrain the wage demands of the labor union, a complicated maneuver for a politician who relied so heavily on labor's electoral support (which he would need again in the looming election of 1964). How unfamiliar this concept sounds—a politician putting aside political concerns so he could do what he felt was right for the country.

Kennedy sent a letter to the United Steelworkers' president, David J. McDonald, that was reprinted in the 1962 *Economic Report*. The letter maintained the president's position on the matter that reflected his desire to secure progressive benefits for all parties involved. Wage increases, Kennedy submitted, could only be realized in the event of increased productivity (and thus, increased industry profits). And the president's plan worked both ways. If the workers were willing to cease their demands for increased wages, so, too, would steel executives be expected to drop their threat of increasing industry prices in order to prevent inflation.

The negotiations orchestrated by the president resulted in an agreement by both sides that wages would be frozen for an entire year, but that there would be a slight increase of 2.5 percent in fringe benefits for the workers (consistent with the growth in industry productivity). The workers' capitulation to the demands of the president and the industry executives was enough for Kennedy to assume that there would be no price increase. As the scholar John Murphy observed, "[Kennedy] and his advisors celebrated, sure that they had slain the inflation dragon in its cradle."[2] But this was not to be; a failure on the part of steel executives to exercise the responsibilities of citizenship would incur the indignation of a president dedicated to the promotion of such principles.

An Unexpected Response

Four days after the steelworkers had signed the contract dropping their demands for increased wages, Roger Blough, the president of United States Steel, the industry giant, paid Kennedy a visit in the Oval Office. To Kennedy's great surprise and unmitigated anger, Blough delivered to the president a soon-to-be-released press statement declaring a 3.5 percent across-the-board price increase in direct contravention of the agreement; Kennedy could not believe what he read.

Kennedy stood up from his desk and unleashed a series of angry remarks toward Blough, alerting the steel executive that he had "made a terrible mistake" by betraying him. Upon Blough's departure, Kennedy telephoned McDonald and told him, "Dave, you've been screwed, and I've been screwed."[3] A remark from the president was deliberately slipped to the press to reveal the intensity of his fury: "My father always told me that all businessmen were sons-of-bitches, but I never believed it till now."[4] Kennedy would later claim to have been misquoted, but regardless, the message had been sent. The president felt that he had been double-crossed in the wake of an apparent deal to hold the line on prices.

Rather than dwell on the fact that he and the labor unions had been deceived, Kennedy went into action. He summoned his brother Bobby, whom he had appointed attorney general, to the White House to discuss what his response should be. He decided to hold a press conference—a favorite tool he used to strengthen his bond with the American public, much the same way Franklin Roosevelt effectively used his famous "fireside chats."

The president showed his brother a draft of the speech he intended to deliver to begin the press conference, prompting several suggestions from the attorney general. Bobby felt that the original draft was "too personal" and that "the President's statement should be one of sorrow for the country and the betrayal of the steel executives rather than on any personal feeling." Bobby's suggestion, therefore, was to include something about "the Sergeants in Vietnam, the reservists who had been called up, the unions that had kept their wage demands down, and the other sacrifices that were being made."[5] This approach would help better frame the president's anger, enabling Kennedy to portray the steel executives as self-centered and greedy businessmen not heeding their obligations of service and citizenship.

The Morality of Citizenship

The president agreed with Bobby's comments. The day after his meeting with Blough, April 11, 1962, Kennedy held the press conference. The increase of steel prices by six dollars per ton, Kennedy announced, was "a wholly unjustifiable and irresponsible defiance of the public interest."[6] The president sought to humiliate the steel industry executives for their lack of concern for the American public by highlighting their transparently selfish motives that reflected a rejection of his notions of citizenship. He began the speech by placing the steel crisis within the context of implicitly more important issues and events. The length of one sentence—133 words—revealed the depth of the president's anger:

> In this serious hour in our nation's history, when we are confronted with grave crises in Berlin and Southeast Asia, when we are devoting our energies to economic recovery and stability, when we are asking Reservists to leave their homes and families for months on end, and servicemen to risk their lives—and four were killed in the last two days in Vietnam—and asking union members to hold down their wage requests, at a time when restraint and sacrifice are being asked of every citizen, the American people will find it hard, as I do, to accept a situation in which a tiny handful of steel executives whose pursuit of private power and profit exceeds their sense of public

responsibility can show such utter contempt for the interests of 185 million Americans.

The rhetoric bore noticeable resemblance to the fiery language used in the inaugural address to summon Americans to service in the name of the national interest. No individual was larger or more important than any other in Kennedy's America. All stood equally before the law; all were supposed to serve in their own capacities to make collective progress for the nation. It was clear that the steel executives were not willing to "pay any price, bear any burden," a guiding mantra from the inaugural address. No, they were not willing to "bear the burden of a long twilight struggle." Their transgressions, in other words, had not been transgressions of law but defiance of the spirit that Kennedy had attempted to inspire with his words and actions.

Kennedy warned of the harmful effects the price increase could have on the economy, which must have occurred to the steel makers, given how evident it was to Kennedy's advisers. The boost "would increase the cost of homes, autos, appliances, and most other items for every American family," he said. "It would increase the cost of machinery and tools to every American businessman and farmer. It would seriously handicap our efforts to prevent an inflationary spiral from eating up the pensions of our older citizens, and our new gains in purchasing power."

Such a price increase, Defense Secretary Robert McNamara had informed the president, would add an estimated $1 billion in expenses to the federal government alone. The increase would also make American goods and products less competitive in foreign markets, making foreign imports more appealing to the American consumer, in turn contributing to a more pronounced national imbalance of trade.

Kennedy then revealed how he had been betrayed. "The facts of the matter are that there is no justification for an increase in the steel prices," the president said. The settlement between the steel executives and the union workers had been "widely acknowledged to be non-inflationary, and the whole purpose and effect of this Administration's role, which both parties understood, was to achieve an agreement which would make unnecessary any increase in prices."

Earlier that morning, Kennedy said, he had been informed by the acting commissioner of the Bureau of Labor Statistics that "employment costs per unit of steel output in 1961 were essentially the same as they were in 1958," which was further proof that a price increase was unwarranted.

The president concluded by striking a careful rhetorical balance, deftly weighing the considerations in play. "Price and wage decisions in this country...are and ought to be freely and privately made," he said, "but the American people have a right to expect in return for that freedom a higher sense of business responsibility for the welfare of their country than has been shown in the last two days." Individual decisions were to be weighed on two scales, Kennedy suggested: what was right for business and what was right for the country. "Some time ago," Kennedy noted, "I asked each American to consider what he would do for his country, and I asked the steel companies. In the last twenty-four hours, we had their answer." This was personal—evoking the famous "ask not" line from the inaugural, Kennedy labeled the steel executives as selfish and unpatriotic—as individuals who were not fulfilling their duties as responsible citizens.

Kennedy viewed the steel-price increase as a political affront and a personal insult—as an effort to belittle his leadership and cause him political embarrassment. He would turn the tables and reinforce his point: no one, in a free society, ought to exploit concessions made in good faith to secure profit to the limit of the law. Kennedy would reach beyond the law for actions in furtherance of the public good.

Behind the scenes, Kennedy's fight against the steel executives was even more brutal. At the behest of the president, Secretary McNamara steered government contracts away from the steel companies that had followed Roger Blough and U.S. Steel's lead, and these very contracts were awarded to companies that had held the line on their prices.

Bobby Kennedy began speaking publicly about "anti-trust actions, price collusion, and grand jury investigations," while simultaneously instructing FBI director J. Edgar Hoover to haul in for questioning steel executives who propagated the price increase.[7] Congressional allies promised investigations in the House and Senate into industry price-fixing and other possible violations of antitrust laws.

Not surprisingly, the big steel tycoons soon backed down and returned to the terms of their original agreement. But Kennedy had clearly made his point: no citizen should put his own interests before those of the public interest under the color of law; no one doing so and going up against President Kennedy would be allowed to do so.

Reinforcing His Message

Kennedy moved quickly to cement the lessons of the steel crisis into public consciousness, again choosing a university commencement as a forum to address, in this instance, future business leaders of the country. The scene was Yale University, two months after the steel crisis.

The speech at Yale served to rebuild the tattered ties that developed between Kennedy and the business community in the aftermath of his handling of the steel crisis (many business leaders took exception to Kennedy's involvement in what many viewed to be a private business issue). Accordingly, Kennedy endeavored to craft a message that both underscored his commitment to the public interest and established means through which business and enterprise could continue to thrive.

To get this point across, Kennedy sought to artfully reposition the public focus on ways in which the private pursuit of individual gain could peacefully coexist with notions of public advancement. To do this required an emphasis on mutual interest and a shared ability to look beyond the prism of contemporary public discourse—the boundaries of which often obscure the real point at hand. "For the great enemy of truth is very often not the lie—deliberate, contrived, and dishonest—but the myth—persistent, persuasive, and unrealistic," Kennedy declared. "Too often we hold fast to the clichés of our fore- bears. We subject all facts to a prefabricated set of interpretations. We enjoy the comfort of opinion without the discomfort of thought."[8]

Kennedy proceeded to dispel the many myths and orthodoxies that corrupted economic thought, including misapprehensions about the degree of federal intrusion and regulation of the private sector. His point was that the private sector enjoyed wide latitude over its deci- sions and policies, as it should, but alongside this latitude came certain corporate and government responsibilities to protect certain vital so- cietal interests. Hence, Kennedy endeavored to speak as a manager of economic prosperity, not as the author of it, and as a citizen interested in seeing the private sector reflect the values being embraced by the country as a whole.

The Yale speech, which in some circles became known as "The Myth and Reality in Our National Economy," provided the framework for a Kennedy attempt, as John Murphy put it, to "justify the government's management of the economy, or, more precisely, the president's man- agement of the economy." Murphy discerned that "[t]he rhetorical force of this text rests in its deployment of linguistic strategies—*ethos*, dissociation, and time—that transformed ideology into action, that recast the terms of the liberal consensus into a powerful public image."[9]

Kennedy's handling of the steel crisis and his subsequent speech at Yale demonstrate key elements of his views on the interplay between civic obligation and the pursuit of private gain. Individuals should be encouraged to seek private advancement, and such efforts ought to be commensurately rewarded. However, no private interest should be advanced at the expense of public good. Government, in Kennedy's America, has an obligation to the people to protect their collective in- terest, and the president is the responsible officer who must fulfill this duty. In other words, the businessman's role is defended by Kennedy, but in a specified context. When the businessman profits at the ex- pense of the public at large, Kennedy reasoned, the government ought to intervene. Kennedy therefore reached for an understanding that went beyond the technical limits of the law, attempting as he would soon say to "make men see right."[10]

Familiar Themes

The interplay between the pursuit of private gain and the protection of the public good is a tension we know well in the twenty-first century. We can debate the causes of the financial crisis that began in 2008 or the role government ought to play or ought not to play in regulating the economy, but what is clear is that there are lingering questions concerning the relationship between public and private action half a century after Kennedy's time—and undoubtedly there will be in the years ahead.

Regardless of the specifics we might debate in times to come, Kennedy's handling of the steel situation offers a context within which we can consider future issues. There is a distinction between legality and morality, he explains. More specifically, to do something that is legal is not necessarily moral. What this means on a personal level is that each of us is tasked with evaluating our actions on two standards: First, are we acting within the law? And second, are our actions morally upright and consistent with the spirit of serving the common good that our citizenship demands?

To Kennedy, being a good citizen requires both. The rule of law must of course govern societal relations; but to be worthy of our citizenship requires more than this. It means that we must also act morally, that we must treat others as we would want to be treated if the situation were reversed, that we must take actions that reveal our values as a people. This was the failure of the steel executives—a breach of the public trust, a higher law—and this is the most important takeaway from that episode.

Kennedy's message is intended to challenge us, even now, half a century later, to live up to this creed. It goes beyond the particulars of the issue at hand. It is a mindset. If we adopt this universal truth in our endeavors, we will be fulfilling our potential as citizens and doing our public duty.

The Arts

John Kennedy's handling of the steel crisis helped crystallize a set of societal values he had been defining for some time. Along with the privilege of American citizenship came personal responsibility, and at times this truth required individual sacrifice. It also meant there were certain goals that merited public support—goals that perhaps were un-related to the economic interests of individuals or the nation but that nonetheless advanced the cause of citizenship and improved public life. For Kennedy, this cause included an active promotion of the arts and culture generally, and he directed public support toward such ini-tiatives with the aim of increasing national prestige.

Kennedy signaled this commitment by inviting the celebrated poet Robert Frost, eighty-six at the time, to deliver a poem at the inaugural ceremonies, in contrast from previous inaugurations. "If you can bear at your age the honor of being made President of the United States," Frost wrote the president-elect, "I ought to be able at my age to bear the honor of taking some part in your inauguration. I may not be equal to it but I can accept it for my cause—the arts, poetry, now for the first time taken into the affairs of the statesmen."[11]

Transforming Washington

In short order, the new president and his wife, Jacqueline, began other endeavors that contributed heavily to the aura of Camelot and the advancement of Kennedy's conceptions of citizenship. First, the Kennedys sought to change the role of the White House. No longer would it be used simply as a residence for the president's family and an office to house government officials; it would become a new symbol of the cultural dominance that the United States would attain in the thousand days of Kennedy's presidency.

The president's secretary, Evelyn Lincoln, remembered that the Kennedys had barely moved into the White House, and they were already discovering the changes they wanted to make. "They were concerned not only with their own comfort and convenience and acute sense of beauty; they also wanted to make the White House a national shrine of historical interest to all Americans."[12]

To change the atmosphere of the executive mansion required changes both to the appearance of the house as well as to the spirit that lived inside. Old decorative styles would be replaced with the latest that high fashion had to offer. The perceived dullness of the Eisenhower years would be swapped out in favor of the chic and classy. Changes large and small would be made to make everything more charming, more regal. There would be action and energy.

In observing the new presence in Washington in 1961, British Prime Minister Harold Macmillan commented that Americans

> certainly have acquired something we have lost—a casual sort of grandeur about their evenings, always at the end of the day's business, the promise of parties, and pretty women, and music and beautiful clothes, and champagne, and all that. I must say there is something very eighteenth century about your new young man, an aristocratic touch.[13]

Surely a renewed sense of youth and vigor lay at the heart of the New Frontier. But this was only part of a larger transformation that was intended to morph Washington, D.C., into a modern-day Athens. In his famed funeral oration, Pericles had suggested that all things flow into the city because of the city's greatness. Kennedy's conception was no different. If the United States were to remain at the forefront of progress and growth in the twentieth century and beyond, Washington would have to be a locus not only of political preeminence but of creativity and culture, as well. And again, the prestige factors were significant. A revitalized capital city increased citizens' pride in their country, and pride was a vital component of one's willingness to be involved, to contribute to society.

The First Lady Takes Charge

Jackie's most important project quickly came to light: she would lead an official White House restoration, transforming the mansion into the most revered residential museum in the nation. The First Lady soon realized that this would be a massive undertaking—and with limited funding—so she made her first task that of persuading Congress to permit the White House to accept tax-deductible donations from the American public in efforts to beautify and re-adorn the mansion. A Committee of the Fine Arts Commission was established to provide aesthetic and cultural expertise and support.

Jackie discovered a treasure trove of materials by sifting through presidential storage in the White House basement. Forgotten pieces of china, art, and furniture had been put away for years, and the First Lady had an eye for identifying pieces that would stand out in her new design. Meanwhile, the president made contributions, too. On his daily walks along the portico outside the West Wing, he noticed that the so-called Rose Garden did not actually have many roses. He directed his assistants to plant roses and other flowers all along the walk, and whenever the flowers began to wilt, he instructed, he wanted new flowers planted immediately. The image of beauty and vitality was critical. In projecting this aura, the prestige of the presidency and therefore the nation would increase and manifest itself in the form of renewed national pride.

The First Lady's task was more daunting, but with time, Jackie's undertaking became an important aspect of the administration. During this effort, the Kennedy "touch" began to emerge as Jackie redecorated nearly every room in the house: fireplaces were installed (and during the winter, fires were always burning), flowers and plants lined the hallways, and paintings new and old graced the walls of the sacred mansion. All efforts were designed to elicit the sense that something interesting was happening, which invited curiosity and even awe.

Yet simply restoring and beautifying the White House was not the First Lady's only aim; Jackie sought to turn the cultural improvements into a sort of political currency that could be flaunted and used. Early on in the project, Jackie switched her focus from the private rooms in the residence to the public state rooms, "a political stage on which to enact the drama of the Kennedy presidency."[14] The White House, "which Jackie had once believed ought to be comfortable, cozy, and inviting, would be deliberately formal, finished, and above all intimidating. Rather than putting people at ease, those rooms would impress upon them the grandeur and power of the presidency—and of Jack."[15]

Not only was Jackie intent on unearthing old and forgotten treasures such as the 1817 set of china made for James Monroe by the French government, but she also wanted to rearrange items already on display in the White House. An old portrait of Abraham Lincoln, for instance, was moved to the State Dining Room at Jackie's request. "Hanging over the marble mantelpiece," Barbara Leaming noted, "it would offer a reminder of America's own Civil War, fought to liberate an oppressed segment of the population."[16] The inclusion of this piece (with no other painting in the room to compete with it) would serve as a political instrument by which the president could push his Latin American agenda centered on the Alliance for Progress—Lincoln's role as emancipator was an apt historical analogue for conversations concerning Latin American freedom over dinners with foreign leaders. Jackie also refurbished the 2,500-volume White House library as well as the Treaty Room where American presidents have traditionally signed official alliances and treaties with nations around the world.

Her restoration of the White House culminated in an official White House tour that was filmed on January 15, 1962, and which aired a month later on Valentine's Day. In the commercial-less program, Jackie strolled through the White House and offered a history of the building, explaining the significance of specific rooms and their functions as she walked through them. Charles Dickens, she noted, had called the White House an "English clubhouse," yet when funds were low, it became known as the "public shabby house."[17] Thomas Jefferson gave dinner parties in the East Room, Jackie said, and she explained the many themes each room embodied (such as Ulysses Grant's "ancient Greek and Mississippi riverboat" style in the East Room).[18]

The White House tour was a dazzling success. Some 46.5 million Americans—an astonishing 75 percent of the television audience—viewed the tour; it aired on CBS and NBC on Valentine's Day, and 10 million more viewers watched the program on ABC days later.[19]

Jackie's performance had been masterful. Her regal tone and engaging demeanor gracefully complemented the beauty she exuded despite the black-and-white picture that recorded her tour. As she walked slowly through the mansion's corridors with natural ease, viewers quickly became infatuated with her poise and control—all this reinforced the feeling that something special indeed was occurring inside these famous walls.

"The things people had once held against her," Arthur Schlesinger Jr. noted, "the unconventional beauty, the un-American elegance, the taste for French clothes and French food—were suddenly no longer liabilities but assets. She represented all at once not a negation of her country but a possible fulfillment of it, a suggestion that America was not to be trapped forever in the bourgeois ideal, a dream of civilization and beauty."[20] In other words, it was real—romantic aspirations of royalty now realized; the strength behind the grace and power.

In the aftermath of the tour, the number of people taking White House tours grew exponentially. By the end of 1962, the total number of guests was nearly two-thirds greater than the number of people who had visited the mansion in 1960.[21] Excitement was back, and power was popular. People wanted to see it and believe it and be part of it.

Central to her success in the tour and the subsequent adulation Jackie enjoyed was her keen sense of style. Her famous bouffant hairdo initiated a wave of hairstyle imitations that pervaded the nation and influenced the manner in which countless hairstylists worked with their customers. The pearls she famously wore became a symbol of her status and power that revealed the refined aspects of her taste. Her elegant wardrobe not only spurred revolutions in American fashion but also served to highlight her image as queen of American society.

As early as her husband's first days as president-elect, Jackie had hired fashion designer Oleg Cassini to craft an image that would bestow upon her a kind of regal status. Such an image, she hoped, would contribute to a new sense of grandeur around the presidential couple, offering a sort of American Versailles that emphasized youth and sophistication in the wake of 1950s conservatism—that, again, would reinforce national pride and lift American prestige. Sally Bedell Smith noted that "in a letter to the designer summarizing her goals, she asked for designs 'that I would wear if Jack were President of France.'"[22] It was all intentional.

The president, too, would be fashioned with a new wardrobe. At Jackie's behest, Jack wore formal tails on his coats for certain ceremonial events. The First Lady understood that "just as the White House must look like the residence of a man of power, she and Jack, more than seeming just young and attractive, must appear truly out of the ordinary."[23]

The Cultural Revival

The Kennedy "touch" translated into a new atmosphere in the nation's capital, reaffirming, in a sense, America's greatness. What did this mean for Washington?

The White House and the capital city "became both a showplace and a dwelling place for the distinctive, the creative and the cultivated."[24] Shakespeare's plays were performed at the presidential mansion, state dinners were common, and world-renowned musicians performed there. There were ballet shows, dance troupes, musical comedies, and a dinner for Nobel Prize winners.

Pablo Casals, the renowned cellist, performed in the East Room after a state dinner. In inviting him to perform, Kennedy had written to Casals, "We feel that your performance as one of the world's greatest artists would lend distinction to the entertainment of our invited guests."[25] The presence of the artist, in other words, increased the stature of the evening.

The cultural revival went beyond the president's home. In fact, "[a] wave of intellectual interest and excitement rippled out from the White House. Learning and culture were in style."[26] As he would later note in a speech at Amherst College, Kennedy believed that a nation defines itself by the citizens it honors and the kinds of rewards bestowed upon them. Accordingly, he promoted the New Freedom Medal, an annual civilian honors list that recognizes great individual achievement. Those contributing to the artistic and cultural merits of an appreciative nation were important pioneers in Kennedy's New Frontier.

Ted Sorensen observed that Jack

> was a President who pursued excellence, and excellence in creative activity, he believed, was essential to excellence in the nation now and generations from now. "If we can make our country one of the great schools of civilization" like Athens, he said, "then on that achievement will surely rest our claim to the ultimate gratitude of mankind.... I am certain that, after the dust of centuries has passed over our cities, we will be remembered not for victories or defeats in battle or in politics but for our contributions to the human spirit."[27]

In Appreciation of the Artist

In a famed speech in October 1963, President Kennedy explained what this new cultural emphasis meant in the national context. Robert Frost had died earlier that year, and Amherst College subsequently sought to honor the poet's life by dedicating the school's new main library in his memory. To underscore the depth of Frost's achievements—including his winning of four Pulitzer Prizes—Amherst invited Kennedy to speak at the ceremony.

A thousand days earlier, Frost had stood on the inaugural podium with the new president to deliver the poem he had composed for the occasion. The intense glare of the sunlight that frigid day prevented Frost from being able to read the text of his poem, and so he recited a well-loved alternative, "The Gift Outright," from memory. Now a relic of history, the text of "Dedication," the poem he had intended to deliver, prophesied "A golden age of poetry and power / Of which this noonday's the beginning hour."[28]

Speaking at Amherst, Kennedy eulogized Frost, but in a greater sense, the encomium to Frost's life became a defense of the artist in general and a meditation on the contributions of the arts to a free and democratic society.

The library being dedicated that day and Amherst College itself, Kennedy submitted, were not there purely to give the school's students an advantage in the life struggle; it did do this, but there was also a greater purpose. He continued, the theme familiar, "[I]n return for the great opportunity which society gives the graduates of this and related schools, it seems to me incumbent upon this and other schools' graduates to recognize their responsibility to the public interest."[29]

"Privilege is here, and with privilege goes responsibility." These privileged few had an obligation to give back, and their country required their best efforts to satisfy the general imperative of service. "There is inherited wealth in this country and also inherited poverty," he stated, and the stakes were clear: "[U]nless the graduates of this college and other colleges like it who are given a running start in life—unless they are willing to put back into our society those talents, the broad sympathy, the understanding, the compassion—unless they are willing to put those qualities back into the service of the Great Republic," Kennedy reasoned, "then obviously the presuppositions upon which our democracy are based are bound to be fallible." The privileged members of society shouldered more of the national burden, he implied.

He was proud to come to Amherst, he said, where he knew that the students recognized such an obligation. Kennedy noted that it was Frost who had written: "Two roads diverged in a wood, and I—I took the one less traveled by, and that has made all the difference." Kennedy hoped that this route—the route of service—would not be the one less traveled by.

Frost "was supremely two things: an artist and an American. A nation reveals itself not only by the men it produces but also by the men it honors, the men it remembers." In other words, the public celebration of virtues and actions is indicative of the underlying values a society seeks to promote. In honoring individuals who fulfill this aim, a society simultaneously rewards such individuals and holds them out as models to others, inviting emulation and praise. The nations with the best rewards for public virtue have the best citizens—such recognition deepens individual pride and patriotism, thereby reinforcing one's willingness to accept responsibility and serve the public interest.

American heroes, Kennedy asserted, are traditionally individuals of large accomplishments. But Robert Frost is a different kind of hero—a hero "whose contribution was not to our size but to our spirit, not to our political beliefs but to our insight, not to our self-esteem, but to our self-comprehension."

"In honoring Robert Frost, we therefore can pay honor to the deepest sources of our national strength. That strength takes many forms, and the most obvious forms are not always the most significant," Kennedy maintained. "The men who create power make an indispensable contribution to the nation's greatness, but the men who question power make a contribution just as indispensable, especially when that questioning is disinterested, for they determine whether we use power or power uses us." Less obvious forms of strength, such as the arts and humanities—and those who fight the status quo—enhance a society and help form its greatness.

"Our national strength matters, but the spirit which informs and controls our strength matters just as much," he continued—such was the "special significance" of Frost. The spirit behind the strength, in other words, reinforced the strength itself—neither was possible without the other. This fact explains Frost's "special significance," for his poetry mastered and embodied the American spirit. Here, Kennedy saw a relationship between the stature of the public official and the thrust of the national spirit within.

The most basic connection Kennedy envisioned between politicians and artists was that they shared the role of public servant. A true public servant is one who not only serves his community, but who also places the good of his community before his own well-being. An artist shares a similar accountability to the public; for the artist's creation says much about the society in which he lives.

Frost appreciated this connection, seeing poetry as a counterforce to power. "When power leads men toward arrogance, poetry reminds him of his limitations," Kennedy continued. "When power narrows the areas of man's concern, poetry reminds him of the richness and diversity of his existence. When power corrupts, poetry cleanses. For art establishes the basic human truth which must serve as the touchstone of our judgment." Poetry and power, Kennedy asserted, stand as balancing elements of a society in order to help guide its citizens toward a more fruitful existence. For the artist reminds others "that our nation falls short of its highest potential." He reminds us that we can do better.

A Legacy That Still Resonates

In less than three years, the Kennedys worked a transformation in the spirit of Washington and the nation that remains with us today. Thereafter, both would strive to be centers of excellence, of artistic and intellectual attainments, and both would impart a fresh concern for quality of life, for self-improvement, and above all, for striving for greatness. These are legacies that powerfully reinforce the political and social legacies of the Kennedy era; it requires largeness of spirit to grasp the wider whole. And in the final analysis, these are closely connected with Kennedy's efforts to invoke classical themes of citizenship and heroism. The status quo does not require imagination, but democracies do not stand still. Imagination is nurtured by intellectual and moral endeavors and, above all, courage in the pursuit of honors in a society willing to bestow them.

These notions are as true now as they were when Kennedy expressed them. We can embrace this spirit here in the twenty-first century by similarly appreciating the role that the arts play in society and the manner in which they reflect our progress.

Historically speaking, when we look back at earlier societies, we pay less attention to ideological rivalry, to who won elections and what differences divided people; we focus more on the impact such societies had on future cultures and future generations. Promotion of the humanities underscores this basic point—generations from now, as Kennedy suggested, we will indeed be remembered for the contributions we made to the human spirit.

This perspective demonstrates how we ought to measure progress in our own time—not by which political party is in power, or by the issues that divide us—but by assessing who we are as a people and the values we promote. We do not have to pursue a career in the arts to recognize its wider importance. But neither should we refrain from promoting and supporting this important field through public recognition for artistic achievement.

And there are many ways to do so. We can visit museums, make donations to cultural institutions, go to the theater, attend poetry readings, see the ballet or the opera, give prizes to students who pursue these endeavors, bestow these professionals with awards for exceptional work, encourage children to express their creativity in the form of art and music, and have ceremonies honoring great achievements. These efforts are means of exercising our freedom and our citizenship; this spirit is what attracts people from all over the world to our country. Kennedy's legacy in this regard instructs that we should not take any of this for granted; we should treasure our uniqueness and take pride in our humanity.

Civil Rights

The path to civil rights in the United States was long and arduous, and there were many false starts. Indeed, how and in what ways effective civil rights legislation might take shape changed over time, affected as it was by tectonic shifts in the political landscape and new perspectives formed around common understandings.

John Kennedy's efforts in 1963 were intended to use such mutual accords as a basis for the platform of the individual equality he sought to advance—all predicated on the concept of citizenship. His push for global peace at American University had provided the framework within which these new understandings could be forged, and fresh momentum had transformed the once-fledgling movement into an all-out attack on inequality—sponsored, as it came to be, by the most powerful leader in the world. On both personal and historical levels, it had been a momentous transformation.

In considering the course of these events, one can readily observe a consistent intellectual thrust that guided Kennedy's actions and formed the basis upon which his rhetorical arguments were made. In short, the new urgency Kennedy lent to the quest for equal rights became the most apparent and the most forceful sphere in which his promotion of citizenship could be achieved. Such efforts offered the most visible climax and realization of the ideals he had learned through his reading earlier in life and that became the underlying core premise of his presidency. To be sure, the strategic reasoning Kennedy employed in his actions and remarks in this context sheds valuable light on all of his other endeavors—highlighting most profoundly the paradigms of civic obligation and citizenship in ways perhaps no other circumstances could.

Tepid Support

The issue of civil rights long predated Kennedy, but it was a concern that became increasingly pressing in the public arena as Kennedy entered elective office. In Congress, Kennedy had been a consistent but relatively low-key supporter of the movement. By 1956, Kennedy had insisted that the Democratic Party could not waver on its commitment to civil rights on legal grounds in the wake of *Brown v. Board of Ed.* Thus, while Kennedy's moral inclinations were sympathetic to the cause, it was clear that his support would remain tepid, couching justification for the movement in legal terms in a fashion that contrasted with the moral urgency espoused by the more liberal wing of his party. By the same token, his approach implied that changes in law and attitude would be necessary to cultivate the kind of responsible citizenship he would later advocate.

By the 1960 campaign, Kennedy's efforts remained lukewarm. While the movement continued to pick up steam, Kennedy was cognizant of the political reality confronting the Democratic Party's nominee: a strong civil rights platform would be at the expense of Southern conservatives' support, and with the electoral college map shaping up as it was, Nixon would be president if he could win over a region that had remained a fractious component of Democratic coalitions for generations.

Yet in the first televised debate with Nixon, Kennedy nonetheless used a portion of his opening remarks to highlight this issue, underscoring his willingness to look past politics. "I'm not satisfied until every American enjoys his full constitutional rights," he declared.[30] A black baby born in 1960, he indicated, had a fraction of the chances of a white baby to graduate from college, to work in professional fields, or to buy a house. While individuals must bear a burden to lift themselves up out of this sad reality, he said, he believed "there is also a national responsibility" to rectify these problems.

At his inauguration three months later, he noticed during the inaugural parade that there had been no blacks marching in the group of servicemen in the Coast Guard. He wanted this fixed immediately.

After the parade, Kennedy called new Treasury Secretary Douglas Dillon, under whose jurisdiction the Coast Guard fell.[31] From Kennedy came orders to Dillon to make sure that blacks were included in all future ceremonies.

Similarly, in Kennedy's first cabinet meeting, he ordered all department heads to be aware of race when hiring and to ensure equal opportunity for anyone, regardless of color, to apply for and obtain jobs. Andrew Hatcher, associate press secretary under Pierre Salinger, and Robert Weaver, housing and home finance administrator, both black men, became members of the administration. Kennedy also appointed blacks to judgeships and ambassadorial posts consistent with his instructions to the cabinet secretaries.

Kennedy would soon be put to the test. On the campaign trail, he had rallied support among blacks by declaring that he would desegregate federally financed housing "with the stroke of a pen."[32] When he did not do so upon entering office, the delay prompted thousands of people to send pens to the White House to sarcastically remind the president of his unfulfilled pledge. Meanwhile, growing unrest in the South led to a new wave of violence, and leaders of the movement were becoming justifiably impatient.

A Fast Escalation

Birmingham, Alabama, became the primary city of conflict—"the most thoroughly segregated city in America," Dr. Martin Luther King Jr. called it.[33] The year 1962 had been marked by several demonstrations in the city led by King, dramatized by King's multiple arrests by Eugene "Bull" Connor, the city's commissioner of public safety.

The situation continued to deteriorate as "city voters approved of a change in government from a board of commissioners to a mayor-council form," which left citizens in a state of confusion as to whether Connor was in control or Mayor-elect Albert Boutwell had the reins.[34] It was Connor, however, who maintained control of the city's police and fire departments, and it would be Connor who would emerge as the primary figure in the Birmingham confrontations early the following year.

In early 1963, King continued to organize protests and demonstrations. In what turned out to be the most notable protest, he arranged for thousands of young people to join in the action. When King and the protesters departed from a church—the organized gathering point—Connor ordered the police and fire departments to spray water at the protesting children, signifying his steadfast refusal to give in to demands of equal opportunity and equal citizenship.

Though hundreds were arrested on Thursday, May 2, 1963, the first day of the protest, the demonstration resumed the following day with greater force and determination. Only this time Connor ordered his subordinates to increase the pressure on their hoses with every step closer that the children took. As the children advanced out of the church, the police and fire departments unleashed a barrage of hose spray that resembled a small brigade of cannons firing on defenseless children. The force of the hoses—which were strong enough to break through brick-and-mortar walls—hurled the small children into the air and down the street.[35] The protesters began throwing rocks at the police, and Connor responded by releasing police dogs to stop them.

Things Were Different This Time

Under normal conditions, such events might only be reported in newspapers and brushed aside by readers as "just" another civil rights demonstration in the South. But this time it was different. The entire "battle" between Connor's cronies and the civil rights defenders was caught on tape by television news cameras, and the footage of what had happened in Birmingham was immediately sent to the major broadcasting networks to be shown across the country. The collection of images was ugly, "something [Connor and his allies] wanted no one in the world to see."[36]

Kennedy detested this display of unprovoked brutality. Nonetheless, for the moment, he affirmed that law and order was indeed a state issue and that the practices in question were beyond the reach of the federal police power. King responded with a definitive statement on national television, stating that the time had come for the federal government to publicly "take a forthright stand on segregation in the United States"— it was time, he suggested, for the president "to issue a Lincolnesque proclamation."[37]

Kennedy finally agreed. Television had changed the entire situation and had handed him his best opportunity to act. As the historian Richard Reeves observed, "[T]he torch of communications was being passed to a new generation of technology, speeding up cycles of event-action-reaction-backlash, changing what people knew and when they knew it."[38] Such a transition took power out of the hands of state and local officials, vesting it in Kennedy's hands. Public officials could no longer conceal the realities of what had occurred; citizens could now supply their own proverbial thousand words for every picture viewed, and Kennedy would supply several more.

On May 8, 1963, Kennedy held a press conference to discuss the events in Birmingham. The problem, Kennedy noted, was that there was no precedent for federal action in such instances. In Little Rock, Arkansas, in 1957, Eisenhower had called in the 101st Airborne Division, but only reluctantly and after much deliberation—and the handling of that crisis did not make explicitly clear under whose jurisdiction such conflict belonged.

Meanwhile, George Reedy, an aide to Lyndon Johnson, wrote an extensive memorandum to the vice president that outlined the situation as he saw it. "The Negroes are going to be satisfied with nothing less than a convincing demonstration that the President is on their side," he wrote. "The backbone of white resistance is not going to be broken until the segregationists realize that the total moral force of the United

States is arrayed against them."[39] In other words, the president must take a stand on civil rights, whether it meant proposing new legislation or using force. Others in his administration were now saying it, including Southerners; Kennedy would say it very soon.

Mounting Tension

Kennedy's course was straightforward. In the news at that moment was a school case in Alabama of the standard type; the federal courts had ordered the University of Alabama to integrate its graduate programs, and Alabama governor George Wallace was vowing to defy this federal edict. Once again, Kennedy faced the standard school crisis calling forth the standard remedies of National Guard and regular Army forces to integrate a Southern school by force. But the outcome this time would be anything but standard; for this time, the relationship between the president and similar disturbances would be altered by Kennedy, who saw his opportunity to move on the school question and a good deal more. In short order, he resolved to use the university crisis as the pretext for a speech designed first to advance legislative proposals, and second, to redefine the relationship between states and the federal government on all social questions, particularly between black and white Americans.

In early June, Kennedy contemplated what such a speech would entail. His only planned address was the upcoming commencement at American University on June 10, a speech that would not mention the civil rights movement beyond contextual references to freedom at home. But events out of his control would soon force him to change that.

Two black students were to be enrolled at the University of Alabama on the following day, June 11. Yet Governor Wallace swore that he would uphold his belief of "Segregation now—Segregation tomorrow—Segregation forever" and would refuse to permit their matriculation.[40] The governor controlled the police force, and he was prepared to use them to physically prevent the students, James Hood and Vivian Malone, from entering the university. The private politicking Kennedy had employed with Wallace would not ameliorate the conflict. Wallace was prepared for a confrontation.

At the University of Alabama, Kennedy faced a familiar scenario, much like the Oxford, Mississippi, crisis of October 1962. In that situation, the University of Mississippi had accepted James Meredith, a black student, but university officials did not permit him to enroll in the school because of his race. After hours of exhausting negotiations, Meredith had finally been permitted to enroll in classes, but in the ensuing disturbances, two were killed and millions of dollars in damage was incurred in a pitched battle between guardsmen and die-hard segregationists defending what they believed to be their state sovereignty. What was now to change was Kennedy's handling of the crisis.

Game Change

Like Eisenhower in 1957, Kennedy had managed the disturbances with his eye principally fixed on the need to enforce the edicts of a federal court and to mediate a peace between the warring factions. This studied neutrality had served a vital purpose in 1957 and 1962; obstructionists were isolated as lawbreakers, and the national authority was intervening to prevent anarchy. But this posture implied moral neutrality, positioning the presidency between the extremists of the right and left. Whatever the usefulness of neutrality in the past, it was about to end, and it ended with Kennedy's decision to supply one missing word to describe the growing crisis over civil rights: "moral."

By defining the crisis as a moral crisis, Kennedy declared in effect that civil rights was a problem that transcended the usual give-and-take of legislative and executive action; moral questions are not, by their nature, to be compromised—instead they divide the electorate along a clear fault line of right and wrong. By his application of the word "moral," Kennedy would finally substitute the civil rights fault line for the predominant Cold War fault line that, for more than a decade, had placed all Americans on the side of right. By 1963, only some Americans were on the side of right in the context of civil rights. Others were plainly on the side of wrong, and the citizenry as a whole was to be asked to choose: which side were they on?

Wallace's threatened action transformed the expected enrollment—the date that had been approved and confirmed by the courts—into the crisis Kennedy wanted. Kennedy learned of the developing situation through his deputy attorney general, Nicholas Katzenbach, who reported that Wallace was willing to block the entrance of the school in order to stand by his initial stance in support of segregation. Bobby Kennedy reminded his brother of the political delicacy of the ensuing confrontation that was a predicament insofar as Wallace was a Democrat and a governor.

Kennedy initially hesitated. Eager to intervene on behalf of the courts and against Wallace, he felt some reluctance about making Wallace into a "white martyr across the South."[41] The specific concern was that Wallace would defy Katzenbach and oblige the federal authorities to arrest him, obligating Kennedy in turn to impose a form of twentieth-century Reconstruction on Alabama and the South. The 1964 election was in question. Did Kennedy foresee that such a maneuver would put the South into Republican hands for generations? Wallace certainly did, and so the governor stuck by his planned defiance, facing off against President Kennedy, who had resolved that such an expenditure of political capital on his part was justified by the promised result of effective civil rights legislation, no matter what the consequences (the very kind of action he had lauded in *Profiles in Courage*). Sorensen suggested the idea of doing a televised address to explain the crisis and to use it for the purpose of proposing civil rights legislation.

On the morning of June 11, Katzenbach prepared to escort the two black students to their dormitories. Upon reaching the main entrance to the university—and amidst the command of Wallace to

"Stop!"—Katzenbach read a message on behalf of the president insisting that Wallace cease and desist from his illegal obstructions.

The governor responded by reading a prepared statement of his own, not only to Katzenbach, but also to the many television cameras on site, declaring that he denounced the "illegal and unwanted action by the central government" that was suppressing the sovereignty of his state.[42]

This was Kennedy's cue to federalize the Alabama National Guard, thereby transferring the command of the troops from Governor Wallace to himself. At such time, Brigadier General Henry Graham and one hundred of his men marched onto campus to enforce the president's orders; Wallace saluted Graham and stepped aside.[43] By noon, Kennedy had requested airtime. At eight o'clock that night, he spoke.

The Speech

Kennedy's speech had undergone a series of revisions all day and was not entirely complete by the time he began speaking live. It was written to take into account the outcome in Alabama—the successful registration of the two students that had proceeded peacefully after Wallace stepped aside. Kennedy was direct:

> I hope that every American, regardless of where he lives, will stop and examine his conscience about this and other related incidents. This nation was…founded on the principle that all men are created equal, and that the rights of every man are diminished when the rights of one man are threatened. Today we are committed to a worldwide struggle to promote and protect the rights of all who wish to be free. And when Americans are sent to Vietnam or West Berlin, we do not ask for whites only. It ought to be possible, therefore, for American students of any color to attend any public institution they select without having to be backed up by troops.[44]

Americans of all races, Kennedy said, deserved equal service in places of public accommodation. Every American deserved "to enjoy the privileges of being American without regard to his race or his color" and to be "treated as he would wish to be treated." But such was not the case. In other words, Americans were failing to exercise the responsibilities of their citizenship that by nature required a commitment to equality.

Kennedy endeavored to outline the basics of the problem:

> The Negro baby born in America today...has about one-half as much chance of completing high school as a white baby born in the same place on the same day, one-third as much chance of completing college, one-third as much chance of becoming a professional man, twice as much chance of becoming unemployed, about one-seventh as much chance of earning $10,000 a year, a life expectancy which is 7 years shorter, and the prospects of earning only half as much.

Thus Kennedy defined the problem: the systematic deprivation of equal rights, proven by dry statistics, of fully a tenth of the nation's people.

"This is not a sectional issue," he continued. The dilemma concerning civil rights was not simply a Southern problem; it was not a question of "red" states and "blue" states; it was an *American* problem.

> In a time of domestic crisis, men of good will and generosity should be able to unite regardless of party or politics. This is not even a legal or legislative issue alone. It is better to settle these matters in the courts than on the streets, and new laws are needed at every level, but law alone cannot make men see right.

Kennedy, in other words, had intervened on behalf of the execution of the just decrees of the federal courts in Alabama, yet he was using the occasion to reflect on a new and unexplored problem: the effect and enforcement of unjust laws that constituted the "separate but equal" policy of status quo.

"We are confronted primarily with a moral issue," he proceeded. "It is as old as the scriptures and is as clear as the American Constitution. The heart of the question is whether all Americans are to be afforded equal rights and equal opportunities, whether we are going to treat our fellow Americans as we want to be treated."

Kennedy proceeded to ask his audience to imagine the world as the black American saw it:

> If an American, because his skin is dark, cannot eat lunch in a restaurant open to the public, if he cannot send his children to the best public school available, if he cannot vote for the public officials who will represent him, if, in short, he cannot enjoy the full and free life which all of us want, then who among us would be content to have the color of his skin changed and stand in his place? Who among us would then be content with the counsels of patience and delay?

To this point, Kennedy had innovated in another sense in the way he depicted blacks who were bidding for equal rights. Throughout the address, blacks were presented as deserving of the changes Kennedy sought: blacks served in the military, they had identical aspirations as whites, they were citizens on the threshold of full recognition of rights they had earned—and deserved. They were not poor, necessarily, or deprived or in any way in need of assistance other than the assistance of fair-minded Americans willing to acknowledge their equal rights. The barrier, in a word, was prejudice, like the prejudice so familiar in American history directed at other groups in other times.

This positive picture that Kennedy painted raises a key point of "audience." On which side of the moral divide he was defining that night did Kennedy stand? And what was the predictable effect of his words on the blacks who stood there with him? Indignation, for sure, and a renewed determination to be impatient and to demand equal rights now. Simultaneously, by casting aspersions on unjust laws and by expressing empathy with those who would violate unjust laws, Kennedy clarified a crucial point. Federal troops were available to enforce desegregation in the name of law and order and preventing anarchy; they were *not* available to enforce injustice. If the various states were to persist in perpetuating injustice, he implied, they would leave themselves exposed to the mercies of fate—denied help or even sympathy.

Kennedy invited empathy vis-à-vis the rhetorical questions he posed. Who would change places with blacks? The answer was obvious: no one would subject himself to the same kinds of treatment given to blacks, an answer that illustrated his basic point. We recall Kennedy's tour of Latin America, in which he supported the move toward equal rights and opportunities in countries long in the sway of land-holding oligarchs—concepts that did not receive objections at home. But in a matter of months and years, the consensus behind segregation had turned into a consensus for something else. Kennedy merely voiced the truisms derived from America's hard-won experience in the global struggle against injustice.

Essentially that night Kennedy was employing the same rhetorical maneuver, in which he symbolically transposed the privileged into the shoes of the less fortunate. As Atticus Finch said in our earlier example: "You never really understand a person until you consider things from his point of view—until you climb inside his skin and walk around in it."[45] Kennedy's imagery confronted those who saw alternatives to civil rights, forcing them to consider the experiences of injustice elsewhere.

Having rhetorically destroyed Jim Crow, Kennedy turned to the question of urgency about filling the vacuum left by Jim Crow with laws and regulations that reflected the wider sense of fairness. A century had passed since Lincoln had freed the slaves, he said, "yet their heirs, their grandsons, are not fully free. They are not yet freed from the bonds of injustice. They are not yet freed from social and economic oppression. And this nation, for all its hopes and all its boasts, will not be fully free until all its citizens are free."

He continued:

We face, therefore, a moral crisis as a country and as a people. It cannot be met by repressive police action. It cannot be left to increased demonstrations in the streets. It cannot be quieted by token moves or talk. It is time to act in the Congress, in your state and local legislative body and, above all, in all of our daily lives.

In the balance of his text, Kennedy examined the practical measures available to redress the shortcomings of the law. Within the week, he would ask Congress to act and pass new laws addressing public accommodations as well as voting rights and schools—the whole panoply of equal rights. The federal judiciary has since upheld that proposition in the conduct of its affairs, including the employment of federal personnel, the use of federal facilities, and the sale of federally financed housing.

And so it went. Kennedy had finally made the push necessary by a president to initiate such action in Congress.

Reconsidering Familiar Themes

Now that Kennedy had redefined the struggle in the United States as one concerning civil rights (and not the Cold War with the Soviets), let us once again revisit the key themes of his inaugural address. If we alter the context in which the speech is viewed, it is conceivable to consider "both sides" that he refers to not as the United States and the Soviet Union, but as the two sides in the quest for civil rights.

"Let both sides explore what problems unite us instead of belaboring those problems which divide us." The Kennedy rhetoric of *transcendence* seeks to unite the nation in the fulfillment of its duty, which is to promote equality and unity, not segregation and division. "Let us begin anew," for this is "an end as well as a beginning—signifying renewal as well as change." It is "the same revolutionary beliefs for which our forebears fought" that will characterize the next struggle—the next mission—in America. "We dare not forget today that we are the heirs of that first revolution." We are a generation "unwilling to witness or permit the slow undoing of those human rights to which this nation has always been committed, and to which we are committed today at home and around the world." It is time for us to "pay any price, bear any burden, meet any hardship, support any friend, oppose any foe, in order to assure the survival and the success of liberty."

Liberty. Liberty is the key to everything—it lies at the core of all the success that the United States has enjoyed in its glorious history.

He also stressed in his inaugural address the importance of working together. "United, there is little we cannot do in a host of cooperative ventures. Divided there is little we can do—for we dare not meet a powerful challenge at odds and split asunder." All this must be done, for "one form of colonial control shall not have passed away merely to be replaced by a far more iron tyranny." The American colonists did not wage a revolution against the British only to suppress again the freedoms that they so desperately sought. The "heirs of that first revolution" cannot forget why it was that the United States broke away in the first place.

Kennedy noted that those who stand in opposition to our views—which would include those on civil rights—would not always agree with this: "We shall not always expect to find them supporting our view. But we shall always hope to find them strongly supporting their own freedom—and to remember that, in the past, those who foolishly sought power by riding the back of the tiger ended up inside."

And consider these words as a message to those against civil rights: "Finally, to those...who would make themselves our adversary, we offer not a pledge but a request: that both sides begin anew the quest for peace, before the dark powers of destruction...engulf all humanity in planned or accidental self-destruction."

We cannot afford to be on opposing sides of the new dividing line in human affairs; not between communists and noncommunists, but between humanity and the "common enemies of man: tyranny, poverty, disease, and war itself."

"Let both sides *unite* to heed in all corners of the Earth the command of Isaiah—to 'undo the heavy burdens...[and] let the oppressed go free.'" What could be more powerful than the use of biblical imagery to strengthen his assertion?

And in sum: "In the long history of the world, only a few generations have been granted the role of defending freedom in its hour of maximum danger. I do not shrink from this responsibility—I welcome it." We have tremendous opportunity here, Kennedy says. This is our time. This is our calling. This is our purpose. We are unique. Such an opportunity does not present itself very often, and we can be the ones to make a difference. "The energy, the faith, the devotion which we bring to this endeavor will light our country and all who serve it—and the glow from that fire can truly light the world. And so my fellow Americans: ask not what your country can do for you—ask what you can do for your country."

Kennedy reminds us that it is our duty as Americans to place the ideals on which this nation was founded ahead of personal gain or individual advancement. For if we do not have success as a nation, how can one be content to have success for himself? Can one truly have individual success if the state fails? What does that individual success count for in a state that knows nothing but failure? What power is granted to the individual in the state that has no genuine power?

Let us revisit a key inaugural line: "If a free society cannot help the many who are poor, it cannot save the few who are rich." Kennedy argued that the freedoms enjoyed by some automatically become jeopardized when all do not enjoy them. Indeed, he said, the grotesque social and economic oppression of individuals based on the color of their skin—or any other dividing factor—had no place in America. And in fact, such inequality diminished the standing of all freedom-loving people, regardless of who they were or where they came from. Hence, "this nation...will not be fully free until all its citizens are free." By affirming unity and progress at home, America would loosen the bonds of injustice and become a more righteous, dignified, and worthy place.

View the inaugural address in these terms, and we may just begin to understand the true message of Kennedy's most historic speech and his presidency generally. On the surface, yes, the speech is about the Cold War. It is about foreign policy and renewed requests for peace. But its terms are intended to be seen in many lights, and through Kennedy's rhetorical transcendence, we observe something far more important than Cold War rhetoric: the president's request for a better America. The man elected in 1960 is not content with what he sees. Reforms are necessary, change is inevitable and required, and anything less than a full effort will not do.

The struggles of which he spoke in his convention speech were not over—the problems were not all solved, and the battles were not all won. There was a New Frontier indeed.

For all that he said, for all that he did, for everything he stood for, Kennedy's message on the night of June 11, 1963, the culmination of his presidency, came to stand for what, in his eyes, was meant by the idea of citizenship. And by it, Kennedy defined the civil rights movement, and, as in others, the movement came to define him. Civil rights and human rights were not concessions of governments or conferred by the grace of superiors, he understood; they were the natural attributes of free citizens of a republic and conferred by the hand of God.

Civil Rights Today

Kennedy's efforts culminated in the historic passage of the Civil Rights Act of 1964 and the Voting Rights Act of 1965 after he died. A critical facet of his legacy in this regard is the framework he established for us to approach issues in any generation. Regardless of the circumstances, we should approach issues within this construct: if an individual or group of people is being treated in a way that we would not wish to be treated if in their position, then we have a responsibility to help them fight for their rights. This duty is an obligation of our citizenship and reflects the basic premise of equality that underscored Kennedy's promotion of this theme. When the rights of one are threatened, the rights of all are jeopardized. Therefore, we protect the public good.

There is an inclusive nature to this model that is instinctively appealing. We are part of something bigger than ourselves, and we belong to a community. By serving the public interest and protecting the vulnerable among us, we are in fact looking after our own affairs at the same time. This is why we ask what we can do for our country. Because we are at our strongest and our best when we stand together and put forth a collective effort that highlights our common concern. Here, Kennedy's emphasis on citizenship remains particularly enlightening.

PART III

THE CITIZEN OF TODAY

JFK evokes the spirit of the Founding Fathers by speaking in front of Independence Hall in Philadelphia on July 4, 1962. The principles of service and sacrifice that defined the nation's first generation, Kennedy reminded Americans, were necessary elements of national progress in any age.

CHAPTER 7

The Next Frontier

"Let us not despair but act. Let us not seek the Republican answer or the Democratic answer but the right answer. Let us not seek to fix the blame for the past—let us accept our own responsibility for the future."

— JOHN F. KENNEDY,
remarks at Loyola College alumni banquet, February 18, 1958

WHEN JOHN KENNEDY gave his vision for America in his acceptance speech at the July 1960 Democratic National Convention, the New Frontier, as he called it, signified a need for new exploration, a renewed spirit of adventure, a fresh desire for progress, and a sense that the unknown could be harnessed to help a worthy nation achieve great things. At the core of this message was the concept of citizenship, in which Americans were asked to consider what role they each played in an individual capacity as the nation faced great challenges.

As we've seen in looking over certain actions of his presidency and the driving force behind these deeds, citizenship in Kennedy's America was not an abstract idea discussed among academics. Instead, it was a discernible essence that highlighted the major truths of a free and successful society: that our fate, as individuals, is tied to that of our neighbors, that members of the same community have common aspirations and fears, and that our actions can and do affect the lives of others. Citizenship therefore was—and is—a concrete calling that highlights the interconnectivity of individuals and the nation, borne out in the ways in which individuals embrace certain responsibilities. In short, it is a call to service—service in the name of one's community, service in the name of one's country, service in the name of one's generation.

The concept of service invokes different thoughts in each individual. For many people, it is a reminder of projects we worked on as students—volunteering our time for a charity, working at a school bake sale, organizing a toy drive for underserved children, or other similar initiatives. Perhaps it was a school requirement—that in order to be a member of an honor society or in order to graduate, for instance, one had to perform a certain number of hours of community service.

Kennedy's concept of service goes deeper. It speaks not only to the actions he hoped to elicit but also to the spirit he aimed to foster. Service in the New Frontier was more than a series of actions that in the aggregate would change the nation. Service became an attitude, a disposition, a willingness to see people and issues from a more nuanced perspective that invited mutual cooperation and understanding. In this light, problems could be cast in more favorable ways intended to underscore uniting factors that brought people together, such as their hopes and dreams and their sense of patriotism—rather than factors that divided them, such as the political party to which they belonged, the color of their skin, or where they were from.

There were tangible examples of these efforts in the initiatives on which Kennedy embarked. In establishing the Peace Corps, for instance, he did not ask all Americans to consider joining the organization and living overseas in foreign lands. What he did ask was for Americans to assess the merits of such efforts and to partake in such endeavors in spirit—by supporting the program, by thinking about how helping developing nations abroad served to advance American goals, and by recognizing the interrelatedness of human concern among nations. One does not have to be a member of the Peace Corps to embody the spirit it represents; if an individual believes in the concept of sacrifice and helping others, such individual can find other ways to make similar contributions. Service in this program was merely one means of demonstrating such commitment.

Similarly, in the mission to go to the moon, individuals were not expected to quit their jobs to go to work for NASA. But individuals could embrace the spirit of exploration underlying space efforts in other aspects of their lives—a spirit that symbolized stepping out of the proverbial "comfort zone" to expand the scope of our reach to new communities. A teacher who is willing to share her talents with underserved children, for example, might seek to work in an unfamiliar neighborhood with different demographics because she recognizes the difference she can make there. Clergy and lay leaders of religious institutions might seek out new interfaith solidarity initiatives or engage in more collective community service projects than they have done before.

Such efforts symbolize one's willingness to see past traditional obstacles—to personify a more enlightened perspective while seeking to expand the richness and diversity of our existence as individuals with common concerns. When he announced the goal of landing on the moon, Kennedy gave voice to this collective effort: "In a very real sense, it will not be one man going to the moon. If we make this judgment affirmatively, it will be an entire nation. For all of us must work to put him there."[1]

In the quest for civil rights, not all individuals were expected to join the Freedom Rides or participate in sit-ins. But citizens could consider how they could be more tolerant in their own lives, how they could make their own communities better, how they could be examples of justice and righteousness on a personal level.

Similarly, in chastising the executives in the steel industry, Kennedy's message was in fact for a much wider audience. Americans were being asked to consider what kind of sacrifice they could make in their own lives that would benefit the national and local interest amidst trying times. Were they being good citizens? Were they being selfish at the expense of their community? Would they be proud if their individual actions were broadcast in their local newspaper for their neighbors to see?

With the goal of producing a more informed citizenry, Kennedy could advance his goals in a universal paradigm of national progress. All individuals could participate, all individuals could benefit, and each person played a role in advancing the country's objectives. This premise helped justify the outsized goals of his presidency. Because the potential of the American people is limitless, his words suggested, so too is the possibility for progress. In espousing a powerful national spirit of service borne out on a local level, previously intractable problems could be solved and new advances achieved. Such was the uniting element of Kennedy's rhetoric and the position from which the challenges of the New Frontier could be addressed.

In his famed commencement speech at American University, Kennedy articulated this underlying theme: "For, in the final analysis, our most basic common link is that we all inhabit this small planet. We all breathe the same air. We all cherish our children's futures. And we are all mortal."[2]

New Frontiers of Today

With Kennedy's view of citizenship in mind, we have a universal construct within which we can seek progress in our time. If we adopt the approach Kennedy envisioned, we are better positioned to solve the problems of our day. Pursuing the mission of service he summoned can form the basis of how we approach the trials of the twenty-first century.

A Different World

The world we inhabit today is very different from the one Kennedy led in the 1960s. Indeed, many of the issues and concerns of the Kennedy era have changed markedly or even vanished. The Cold War is over. Vietnam is, in many ways, a distant war of the past. Sweeping health care legislation, absent in Kennedy's time though a lurking concern, has been fiercely debated but nonetheless has changed how citizens are insured. The spread of communism has been contained, and "domino" theory fears in Southeast Asia and elsewhere have similarly evaporated. Germany has been reunited. Civil rights legislation was passed. Cuba is no longer perceived to be the threat it once was. Latin American nations are no longer as weak and susceptible to the communistic impulses that had enveloped Cuba, and the need for a program like the Alliance for Progress in its 1960s meaning seems outdated, or at least self-evident, today.

Instead, new realities define our world. Advances in science and technology have revolutionized all facets of daily and national life. Innovations in social media have transformed the way we relate to each other. Globalization has redefined the world order and changed the way we communicate, how we conduct business, and how we engage in geopolitical discourse. Terrorism has dramatically altered the world we inhabit. We know more about our planet and our place in the universe. We know more about each other. We have traveled further in space. Health care has improved. Educational needs have changed. Continued dependence on foreign oil has spurred discussions of developing alternative resources of energy to help create jobs and protect the environment more effectively. A burgeoning economic and political rivalry with China has been afoot for some time. And a good deal more.

Additionally, new initiatives hardly envisioned during Kennedy's time have been launched in the wake of new knowledge and better understandings of what is possible. Such efforts include, for instance, the global effort to combat HIV/AIDS, domestic efforts to fight childhood obesity, and new struggles to assist individuals with special needs. These issues—and many others—represent a host of challenges that form the basis of the New Frontiers of the twenty-first century.

Meeting Our Challenges

One pivotal frontier we face today is determining what course to take to keep the United States as the most potent economic power in the world. Coming out of a recession in which jobs are scarce, dependence on foreign oil remains high, our Asian trade imbalance still exists, and the economy is still recovering from the recent financial crisis, we are forced to consider what the priorities of our country will be in the years ahead. Will we focus additional money and efforts on developing alternative energy solutions? Will we emphasize the need to rebuild our teetering infrastructure with new roads and bridges to simultaneously create jobs and stimulate the economy? Will we concentrate efforts on training the next generation of entrepreneurs and work to increase the number of individuals pursuing careers in science, math, and technology?

Another lurking frontier is establishing how our actions show what we as a country value. Questions of humanity abound: Will we provide sufficient care for our military veterans, both in terms of health care needs and economic and job-related needs? Will we take care of our seniors and maintain and/or modify Social Security, Medicare, and Medicaid? Will we work harder to end hunger? Will we adequately deal with privacy issues related to our innovations in technology and social media? Will we combat bullying, both at school and in the cyber world? Will we assist the roughly 50 million Americans with disabilities and/or special needs? Will we advance in the battle against obesity and in how we treat mental illness? Will we protect and/or expand the civil rights accorded to our citizens, regardless of the color of their skin, where they come from, what they do, or whom they love? Will we continue to fight prejudice and discrimination? Will we successfully address immigration issues?

And there is the frontier of global issues and safety concerns, from which more questions arise: Will we seek to understand the issues of climate change and make efforts to further protect the environment? Will we keep Americans safe and secure, both at home and abroad? Will we contain nuclear threats around the globe such as those posed by Iran and North Korea?

Another frontier speaks to our national spirit, about which we ask: Will we promote the arts and humanities? Will we devote resources to increasing our awareness and appreciation of the human condition in the form of medical and scientific research? Will we continue to explore space and one day land a person on Mars? Will we gain a more civil public discourse? Will we uphold the inalienable rights outlined in our sacred Constitution? Will we fix our atmosphere of political bickering? Will we elect new leaders who are not part of the old rivalries and who are serious about bringing about the changes we need? Will we be ever mindful of helping one another and encourage the sense of community that underscored the thrust of Kennedy's efforts? Will we determine ways to more effectively handle our disagreements rather than by suffering through partisan stalemates each time the political parties choose not to compromise?

And what about the frontier of education and health care? We must consider how America's ranking in overall global competitiveness has dropped to seventh,[3] with recent data indicating that America is ranked eleventh worldwide in fourth-grade math, tenth in eighth-grade science, and seventeenth overall in education.[4] Will we reverse this perceived decline of American competitiveness in the world? In terms of health care, relative to other developed nations in the Organization for Economic Co-operation and Development (OCED), which was established during Kennedy's presidency, we have much higher health care costs than the average OCED country, fewer physicians, fewer hospital beds, and lower life expectancy.[5]

Will we continue to examine and improve our health care, providing better access and lower costs?

And the concerns go on, demonstrating clearly that the new frontiers of today—as they were in the 1960s—are vast.

The spirit of service and sacrifice Kennedy expressed does not provide solutions for all of these challenges. But it provides us with a means of approaching them. It offers a bridge between our questions and our answers—that is, if we are willing to grapple with the difficult issues at hand according to certain unbending principles and if we can work collectively toward common goals, regardless of the differences that divide us. It is our responsibility to embrace the spirit of the New Frontier in our own lives so we can meet the challenges of our time; it is time to embrace our obligations as citizens so we can take action and embody the spirit of service our country needs.

Seeking a More Civil Public Discourse

Rededicating ourselves to the principles of service and public betterment will position us well for facing the challenges of our times head on. Yet to do so, we must overcome a considerable obstacle: the partisan divisiveness that marks our public discourse. How can we tackle all the myriad problems if we do not work together? As Abraham Lincoln said, "A house divided against itself cannot stand"—let alone solve the issues at hand.[6]

We as a nation have somehow forgotten that we're on the same team. Our society seems to have moved away from the civility and cohesiveness that a spirit of shared sacrifice brings forth; we have departed in some sense from Kennedy's message of citizenship. This reality undermines the work we hope to do as a people; it weakens our sense of community and impedes our resolve. A renewed emphasis on collective effort highlights the need for mutual cooperation, and therefore we need to make the public exchange of ideas more dignified and more functional.

The shift in the tone of public dialogue is most visible in the bitter climate of narrow-mindedness that defines our political atmosphere—particularly among many of our elected officials who show such disdain for those with opposing views that at times it seems like there is barely a dialogue at all. We live in an era in which our representatives in government appear to be more focused on reelections than results. They disparage one another; they vote for or against legislation on the basis of who proposed it, not whether the legislation is good or bad or right for the country. They would rather score political points than engage in an honest exchange of ideas predicated on the belief that we all love our nation and want to make it better for the next generation. There is little spirit of compromise or mutual cooperation, which we very badly need. This environment divides us; it hinders our ability to make advances as a nation.

Fixing the Mess

Solving the partisan gridlock in Washington and elsewhere is a common desire. Pundits talk about it, journalists write about it, people want it, and even politicians are quick to agree that it ought to be a top priority. Yet we haven't made progress on this issue in some time, and in a basic sense, this is because the spirit of service and citizenship that underscored Kennedy's rhetoric is not being heeded in constructive ways.

Kennedy's brand of citizenship suggests that there are certain principles to which we must adhere if we are going to bring about a more fruitful public dialogue. A return to these ideals is in fact the means by which we will achieve this aim. This is so because being a good citizen—doing what is right for our country and accepting individual responsibility—by nature invites a more civil exchange of ideas. It means being tolerant of others, even if we disagree—that we must make efforts to disagree without being distasteful in how we express that divergence in view.

This is not to suggest that Kennedy was not a partisan figure in his time or that those with opposing views did not fiercely contest the issues of the 1960s. Kennedy lived in partisan times, too. But there was a different tone underlying political debate. Individuals and parties attacked one another's positions—yet there was a genteel element in such exchanges that suggested politics had parameters, it had rules. This spirit existed well into the 1980s, when Republican president Ronald Reagan and Democratic house speaker Tip O'Neill battled over policy and legislation but found ways to compromise for the sake of making national progress, despite their personal differences. (In fact, Reagan and O'Neill used to joke with one another that they would argue fiercely during the day, but after 6 P.M., they were friends.[7]) Today, this concept seems foreign. People reject the views of others because of which party they belong to, not the merits of the actual views being voiced. They attack the person, not the position. They are adversaries, not friends.

To meet the host of challenges on the horizon requires that we behave in certain ways. We should not be acting merely out of convenience, or self-preservation, or in search of popularity. We should not be fostering the "me first" mentality that our politics encourages—a mentality that manifests itself in ways even outside the political arena by affecting how we relate to one another in our daily lives. We should be acting in ways that reveal our understanding and compassion and common love of country. We should be acting in ways that live up to our potential to work together and be partners in addressing causes of common concern. We should be focused on finding ways to bring people together, not drive them apart for the sake of winning elections. This is the kind of ethos that brings about national progress; this is what it means to fulfill our obligations as individual citizens, and we can fix the problems with our political dialogue by embracing these aims.

Guiding Principles

A key lesson, and among the most important, is to accept that none of us, and neither major political party, has the answer to every looming question or problem. Naturally, this fact suggests that there is a persistent need for mutual cooperation—that the first step in achieving progress is identifying certain goals and the obstacles that stand in their way. Partisanship may have its purposes, but blind party loyalty is not in and of itself helpful or constructive—it divides rather than unites. And if we look toward our commonalities as citizens of a great republic, the fog of partisanship and division can disappear in favor of more robust and honest debate, which in turn can lead us toward the destinations of health, happiness, and security that we all want to give to the next generation.

To look deeper than party labels requires insight and patience, but there are tangible rewards for doing so. To look beyond labels is to reveal that less divides us than our politics suggest, and more unites us than our rhetoric implies. When the economy is in recession, we all feel the brunt of it. When we go to war, Republicans and Democrats fight alongside one another passionately and loyally—and when bullets are flying, no one asks who his comrades voted for in the last election. When our national pride is wounded after years of foreign wars, we all feel it. When divisions in our national politics prevent the progress we covet, we are all frustrated. There are Democrats who believe in low taxes and who are against abortion, just as there are Republicans who are gay and in favor of gun control. To be from a "blue" state does not mean you are a Democrat or a believer only in Democratic values, and to be from a "red" state does not mean you are a Republican or a believer only in Republican values.

Hence, Kennedy could advocate the need for government regulation of the economy while also submitting legislation that would lower taxes. Similarly, he could distrust the military apparatus and remain skeptical of its recommendations while still appearing hawkish in his tendencies and certain actions he undertook. He could be a fierce Cold Warrior but sound the voice of reason, logic, and peace. He could argue for a higher minimum wage while seeking to help American businesses remain competitive and strong. At the heart of these notions is the idea that a civil public discourse permits the kind of debate needed to make compromises and move our nation forward.

We do not need to accept the modern political atmosphere as the status quo of the twenty-first century. Individual citizens can work together to elect better leaders who are more committed to bipartisanship and the almost elementary concept of teamwork. Accordingly, we must demand a more constructive spirit of compromise and cooperation from our public officials, regardless of their party affiliation. When extremist voices in either political party threaten the peaceful and otherwise cordial exchange of ideas vis-à-vis political debate, turning it into sound bites and attacks instead, it is incumbent upon that party's mainstream leaders to condemn those efforts and bring renewed focus to maintaining the civility in public life that we seek. Those so-called moderates who permit this behavior are as guilty as the perpetrators of a bitter discourse who seek to divide and delegitimize opponents rather than argue the merits of their positions. We are reminded of the adage: "Every country has the government it deserves."[8] We should act in a way that shows we deserve better. And if the adage holds true, then we will reap what we sow.

Embracing Kennedy's Legacy

Key to grasping for more individual responsibility is a better understanding of the obligations of citizenship that Kennedy made a cornerstone of the New Frontier. To be inspired by the thrust of the Kennedy presidency, then or now, is to relate to classical understandings of human existence. To the Greeks and Romans, there was no deeper inclination than the desire to belong, to be a part of society and seek happiness together with one's family and neighbors. Threats to community life were threats to all citizens; conversely, all could share the fruits of an individual's progress in developing new means of living more productively. Kennedy suggested that the same realities govern the modern world. Therefore, we participate in public affairs both as an obligation to our society and so that we can each reap the benefits of living in it. Certain responsibilities, then, should be self-evident.

For one, individuals should strive to fulfill their potential. To contribute to a nation's prestige and welfare is to contribute one's skills and talents to society—there is no replacement for an individual who does not use whatever skills and talents he has. We are not widgets; we are each unique. Though individual honors may be bestowed—and such honors should be encouraged as a means of eliciting the best kinds of individual action—such efforts should aim toward the larger purpose of securing and ensuring national progress. Accordingly, the more basic theme is that one should seek to be involved in society; participation in public affairs is the most fundamental realization of one's citizenship.

For some, this may mean being involved in politics or seeking public office; for others, it may mean following the news and being engaged in the issues of the day and exercising one's right to vote; for still others it may simply mean going about their business, in whatever profession in which they work, public or private, to play an important role in their communities. Perhaps this includes coaching a youth soccer team and teaching children about the virtues of sportsmanship and strong character. Maybe it is volunteering time to help an organization achieve its goals, donating money to charity, or assisting an elderly neighbor with the groceries or mowing the lawn. On some level and at certain times, it means putting public interest above private comfort.

By the same token, we must hold ourselves accountable for the actions of our communities. Whether we are our brother's keeper may be debated, but our communities are undoubtedly reflections of the values and objectives we seek to promote. To stand idly by while one's community drifts away from these values and objectives is to reject one's civic obligation to participate and to avoid fulfillment of our sacred duty to give to the next generation a world better than the one we inherited. Certain collective values and objectives may change over time, but there are certain basic truths that never change. Kennedy's rhetoric—and the spirit that adorned his words—was successful and inspiring for this reason.

In his farewell address to the Massachusetts State Legislature in January 1961, just days before his inauguration, Kennedy enunciated the new vision of citizenship he had begun to present on the campaign trail—a vision based on classical precepts that would form the basis of action in the New Frontier. What Pericles said to his fellow Athenians, Kennedy said, was equally true of the commonwealth where he had been raised: "We do not imitate—for we are a model to others."[9]

Model Citizens

As the Greeks understood, world leadership is something that is earned by model behavior. To be the envy of the world requires higher standards of living and responsibility, and to invite emulation implies that certain actions are worthy of imitation. America, too, Kennedy suggested, could be a lesson to the world if it channeled its energies toward the right goals and focused on an older brand of citizenship.

This notion had broad implications. It meant that Americans would need to respond to certain challenges in ways other nations would not. It implied that global progress hinged on the progress of its leading nation. It signified that if America could not do something, no nation could, and therefore America was indeed the last best hope of Earth for seeking and building a better world.

To live up to this reputation—to truly be the subject of emulation, praise, and even envy—required a recommitment to certain common themes. "For of those to whom much is given," Kennedy continued in his speech before the Massachusetts State Legislature, "much is required." To inherit wealth and power, in other words, comes with certain attendant obligations that cannot be avoided if that wealth and power are to be maintained; and such resources are to be used constructively for the betterment of the human condition. The actions we take will be remembered and judged. And with the world's eyes upon us, this rhetoric implied, Americans can and must live by certain rules, by certain values—values that exude American greatness and invite the emulation that such greatness commands.

Living in these ways—seeking to be a pioneer in the New Frontier—in fact required more than behaving in certain ways. It also required larger imagination—a spirit commensurate with the force underpinning national goals and the collective desire for progress—a willingness to look beyond the prism of today toward a vast future of unknown possibilities. This style—this mode of living—cuts deeper than a dedication to civic obligation. It compels certain understandings of how we ought to relate to one another and how we can identify the goals we, as a society, wish to pursue. Indeed, the realities of the modern world in this era of globalization and interdependence suggest that the standards for remaining "as a city upon a hill" grow ever higher and more challenging. Only in working together—in emphasizing collective progress over individual advancement—can the larger truths of national greatness be affirmed and bestowed for generations to come. Only if we live up to our responsibilities as citizens can the nation we love move toward the destinations we seek.

Camelot Today

Channeling the Kennedy Spirit

Kennedy's America certainly does not solve contemporary problems. In fact, it would seem that the New Frontier raises more questions than it answers; it highlights more problems than solutions. But by the nature of the questions it raises, citizens are asked to consider modifying certain assumptions that can guide a society toward progress. When candidate Kennedy told his fellow citizens that a Kennedy presidency would not be about what he intended to offer the American people but rather what he intended to ask of them, he implied that a changing of attitudes would be necessary to bring forth the changes in policy that were needed. One must accept the responsibilities of individual citizenship before he or she can fully weigh the advantage or necessity of a particular program or initiative, just as an articulation of political priorities requires dedication to a certain set of fundamental societal values. Kennedy's vision emphasized choices over challenges in ways aimed to evoke allegiance to a higher calling.

This is not to say that the Kennedy standard of service and sacrifice can be achieved at any time; it must fit the circumstances. But it suggests that a more basic truth must be universally accepted in order for national progress to be achieved—the notion that the virtues of civic obligation and public betterment must be embodied by each new generation looking to build on past greatness. Kennedy's vision here remains useful.

In addressing the new frontiers of our time, it will be impossible for us to agree on the best approach for every concern. We will also differ on which issues should take precedence over others, and even perhaps who is best equipped to address them. What is important, though, is that we remind ourselves that despite the flaring of passions—despite our disagreements and the issues that highlight our differences—we will always be united by the common elements of our citizenship and the essence of service that Kennedy so eloquently expressed. As Thomas Jefferson said in his first inaugural address: "Every difference of opinion is not a difference of principle. We have called by different names brethren of the same principle. We are all Republicans; we are all [Democrats]."[10]

Photograph by Abbie Rowe, White House Photographs/John F. Kennedy Presidential Library and Museum, Boston.

A central aim of JFK's presidency became challenging Americans to be pioneers in the New Frontier.

We Need Pioneers

While it would be convenient to blame our problems on the partisan divide and the weaknesses of our elected officials, we must also demand more of ourselves as we move toward solving the issues of our generation. The frontiers of the twenty-first century require the same kind of energy and devotion that Kennedy elicited fifty years ago. In fact, as the challenges have increased in scope and complexity, the need for our collective commitment to citizenship has grown, too. Therefore, we must look inward to assess whether each of us is contributing what is expected of us, and we are challenged to think critically in terms of how we can make our communities better.

If we are to effectively meet the challenges of our time, we need to heed Kennedy's message. Though the challenges are great, so are the opportunities, and we can use Kennedy's brand of citizenship as an instructive tool in carving a path forward. To do so, we need individuals to accept responsibility and seek to determine in their own lives how they can best contribute to our progress. We need people to work together toward common goals in the new frontiers of our time, particularly when faced with adversity. In short, we need new pioneers who are willing to be good citizens—individuals who are willing to make a difference in the national quest to secure a better future for the next generation.

We have the ability to answer this call to action. Whether we do so will be reflected in the choices we make and the causes we champion— and the priorities we define in our public discourse. If we commit ourselves to these efforts, decades from now people will be talking about emulating *our* generation and the work that *we* will have done.

Such efforts, Kennedy reminded us, will not be easy. But that truth lies at the very essence of why we make them—because going beyond what is necessary in our individual lives is what makes us, as Americans, different. It is what separates the average American from individuals in other lands—it is the defining element of our citizenship. Indeed, we choose to do these things, as Kennedy said, "not because they are easy, but because they are hard, because [they] serve to organize and measure the best of our energies and skills, because that challenge is one that we are willing to accept, one we are unwilling to postpone, and one which we intend to win."[11]

It is time to get to work and embody the virtues of citizenship that formed the basis of progress in the New Frontier—and which can do so again.

JFK presents Robert Frost with a Congressional Gold Medal. The public bestowing of medals has been used not only to honor individuals of great achievement, but also to highlight for other citizens the need for them to contribute to society.

JFK speaks at a reception for recipients of the Congressional Medal of Honor—the highest military honor in America. These individuals went above and beyond the call of duty. Their actions remind us to consider what each of us can do in our lives to make our country better.

CHAPTER 8

Profiles in Service

"In your hands, my fellow citizens, more than mine, will rest the final success or failure of our course."

—JOHN F. KENNEDY,
inaugural address, January 20, 1961

ON NOVEMBER 13, 1969, President Richard Nixon signed Executive Order 11494 establishing the Presidential Citizens Medal, which recognizes Americans who have "performed exemplary deeds of service for their country or their fellow citizens."[1] The award is bestowed annually by the American president to recipients whom he chooses at his sole discretion for acts of public service outside the course of their regular jobs. It is among the highest civilian honors that the president can bestow.

John Kennedy did not live to see the creation of this medal, but it is an award that is wholly consistent with the thrust of his presidency. It represents the kinds of actions he hoped his bold rhetoric would elicit. It highlights the most salient traits of what it means to be a good citizen.

The winners of this prestigious award have ranged from well-known public figures to everyday heroes. They have come from different backgrounds and different professions; they have been different ages and served in different places; they have worked on different issues and for different kinds of people. Yet all of them have embraced in their own lives, consciously or not, the ideals of which Kennedy spoke and the brand of citizenship he embodied. Each of them personifies what it means to close the "citizenship gap"—that difference between where we are as a society and where we hope to be—and focus on efforts that benefit the wider community.

The Medal Today

The Requirements

According to the White House website, the Presidential Citizens Medal recognizes individuals:

- **Who have a demonstrated commitment to service in their own community or in communities farther from home.** Someone who has engaged in activities that have had an impact in their local community, on a community or communities elsewhere in the United States, or on fellow citizens living or stationed around the world.

- **Who have helped their country or their fellow citizens through one or more extraordinary acts.** Individuals who have demonstrated notable skill and grace, selflessly placed themselves in harm's way, taken unusual risks or steps to protect others, made extraordinary efforts to further a national goal, or otherwise conducted themselves admirably when faced with unusually challenging circumstances.

- **Whose service relates to a long-term or persistent problem.** Individuals who have made efforts to combat stubbornly persistent problems that impact entire communities, for example those who have taken innovative steps to address hunger, homelessness, the dropout crisis, lack of access to health care, and other issues that plague too many Americans.

• **Whose service has had a sustained impact on others' lives and provided inspiration for others to serve.** The ideal nominee for a Citizens Medal is a person whose work has had a meaningful and lasting impact on the lives of others.[2]

In short, these metrics offer a tangible sense of how the government defines citizenship in the ideal. Each individual who lives up to these facets of service fulfills the aim we share of being good citizens; they are among our role models. This collective effort is what propels national progress.

Defining These Values

When the annual award ceremony is conducted, the sitting president describes the actions that brought each medal recipient to the occasion. Such events present an opportunity for the president to define his views on citizenship and what this concept entails.

In a medal ceremony held on February 15, 2013, in the East Room of the White House, President Barack Obama voiced both the importance of public service and the related responsibilities of citizenship. America is home to "people who come from every background, who worship every faith, who hold every single point of view," he said. "But what binds us together, what unites us, is a single, sacred word: citizen."[3]

This idea—that out of many, we are one—that our nationality is the common thread that connects us—is the cornerstone of our national strength. It is not merely a common belief in a system or a love of country, but a more basic feeling that our fate is indeed tied to that of our neighbor; that in helping others, we are doing the right thing, and in fact, such efforts improve our own lives as well. Citizenship entails responsibility—a need to be involved and participatory and concerned with the welfare of our communities.

To accept one's responsibility to one's community is a fulfillment of this obligation. And though we can each endeavor to behave this way, to actually do so requires the kind of sacrifice Kennedy had in mind when he urged Americans not to ask what they could do for themselves but what they could do for their country. Such work is not intended to be easy. If it were easy, it would not be considered sacrifice. It would not separate out those who shoulder more of their community's burdens from those who merely take care of themselves. It would make the idea of being American—which in Kennedy's time meant accepting more responsibility than our laws require—less unique.

This is who we are. "That's what it means to be a citizen of the United States of America," declared Obama in the February 2013 medal ceremony. We're all busy with our personal lives. We each have bills to pay, jobs or school to go to, errands to run, and things we want to do for leisure. As busy as we are, it would be easy—"even understandable," Obama tells us—for each of us to just focus on ourselves, to worry about our own problems, to express a desire to help but feel like we can't do something because the challenges appear too big to make a difference or too burdensome to fit into our schedules. But "that's not who we are," Obama says. "That's not what we do. That's not what built this country. In this country, we look out for one another. We get each other's backs, especially in times of hardship or challenge."

Such are the actions that have earned individuals the prestigious Presidential Citizens Medal.

Medal Recipients

Part of the allure of the Presidential Citizens Medal is the range of the people and acts that have merited the award. Just as Obama noted that U.S. citizens are of all stripes and backgrounds, so, too, have been the recipients: athletes, artists, elected officials, soldiers, teachers, scientists, and more. Some have been famous, some have not. Some have been rich, some have been poor. Some have been young, some have been old. It is worth learning some of their stories, because each story sheds light on the potential we have as individuals and as a country; each story demonstrates how one individual took it upon himself or herself to go beyond the call of duty and work to help others.

ROBERTO CLEMENTE

On May 14, 1973, President Nixon presented the first medal posthumously to the famed athlete Roberto Clemente. Of Puerto Rican descent, Clemente was a Hall of Fame baseball player for the Pittsburgh Pirates and one of the greatest individuals ever to play the game. He was not given the award for his baseball accolades, however, but for the considerable and selfless charitable work he did off the field—work that ultimately cost him his life.

Clemente regularly spent his offseason winters performing charity work. When Nicaragua suffered a massive earthquake just before Christmas in 1972, Clemente, who had visited the country just weeks earlier, immediately began leading relief efforts to aid the people and arranged for the air delivery of various aid packages, including food. When Clemente learned that the packages on the flights were not getting to the victims but were instead being looted by corrupt government officials, he decided to board the next flight in the hope that his presence would ensure that the packages reached the intended recipients. His New Year's Eve flight, however, suffered mechanical failure and crashed into the ocean shortly after taking off from San Juan, Puerto Rico, killing Clemente and the pilot.

Speaking at the inaugural ceremony of the Presidential Citizens Medal, Nixon spoke of Clemente's "selfless dedication to helping those with two strikes against them in life" and how he "set an example for millions."

"As long as athletes and humanitarians are honored," Nixon continued, "Roberto Clemente's memory will live; as long as Citizens

Medals are presented, each will mean a little more because this first one went to him."[4]

Here, Nixon established a benchmark for the kind of action that would qualify as being worthy of the award—"selfless dedication" to helping those less fortunate, and setting an example for others—an important precedent that others would follow in time. In demonstrating to the American people what kinds of works citizens could perform, the award began to carry a tacit message that one can readily identify in Kennedy's rhetoric: past generations had done their part to make our country better; now we must live up to the high standards they set. In other words, as Kennedy said in his inaugural address, "We dare not forget today that we are the heirs of that first revolution."

RAYMOND WEEKS

Dubbed the "Father of Veterans Day," Raymond Weeks was a key force behind the establishment of the national holiday we celebrate each November 11. Before Weeks's efforts, the date November 11 was annually observed as Armistice Day, which commemorated the peace treaty that ended World War I. But when Weeks returned home to Birmingham, Alabama, after serving in World War II, he made a new mission for himself: to convert Armistice Day into a new national holiday honoring American veterans of all wars.

Weeks established a grassroots campaign in Birmingham, which had its kickoff event on Armistice Day in 1947. He organized a parade and other ceremonial festivities for that November day, but he called it "National Veterans Day." Soon the movement caught on. Stirred by Weeks's efforts, Kansas congressman Edward Rees proposed legislation to change the name and purpose of the holiday. The bill passed in 1954 and was signed into law by President Dwight Eisenhower.[5]

In November 1982, President Ronald Reagan recognized Weeks's efforts by awarding him a Presidential Citizens Medal. Weeks had earned the award, Reagan said, for exemplifying "the finest traditions of American voluntarism by his unselfish service to his country." Weeks had "devoted his life to serving others, his community, the American veteran, and his nation." In honoring Weeks, Reagan continued, "we honor the ideals that we hope to live up to."[6]

Reagan's words again reveal the purpose of the medal: to highlight certain values—American values—that personify what it means to be a good citizen. The recognition bestowed simultaneously rewards the recipient and invites others to emulate what that individual has done. By seeing someone extolling the virtues of citizenship, we are prompted to ask ourselves if we are living up to our responsibilities in our own lives—if we are doing as much as we can to help others and make our communities stronger and more vibrant for those who come after us.

More specifically, the recognition of Weeks's efforts to honor the American veteran highlights a critical cause: supporting the members of our dedicated military. In awarding the medal to Weeks, Reagan was also placing emphasis on the underlying cause for which Weeks had fought. In doing so, he underscored the importance of the highest calling of service in the name of our country: military service.

CONSTANCE BAKER MOTLEY

Constance Baker Motley grew up in New Haven, Connecticut, the child of immigrants from the West Indies. After graduating from Columbia Law School, Motley went to work as an attorney at the NAACP Legal Defense and Education Fund, where she began a lifetime of public service. Working closely with prominent civil rights attorneys Thurgood Marshall and Jack Greenberg, Motley argued several winning cases before the Supreme Court and became a legal architect of the civil rights movement. Later, she became the first black woman elected to the New York State Senate, the first woman to be borough president of Manhattan, and the first black woman to be named a federal judge.

Motley's remarkable devotion to public service demonstrates how individuals can make a meaningful difference in their community and country once they have recognized the cause that inspires them. Motley had grown up in the pre–civil rights era and experienced racial discrimination as a child—in a time when the number of women entering professions, including law, was much lower than it is today. Yet she had a mission: to "prove in everything I do that blacks and women are as capable as anyone."[7] She made this creed the central force in her life, and it inspired all of the great work that she did.

In awarding her the Presidential Citizens Medal, President Bill Clinton noted that "as advocate, lawyer, public servant, and judge, she has been far more than capable; she has been superb."[8]

We can glean important lessons from Motley's story. Before choosing in what form of service her efforts would take shape, she identified the underlying cause for which she wanted to work: equality. Once this priority was established, she made decisions that reflected this choice and committed herself to doing what she could to advance her goal.

Another noteworthy observation is that serving the public interest does not necessarily mean doing work free of charge or at one's own expense. In many instances, an individual can work in a profession that by nature is intended to serve the public interest. In Motley's case, her contributions included working for an organization that seeks justice, holding public office, and serving as a judge.

PATRISHA WRIGHT

While training to be an orthopedic surgeon, Patrisha Wright was diagnosed with a degenerative muscle disease that left her with double vision. Her diagnosis highlighted not only the new challenges she would be confronting, but also the challenges that millions of Americans were already facing in the form of discrimination owing to their disabilities. Though Wright could have focused on dealing with her own problems, she endeavored to fight for the rights of others like her across the country and made this the cause of her life.

Wright founded the Disability Rights Education and Defense Fund in Washington, D.C., and from 1979 to 2005, she served as the director of government affairs at the organization. Through her work there, Wright strove to ensure that the rights of individuals with disabilities were treated as civil rights. Such efforts resulted in the enactment of the Handicapped Children's Protection Act of 1986 and revisions to the Fair Housing Act, which barred landlords from discriminating against disabled people. Known affectionately as "the General," she became a central player in the coordinated campaign to pass the historic Americans with Disabilities Act of 1990.[9]

Bill Clinton gave Wright a Presidential Citizens Medal in 2001. "Instead of fixing broken bones," Clinton said at the award ceremony, "she set about to fix what was broken in our system." Though a visual impairment changed her career path, "her dedication to civil rights has changed the path of America and helped more of us to see clearly."[10]

Wright's story reveals a basic truth about citizenship: we each have choices in our lives about what our priorities are going to be and what kinds of efforts we are going to make while we seek to fulfill our goals. We can choose to focus on priorities that benefit us personally, and of course, there are certain individual obligations we each have. But there is always opportunity to choose to make some of our priorities ones that benefit our communities. In some instances, this choice requires that we sacrifice time and effort we would otherwise be putting into our personal concerns. In the face of adversity, Wright chose not to shrink from her responsibilities as someone who could make a difference; she put the best of her energies and skills to work.

SAMUEL HEYMAN

Samuel Heyman graduated from law school in 1963. Inspired by JFK's call to service, Heyman took a job in the Justice Department and served as an assistant U.S. attorney.[11] He later worked in the private sector, where he achieved considerable business success, but he nonetheless retained a core belief that public service was a critical element of national progress. He became a noted philanthropist and focused his efforts on promoting public service at academic institutions, which included supporting public service fellowships at three law schools as well as a public policy center at Duke University.

In 2001—fearing that the generation of public servants inspired by Kennedy would soon be retiring—he formed a nonprofit, nonpartisan organization called the Partnership for Public Service.[12] The purpose of the organization is to revitalize ways in which the federal government operates and to encourage a new generation of Americans to seek civil service jobs. Through comprehensive training and recruitment programs, employee-engagement initiatives, and work on modernizing management systems and structures, the partnership works to provide resources and support to government personnel.

In recognition of his lifetime of service, President George W. Bush presented Heyman a Presidential Citizens Medal in December 2008 for his "steadfast devotion" to America. "By encouraging young leaders to answer the call of public service," the award citation read, "he has helped promote a vibrant Federal workforce. The United States honors Samuel Heyman for his dedication to improving the efficiency, transparency, and accountability of the Federal Government."[13]

Some people volunteer their time. Some donate their money. Some, like Heyman, do both. What is true of everyone who seeks to serve the public interest is that he or she has identified a cause in which they believe—a cause that, if nourished, has the potential to make our country a better place. For Heyman, this cause was improving how our government operates. His work reflects the inspiring campaign pledge Kennedy made in 1960, which motivated him to be active in public life: to get things moving again, to improve the system, to recruit the best and the brightest Americans to partake in civic affairs, and to take actions intended to benefit the generations to follow.

ROBERTA DIAZ BRINTON

For more than twenty years, Roberta Diaz Brinton has devoted her time and energy to improving science and technology education for inner-city youth in Los Angeles, California. Brinton serves as the director of the University of Southern California's Science, Technology and Research (STAR) Program, where she has helped open doors of opportunity to thousands of disadvantaged and minority students through one-on-one mentoring, hands-on learning opportunities, and college scholarships. In her professional research as a neuroscientist, she has dedicated her efforts to designing therapeutic molecules and devices for the treatment of disorders of the nervous system.[14] On August 4, 2010, President Obama announced her as a winner of the Presidential Citizens Medal.

Brinton's work highlights the causes she has chosen to champion in her community. Though the issues she has supported are different from those of the other medal winners profiled here, certain themes should be familiar. Brinton's work stems from a desire to help people— to improve her community and contribute to the well-being of society. She has identified causes she cares about and has directed her efforts in ways that reflect her priorities. When given the opportunity to improve the lives of others, she has chosen to act and give back to help pave the way for the next generation.

Her professional work as a neuroscientist has included seeking knowledge and answers in the face of medical challenges so that lives can be saved and the human condition can be improved. In her work as director of the STAR Program, she is literally training the next generation so that it is better prepared to live up to its potential and make contributions of its own.

As Kennedy made clear, no individual, and no generation, is responsible for solving all problems and meeting all challenges. In speaking of the tasks America faced in January 1961, when he delivered his inaugural address, he noted, "All this will not be finished in the first hundred days. Nor will it be finished in the first thousand days, nor in the life of this Administration, not even perhaps in our lifetime on this planet. But let us begin."[15] What is needed, Kennedy said, is for individuals and communities to strive to build upon the work of past generations with the goal of making progress and giving to the generation that follows a better and more hopeful world—with more work needed to bring certain tasks to completion. This is a fulfillment of the generational imperative to serve and make a difference.

We're Not Expected to Be Medal Winners

These stories of some of the Presidential Citizens Medal recipients demonstrate the diversity of the opportunities that lie before us to make a difference in the lives of others and for our country. They also show how making strides in the spirit of service is an attainable goal. To be a good citizen, these winners' stories make clear, requires no specific set of circumstances or any particular qualifications. There is no magic formula, no common methodology. We can exhibit the virtues of citizenship in whatever environment and at whatever stage of life.

Perhaps you find these stories somewhat daunting—these people have helped communities on a level many of us might not be able to fathom. Keep in mind that while they serve as role models for us, we are not expected to be medal winners—we are, however, expected to do our share. Each of us can be part of something extraordinary by doing ordinary things in our own lives that advance the interests of our community.

Kennedy's famous inaugural command implicitly recognized that each of us has the potential to help our community and make a difference. But he chose his words carefully, and it is worth noting that he did not demand that we take certain actions; he did not delineate specific tasks. He did not insist that we work to change laws, or that we leave our jobs to help the space program, or that we join the military, start a charitable foundation, or begin a national movement. Rather, he asked us to consider shifting our priorities and our perspectives. Instead of focusing on ourselves and on what we can *receive* from society, he implored, we should ask ourselves what we can *give* to society—whether in choosing to work in a profession that benefits the public interest, volunteering our time to help worthy causes, supporting others who perform community service, or finding some other way in our lives to contribute to and improve society.

The words are deeply inspirational for the concepts they capture, but there is also a concrete aim that goes beyond even shifting the priorities. He says people should actually "ask" what they can do for their country. Ask not merely in the abstract, but in specifics: What can I do to make my community and country better? Which tangible actions should I take to achieve these goals? Am I doing enough? Have I truly made the efforts of which I am capable to give back to society in ways commensurate with all that I have received?

A key element of Kennedy's challenge is for individuals to consider the weight of what past generations have done as a means of determining what deeds are expected of them in their own time. This is why he emphasized the notion of generational change and the imperative of service to which each of us is expected to contribute. Part of our rite of passage as citizens is to assess what we each feel we can do to improve the lives of our neighbors.

Most people will not receive medals for their actions. Most, in fact, will receive little, if any, recognition at all for what they do in the name of their communities. But we must make the effort. And though most of us will not change a federal law, start a national organization, or create a federal holiday, our collective effort is what matters and what counts and what provides the foundation for progress. We must choose to make these efforts, and it is up to us to do so.

As JFK instructed in his inaugural address: "In your hands, my fellow citizens, more than mine, will rest the final success or failure of our course. Since this country was founded, each generation of Americans has been summoned to give testimony to its national loyalty." In giving such testimony, we live up to our civic obligations in ways that enable the progress we seek.

The Power of the Individual

Grassroots Progress

Though we recognize certain individuals with honors and awards, much of what propels an entire nation toward greatness are the combined actions of common citizens—individuals whose names we do not know, whose actions we have not heard, whose effects have been purely on a local level that may not be remembered by more than a few even a generation later but which made a difference nonetheless.

National progress requires grassroots efforts; rarely does it occur from the top down. To be sure, the stroke of a pen can change law and set majestic plans in motion, but it is individual effort on a comparably small level that permits the larger plans to take shape. A president could sign civil rights into law, for instance, but integration, compliance with the law, courage, and acceptance of others would be needed in the towns and cities that experienced conflict most deeply. A president could promise to land a man on the moon and commit the dollars to making it happen, but only hard work, ingenuity, and individual adventurous spirits would transform the dream into reality.

While our public heroes are worthy of praise and emulation, it is our private heroes—the men and women who stand up for justice and righteousness in their own communities, the folks who devote their lives to selfless service to others, the individuals who ask what they can do for their country without seeking reward, the people who risk their security for the promise of making their nation and world a better place, and the citizens who trade a higher income for a different kind of work simply because they know they can contribute in other ways—it is these individuals who form the bedrock of our national greatness. It is these individuals who are heirs to the New Frontier.

Meeting Pioneers

We are fortunate to learn some of these stories: Leo McCarthy, whose daughter was killed by an underage drunken driver in Montana, founded Mariah's Challenge to give educational scholarships to kids who pledge not to drink illegally or get into a car with someone who has been drinking, so future tragedies can be avoided. Geoffrey Canada greatly expanded the Harlem Children's Zone's innovative efforts to increase high school and college graduation rates for poverty-stricken kids growing up in Harlem, New York. Desiline Victor, age 102, went to vote in Florida on Election Day in 2012, and even though the wait was an unbelievable six hours, she waited in line because she felt it was her civic duty to make her voice heard through her vote. Pat Tillman was an NFL football player who gave up a promising career and a large professional contract to enlist in the Army Rangers so he could serve his country. Marjorie Margolies, a former U.S. congresswoman, founded Women's Campaign International to give women around the world the tools and training to become political leaders who can shape policy and be more effective advocates for the public good. Members of the faculty at Sandy Hook Elementary School in Newtown, Connecticut, bravely confronted a deranged shooter to try to protect the innocent children who went to school there instead of saving themselves. Countless individuals served their country heroically in response to the tragedies of 9/11, Hurricanes Katrina and Irene, Superstorm Sandy, and so many more.

Many other pioneers, anonymous ones, have advanced the cause of citizenship in their own ways when opportunities arose in their daily lives. People like my sister, Leslie Reich, who could have pursued a more lucrative career after receiving an Ivy League education but chose to enroll in the Teach for America (TFA) program, where she could provide ripples of hope to children in underserved communities (and she still does so years after completing TFA). People like my friend Maria Glorioso, who, along with friends and colleagues, works to address the medical needs of the uninsured by providing free health care ser-vices to individuals in need. People like my high school classmate Billy Cassidy, who courageously volunteered to join the U.S. armed forces and saw action overseas, and my friend Emily Kramer-Golinkoff, who, despite her own fight against cystic fibrosis, decided to make a differ-ence by working with family and friends to found Emily's Entourage, which raises money and awareness in the search for a cure. People like my friend Brian Selander, who left a successful business career to serve in state government because he knew he could make important con-tributions to his community through public service; and my friend Dr. Ellenmorris Tiegerman, who sought to provide educational program-ming for children with language and autism-spectrum disorders and founded the School for Language and Communication Development to make this happen. These people have selflessly worked to improve the lives of others and the communities to which they belong. Each has asked, if not aloud then internally, what they could do to make a difference—to serve others through a sacrifice on their part. They are pioneers in the next generation of New Frontier life—not because they seek praise, which they do not, but because they simply want to leave this world better than they found it.

And there are countless others who have stepped forward in the spirit of service and citizenship: the individuals who volunteer their time to mentor children in the program Big Brothers Big Sisters; the young girl who opens a lemonade stand on her front lawn and do-nates the proceeds to charity; the teenager who shovels snow or picks up groceries for an elderly neighbor free of charge, simply because he wants to help; the mom or dad who joins the PTA and spends countless hours working to empower children to reach their potential; the reli-gious leader who commits to a lifetime of service to others and works well beyond the job's prescribed duties to make a community stronger; the volunteer at the local hospital; the teacher who goes beyond what is required in the classroom to help students succeed; the patriotic cit-izen who joins the armed forces, and his or her family who also bears such a deep and profound sacrifice by giving up shared time together; the individuals who work with children with special needs; the single parent who works two jobs to ensure that his or her child has the same opportunities as others; the businesspeople who donate a portion of their profits to causes in their communities; the doctors who save and improve lives; the lawyers who work free of charge to defend civil rights and protect the interests of the powerless—these people care about their communities and embody the tenets of citizenship.

Years from now, future Americans will ask what the current generation did to make our country better. They, not us, will be the ones who interpret our legacy. However, we each have a chance every day to take steps that will influence what our legacy looks like, and therefore we must each ask: how can I contribute? Our collective response will shape not only our legacy but also the future of our nation.

JFK delivers one of the most memorable inaugural addresses in history with perhaps the most famous line in any presidential speech: "Ask not what your country can do for you—ask what you can do for your country."

CHAPTER 9

Embracing Our Citizenship

"Now the trumpet summons us again....I do not believe that any of us would exchange places with any other people or any other generation. The energy, the faith, the devotion which we bring to this endeavor will light our country and all who serve it, and the glow from that fire can truly light the world. And so, my fellow Americans: ask not what your country can do for you—ask what you can do for your country."

—JOHN F. KENNEDY,
inaugural address, January 20, 1961

JFK CHARGED AMERICANS with the task of being good citizens. Implicit in this challenge was the idea that each of us has a chance in our lives to contribute something to society, and in fact, we have a sacred obligation to do so. The stories of others who have made their contributions and fulfilled their obligations as citizens can be helpful in determining what kinds of efforts each of us in turn might make. These stories can educate, they can inform, they can inspire—but they cannot choose our causes for us, they cannot make us do the work that is needed. For this, each of us must look inward.

By now, you may be considering how Kennedy's message of citizenship relates to your own life. What causes do *you* believe in? How do you think *you* can make a difference? Are you fulfilling the obligations of *your* citizenship? If Kennedy were president today, would *you* be considered a pioneer in his New Frontier?

Getting Started

Many people wonder how they can get started—how they can determine what cause moves them, what kinds of organizations they would like to support, or what kinds of activities they would like to pursue. While each of these represents a personal choice—and there are no right answers or required actions—there are certain things each of us can consider doing to get us on the road to public service.

The scope of the possibilities seems endless, and the needs of our communities are deep. As a first step, think on a small scale and consider what initiative or cause moves you to want to do something. You do not need to change the entire world; you do not need to revolutionize the way we do something or be the first person to champion a cause (though should you feel so inclined, go for it and be a trailblazer!). In short, as the adage goes, "You do not need to reinvent the wheel."

Finding a Cause

How do you find your cause? First, think about your personal strengths and the issues you care about, and consider how your strengths might relate to these issues. Do you have special skills or expertise that could help a government agency, a community service project, or a charitable organization? Are you an attorney, for example, who likes the idea of doing free legal work for low-income individuals at a legal-aid clinic? Are you a doctor in private practice who can volunteer your time at a local hospital? Are you a teacher who wants to offer after-school tutoring to children in need of extra help? Are you an administrator who could assist a charity that seeks to improve how it operates? Are you a scientist or plumber or engineer or banker or civil servant who can spend your spare time helping children and young adults interested in pursuing these careers? Are you a student who can volunteer at a child-care center? Do you have experience working with children with special needs who might be looking for mentors? Are you interested in becoming a volunteer firefighter or a Little League coach? Do you want to help pass legislation that would improve your community?

Or perhaps you want to do something completely different from what you do as a profession—something that caters to other strengths you have. So, for instance, you may be an entrepreneur by day, but maybe you have a talent for painting and you can teach a community painting class, or visit the sick at a local hospital and work on a project together. Or maybe you are a musician who is a great swimmer and can help kids learn how to swim at the local pool. Or maybe you're a writer who has expertise in gardening and can plant flower beds for an elderly neighbor who can't get outside often but would enjoy seeing roses through the window.

If you're having difficulty identifying your strengths, ask your family and friends for input—they will likely have a good sense of your abilities and perhaps even of what form of service might suit you well. Consider what issues get you passionate and energized when you talk about them. Think, too, about whether you're a people-person or you prefer animals or working with things—you may discover, for example, that you enjoy digging wells for an organization that provides clean water to Third World countries or working with rescued animals at a shelter rather than serving people directly. Do you prefer behind-the-scenes work (printing and mailing flyers for a local nonprofit, for instance), or do you thrive in the limelight (such as speaking at charity events about the importance of an organization's work)? If you're so inclined, take Gallup's StrengthFinders test and see what results come back. Working in areas that you're most passionate about and that play to your strengths makes it easier for you to persevere in that pursuit.

Connecting with Your Cause

Once you have identified your cause, consider how you can connect with it. One easy step is to identify a program or project in your community that you believe in, that relates to your cause, and that could benefit from your involvement (again, no need to reinvent the wheel).

The beauty of service is that there is no limit to what we can do together. There is always room for another person to help. There is always a cause that requires a champion. There is always more we can do. If you want to be a leader, be the one who organizes something. If you want to be a volunteer, seek out opportunities that need people to give their time and energy. If you are shy, bring a friend or ask a friend if you could participate in something he or she does. Find a project you can be proud to represent.

How do you find these programs? One of the easiest ways to identify an opportunity is, again, through talking to your family and friends. Are they involved in an organization or charity? Do they volunteer their time somewhere? Do they buy tickets to charitable events and attend to show their support? What issues have they identified as important in their lives? Maybe they would love for you to join them. Maybe an organization they support is looking for new people to get involved. Maybe an upcoming event requires extra volunteers, and you are just what they need.

Let your family and friends tell you about their community service and what they do. Ask them questions to learn more. Find out if it's something you might be interested in. Ask them how they got involved with their cause and what prompted them to do the work they do. If you're interested, have them bring you to an event or project or have them introduce you to the people in charge who can tell you more about the volunteer opportunities that may be available.

Another way to learn about what opportunities are available is to read your local newspaper and look for news articles covering projects in your community. Some newspapers even have entire sections devoted to highlighting local events taking place for the very purpose of spreading the word and seeking assistance.

You can also visit the website of your local government. Many municipal websites, including those of towns and villages, provide detailed information about ongoing outreach initiatives taking place in the community. Often, specific events are advertised with open invitations to the public to join and participate.

While you're online, consider checking out the social media websites you frequent. It is common for organizations to post opportunities to get involved with their efforts on their Facebook and Twitter pages and in other social media outlets.

Keep in mind you do not need to commit to one cause or organization for a lifetime or even to working on a particular project more than once—try something out and see if you like it. If it's not to your liking, then you've lost nothing other than a little time (and it was probably for a good cause anyway, even if it's not the one to which you decide to dedicate yourself for a time). It is very common for people to try a few different kinds of projects or organizations before they find the one that is the right fit for them. Every person has different interests, and sometimes it takes participating in different efforts to learn whether something is truly of interest or not. And perhaps in trying one kind of project, you will be inspired to discover something else toward which you might direct your energies that you had previously not considered.

Until you've found the right cause or project, start small. You can always commit more time and do more work, but at the beginning, it is important to focus and make sure the effort is something you want to be making and that the effort is in fact benefiting the desired recipients in the ways you envision. Then you can build upon it and bring about the change you seek. On a basic level, we are talking about the expression "Think globally, act locally." The collective effort of individuals doing good deeds is what brings about progress.

Creating New Opportunities

If you are ambitious and would like to start your own project, there are many ways to do so. To begin, you might consider brainstorming ideas—with friends, family, or by yourself—for what kind of project you are interested in working on. If you're having difficulty identifying what this project might be, then step back and think about what other kinds of projects are going on around you and if there might be an initiative you can undertake that supplements such efforts.

Alternatively, take a look at the block you live on, or the town or city you live in, and try to identify a need that is not being addressed or a challenge that is not being met. Your idea does not need to be completely novel; in fact, many of the best service projects involve building on what others have done or emulating what others have done someplace else. So, for instance, you might learn about a program that provides transportation for the elderly in a neighboring community, or a "going green" initiative upon which another town has embarked. Does your community have such programs? Does your community *need* such programs? Would such programs be desirable? If so, you may have identified a cause that needs a champion, and if you're motivated enough, you might decide to take the lead in organizing something.

Another possibility is that you may find a program in your community that already exists and is in need of something you can help provide. Perhaps there is a soup kitchen that feeds the hungry, and the soup kitchen needs volunteers, or it needs to find new sources for the food it distributes. Maybe you are the individual who can create a service project with your friends to help achieve these goals. Maybe there is a local health clinic that could benefit from a blood drive, and you are the person who can organize it and recruit people to participate. Or maybe there is a park restoration project that has volunteers lined up but needs help securing tools and supplies, and you are in a position to provide aid.

If you are still unsure where to direct your efforts or how to channel your creative energies, consider a different approach. Think about different activities that occur in your community that you may not think of as community service. Many people find opportunities to participate at the religious institution to which they belong—maybe you can attend events or get involved in a committee that deals with a particular subject you care about. Take a look at your local school district—is there a Parent Teacher Association? Maybe you want to attend a school board meeting and make your beliefs heard in the hope that you will shape a new policy that is being considered. Alternatively, perhaps you will consider donating your time or money to a local bake sale to benefit a charity or an upcoming school trip for local students.

There are also ways to contribute even if you prefer not to be involved in a group activity or a particular cause. You can fulfill one responsibility of your citizenship by voting, by helping to determine who your elected officials will be. Voting is critical; it is the most basic means of exercising one's citizenship. It is a way of saying that you count, that you matter—that you care about society and the people who lead it in government. Voting is a privilege, to be sure, but it is also a right and a responsibility. You improve your community by participating.

Making Service Fun

Community service is important, and Kennedy reminds us that each of us should consider what kind of sacrifice we can make in our lives. It can also be a lot of fun. When you engage your family and friends and participate in a project together or support a cause together, there is no requirement that such opportunities be serious or solemn occasions. Helping others is a good thing, and you can be happy about doing it! Make your cause exciting. Make it inspirational and something you enjoy doing—this will make you want to do it more often, which will in turn increase the impact you are having on your community.

In addition to making your community service fun, there are ways you can motivate yourself and your friends by tying your community service commitment to things you do for leisure. So, for instance, you might make a deal with your friends that you will do one hour of community service for each home run that your favorite baseball player hits (though if you choose this one, hopefully you'll choose a player who actually hits home runs!). Or you might match every hour of television that you DVR with an hour of volunteer work, or for every song you purchase on iTunes, you will do fifteen minutes of something to help someone else. It is all about perspective. Will you do one day of community service for each week of vacation you take? If you play in a recreational sports league, will you challenge your teammates to do one hour of service each time your team wins? If you like Lady Gaga or Beyoncé or Paul McCartney, will you commit to doing a few hours of volunteer work for each new song they release? Will you commit to an hour of service for every ten cups of coffee you drink?

Make it fun; weave your service into other aspects of your life or something you do regularly. You will think about your cause or project more often, and it will become a more meaningful part of who you are. That is a goal here that was present in all of Kennedy's major speeches: to make the ethic of service and sacrifice both attainable and inseparable from who we are as individuals. Our fates are tied together, and we share the proud title of being American citizens— what we do with this special privilege is something we must each answer for ourselves.

Making a difference is also something that can be very personally rewarding. In fact, as many people who give their time or money to good causes will say, you often get back more than you put in. Helping others is gratifying.

Serving by Profession

Instead of volunteering for causes in their free time, some individuals choose to work in professions that further the causes in which they believe. A person looking to share his or her skills and talents with underserved communities around the world, for example, might join the Peace Corps or become a social worker. Someone seeking to ensure that his community and neighbors remain safe might become a police officer, a firefighter, or an emergency medical technician. An individual looking to serve the public interest might seek elected office.

Even if you are not employed in a profession that furthers the causes most important to you, there are steps you can take to increase your community footprint while at work. You can speak to people in your office about making the office more environmentally friendly, including implementing a recycling program, encouraging people to avoid printing out documents when possible, or starting a carpool program. You can have contests in the office relating to who can save the most paper or who can commute the most times in a given period using only mass transit and not their individual cars in order to reduce carbon emissions. You can organize the collections of old cell phones or batteries. You can initiate office-based community projects such as toy or clothing drives; organize the donation of books to a library, hospital, or a local school; or create care packages for those in the military. You can collect money for an important cause. All of these efforts can have a powerful impact on your local community and at the same time can make you and your colleagues feel good about yourselves.

Incorporating Service into Our Lives

Service Takes Many Forms

Another means of embracing the spirit of service and sacrifice that Kennedy requests is to consider what kinds of things you do in your personal life that help others or the community, however small they may be. Do you drive to work every day? Maybe you can carpool for the purpose of protecting the environment, or if you live close enough, maybe you can occasionally commute on your bicycle or walk to work when it's warm outside. Maybe the next car you lease or purchase will be a hybrid that uses less gasoline in our national quest to become less dependent on foreign oil. Maybe you can use less water or less electricity. Perhaps you can commit to recycling glass and plastic containers rather than throwing them out with the rest of your trash.

You can support your local businesses and farmers. Or maybe you can add socially conscious elements to your company that benefit the community.

Do commonsense things such as cleaning up and disposing of litter after outdoor activities, or giving aid to someone who needs help. These might seem like inconsequential things, but an individual who does them reveals his commitment to being a good citizen. An individual who endeavors to clean up waste that she sees, however unglamorous or minor that sounds, is demonstrating that she cares about her community—how it looks, how it feels, how others passing through might view it. It shows a concern for what that community will look like a generation hence for the new children who will inhabit it. It displays such an individual's priorities and shows what is important. Even things like driving slower in one's community, conserving water, or adjusting the thermostat in one's home or office to save energy—these support everyone's welfare and are worthy of our efforts and consideration. They reveal who we are and the respect we have for our community, our fellow citizens, and those who come after us.

Whether it is identifying an organization that could benefit from our help, helping a neighbor in a time of need, or doing something as simple as cleaning up after ourselves, the point should be clear: We can each contribute something to society. We can find ways to make our lives count. We can be good citizens.

Becoming an Advocate

Once you have identified your cause and become involved, consider becoming an advocate for it in whatever way you think is appropriate. Kennedy's brand of citizenship teaches us that there is nothing so powerful as when communities stand together to tackle common problems. "United, there is little we cannot do in a host of cooperative ventures," Kennedy declared in his inaugural address. "Divided, there is little we can do."[1]

Tell others about the cause you have chosen, explaining why it is a good one. Invite friends to join you in your work. Is there an upcoming event in which your friends might be interested in participating? Does the initiative you are supporting have an element that would appeal to someone you know? Spread the word by using social media. Make it part of your social dynamic. If you're working with Habitat for Humanity to build a home, post a picture on Instagram so your network of contacts can actually see the difference you are making. If you're doing a volunteer project for the Red Cross, make it your Facebook status—better yet, post something about it in advance and encourage others to join you. Then post photos afterward and tell people when the next event is going to be. If you're doing something to support our troops through a local office of the United Service Organizations, tweet or blog about it. Write an article for your community newspaper that discusses your volunteer experiences or the cause you hold dear. Discuss what made you want to participate—maybe others will be motivated by the same altruistic inclinations that encouraged you.

Embody the inspiration you seek to impart in ways in which you are comfortable. You do not need to give a rousing speech the way Kennedy did; you do not need to be elected to public office to have a platform that invites respect and admiration. You can be influential. You can be the change you want to see, in whatever form that may take. Empower yourself and those around you to be successful in ways that lift one another up.

Increase your community engagement on issues that matter to you, and do not let others who may be less motivated bring you down. This is what it means to respond to the appeal Kennedy made in his acceptance speech in July 1960: "I'm asking each of you to be pioneers towards that New Frontier," he said. "My call is to the young in heart, regardless of age—to the stout in spirit, regardless of Party, to all who respond to the scriptural call: 'Be strong and of good courage; be not afraid, neither be [thou] dismayed.'"[2]

And remember: there are different degrees of advocacy. Do what you think is appropriate for you, and don't judge yourself by the deeds of others. We all play different roles in society, and we are not all expected to do the same things and on the same levels. Doing good deeds is what matters.

Training the Next Generation

A critical facet of service is ensuring that we teach our children the virtues of citizenship. Whether it is educating kids at home about the importance of community service, bringing them along on service projects of your own, or doing family activities that involve helping others, it is incumbent upon each of us to determine how we can instill the American values we hold so dear in the next generation—and this spirit of service begins at home.

There are many ways to engage children and incorporate service into their lives. They can participate in the Girl Scouts or Boy Scouts and learn about the importance of honor, integrity, and strong character. You might consider taking a family vacation to a less traditional destination, such as to a community that has been ravaged by a natural disaster so that you can help rebuild a home. You can adopt a stretch of highway and commit to cleaning up litter there a few hours each week or month, or you can drive to the beach or a public park with children and do the same thing. Your family can volunteer at a homeless shelter or feed the hungry at a soup kitchen.

Performing good deeds breeds a charitable environment that strengthens the bond we share as citizens of the same community. It makes us more likely to do additional acts of kindness and generosity; it provides the kind of character and experience that we want the next generation to have so that it can continue to thrive and build upon what we have inherited and what we have contributed. This is how we pass the torch of service to the next generation—by demonstrating what we mean when we say that we care about our neighbors and that our lives are connected to one another. This is a fulfillment of one aspect of the generational imperative of which Kennedy spoke: the need not only to do good deeds but also to foster a climate that permits more action and more progress.

Pride Has a Place

Feeling good about ourselves—feeling pride in what we do and in our communities—is what makes it possible to achieve great things together. It is a pivotal and conscious point Kennedy highlighted in his speeches and actions. It is not simply an individual pride, but a pride we take in the accomplishments of others as we remember that, again, we're all on the same team. In 1969, all Americans shared in the collective pride of our astronauts when they set foot on the moon. Ask anyone who watched this tremendous feat on television how utterly proud they were to be American, and they'll tell you. Neil Armstrong captured that unified spirit when he uttered his famous words, "That's one small step for [a] man, one giant leap for mankind."[3]

This shared pride makes us more inclined to help others, to want to give back to society—to realize that we are not just here to take care of ourselves, but that there is something bigger out there to which we all belong. When we feel this way, we are all more likely to do the small things that make our communities better: we help strangers, we bring litter to a garbage can, we hold the door for someone, we are more patient, we are more polite and generally nicer to one another—and these contributions, however small, are us living out what it means to be a citizen.

The opposite of this environment is also true. When we do not feel a shared pride, this sense of community, we are less inclined to do these things for others and are instead apt to cultivate a "me first" mentality. When we do not feel good about ourselves, we are less likely to help others.

Do we want to look out for our neighbors as ourselves or look out only for Number One? Kennedy painted a picture of the clear benefits that come with citizenship in action, and it is obvious which world we should want. Hence, there is a deep importance in increasing our pride as a means of embracing our common humanity. When we do this, our collective action thrusts our country forward. This is what it means to "get the country moving again," as Kennedy said on the 1960 campaign trail. This is what creates the energy and vitality that marked the New Frontier and can shape the world of today. This is what the Founding Fathers meant in the Declaration of Independence when they concluded that magnificent manifesto with these words: "And for the support of this Declaration ... we mutually pledge to each other our Lives, our Fortunes and our sacred Honor."[4]

We mutually pledge to each other. Our fate is tied to that of our neighbors. We share common hopes and dreams. We belong to the same community, and we promise to help one another as we would want to be helped. This is citizenship. This is the foundation upon which the new social contract Kennedy expressed was conditioned. This is our destiny, and it is our greatness—the very essence of who we are as a people.

Remember Atticus Finch

You will recall our familiar example of how the fictional Atticus Finch in *To Kill a Mockingbird* served his community in small yet discernible ways. He found a cause that was important to him—protecting the rule of law and an innocent man in a time and place where circumstances made it difficult to do so. Once he found his cause, he became passionate about it; he poured his efforts into it as though someone's life depended upon it (which, in his case, it did).

Finch did not seek to change the law or go beyond the scope of his duty; similarly, he did not take on other causes while he was working on his case. He was focused, and he wanted to do a good job on the task at hand, which required his best efforts. He did not seek praise or recognition; he did it because he believed in it and thought it was right.

Such action reflects a basic truth in Kennedy's America that we can embrace today: while service is an imperative that we are all called upon to fulfill, we are not expected to do more than our fair share. We do not need to place more responsibility on ourselves than what is required of us. When each of us lives up to our responsibilities—when each of us lives up to our potential—we are fulfilling our obligations as citizens. It is our collective effort—of millions of people across this land we love doing what we can to contribute—that is the underlying force of national progress. Such is the scale on which our generation's contributions will be measured, and such is the scope of the need to do things in our individual lives that prove us worthy of the generations who came before us.

A New Call to Action

The sound of Kennedy's trumpet is summoning us again. We would be well served to recall his bold inaugural words: "Let the word go forth, from this time and place, to friend and foe alike, that the torch has been passed to a new generation of Americans." It is time once again for the torch to be passed. A new generation must fulfill the obligations of citizenship and bear testimony to its national loyalty. A new generation must rededicate this country to the principles upon which it was founded. A new generation must seize the reins of leadership. A new generation must focus on solving common problems and building the better future we all desire. A new generation must answer the critical call to service that beckons us all.

Perhaps a revival of these themes is already afoot. In his second inaugural address, Barack Obama declared, "You and I, *as citizens*, have the power to set this country's course. You and I, *as citizens*, have the obligation to shape the debates of our time—not only with the votes we cast, but with the voices we lift in defense of our most ancient values and enduring ideals."[5] (Emphasis added.) Subsequently, in his 2013 State of the Union address, Obama again sought to channel the fundamental theme of Kennedy's spirit. He opened his remarks to the nation by quoting a line from one of Kennedy's similar addresses—an overt acknowledgment to the legacy he was embracing—and he concluded with a refrain about the basic concept of citizenship that one can easily connect to Kennedy's words. Despite our differences, Obama suggested, "we all share the same proud title: we are citizens."[6] This underlying, uniting factor cuts across all other distinctions:

> It's a word that doesn't just describe our nationality or legal status. It describes the way we're made. It describes what we believe. It captures the enduring idea that this country only works when we accept certain obligations to one another and to future generations; that our rights are wrapped up in the rights of others; and that well into our third century as a nation, it remains the task of us all, as citizens of these United States, to be the authors of the next great chapter in our American story.

Similarly, in his speech at the April 2013 dedication ceremony for the presidential library that bears his name, George W. Bush noted: "A free society thrives when neighbors help neighbors and the strong protect the weak and public policies promote private compassion.... Ultimately, the success of a nation depends on the character of its citizens."[7]

Let this be a new call to action—not because Kennedy said it or because Obama or Bush said it, but because we *need* it; because it is right; because the precepts of citizenship in which we ask what we can do for our country form the foundation of our national greatness. It is not about the individual; it is about the community, about something bigger than each of us. It is about striving for collective prosperity and behaving in ways that recognize the obligations we have toward one another. It is about doing what each of us can to make this union more perfect.

This is not a partisan imperative. No political party has a monopoly on good ideas, and no political party owns the notion of public service. It is universal and American to its core. For just as Democrats have summoned citizens toward public service, so too have Republicans. And just as Republicans have spoken about individual responsibility in the wider quest for progress, so too have Democrats. Dwight Eisenhower gave voice to a premise on which both parties agree: "A people that values its privileges above its principles soon loses both."[8] We must, therefore, reinvigorate our allegiance to these critical principles.

All are summoned forward in this new call to action, regardless of age, background, or station in life; this call is to the young at heart, to all who love America and want to lift its greatness to new heights.

This country, Franklin Roosevelt reminded us, has a rendezvous with destiny, implying that each generation has obligations it must meet. It is up to us to fulfill the responsibilities of our generation, because in America, the responsibilities of citizenship are preordained. This generational imperative is not merely a rite of passage, but rather, it beckons all who love our nation and believe in its future. For the test of our patriotism is not whether we belong to a particular political party or support a particular candidate, but whether we cherish our country and are willing to accept sacrifice on her behalf.

Let that be what we teach in our schools. Let that be what defines the American spirit in an age of community and interdependence. Let that be the legacy we leave to generations not yet born, from whom we have borrowed this sacred world.

The challenges we face are serious, and the work that lies ahead will not be easy. We live in an age of conflict, struggle, and difficult choices. And yet with every sobering reminder of destruction and despair, we are confronted with a choice: we can shrink from the responsibilities that lie before us and curse the darkness in our midst. Or we can bring new energy and new focus and new devotion toward common efforts by lighting small candles of hope—hope for our country, hope for the future, hope for the dreams of our children. And as we continue to nourish the dream that began in that small brick building in Philadelphia where a certain Declaration was signed, the flame of American progress burns lighter and brighter, and the glow from that fire will light the world of tomorrow.

The historian's pen is in our hands, and it is time indeed to write a new chapter in the story of America. We have it in our power to embark on a new journey restricted only by the boundaries of our imagination and the limits we ourselves impose—a journey in which we never let our pursuit of private happiness blur our sense of public duty. That we live in this great country may be a matter of chance, but how we conduct ourselves and the kinds of efforts we make are entirely our choice. The British poet Alfred, Lord Tennyson's words of long ago—which Kennedy knew well—still ring true today: "Come, my friends, / 'Tis not too late to seek a newer world."9

The torch has been passed in the expectation that a new generation will hold it higher, make it shine brighter, and carry it farther than ever before. So let us go forth to lead the land we love. Let us volunteer our time in worthy causes. Let us get involved in charity work. Let us be engaged in public affairs. Let us be generous in spirit. Let us use the skills and talents we are fortunate to have in ways that are constructive for the communities we treasure. In short, let us answer the call to service to which we are rightfully summoned.

Now is our generation's moment. This is Camelot for our time. This is the power of citizenship.

EPILOGUE

ON THE TWENTIETH anniversary of the issuance of the Atlantic Charter—the important policy statement drafted in August 1941 by Franklin Roosevelt and Winston Churchill identifying a set of objectives for the postwar world waiting in the distance—John Kennedy wired a message to the former prime minister. "Time has not changed and events have not dimmed the historic principles you there expressed...your own name will endure as long as free men survive to recall these words."[1] It was a message befitting a wordsmith like Churchill, the president's hero from his days in Britain as a young adult. Yet the same sentiment might be true of the man who wrote these words.

Kennedy served as president for just over a thousand days. He did not accomplish everything he set out to achieve; he did not solve all of the problems he identified in his historic 1960 campaign; the world he left behind in November 1963 was imperfect. But he had success. He reshaped our understanding of civic obligation in ways that were fresh and innovative. He gave voice to a new generation of Americans looking to contribute, and he helped define their aspirations in the new world he sought. He spoke to our hopes and not to our fears. He advanced the cause of citizenship. He made it seem like anything was possible. He made us feel good, and he left us with a romantic image of Camelot—an image we collectively still cherish today.

When he died, it felt like America was cut down in its prime, just as he was. Gone were the dreams of a generation; lost, directionless, and stunned were citizens struggling to comprehend what had happened. How could the forces of evil triumph over this man, this attractive and vigorous leader? This is a question we never seem to answer.

The idea of Camelot, in a sense, is its own form of eulogy. It focuses on the triumphs; it holds out the promise of better days; it reminds us of our potential. It makes us yearn for that special time. Fifty years later, no formal eulogy is necessary. We remember this president for who he was and what he represented; the Kennedy era is now more a symbol than a reality. No matter. As Pericles said, "[T]o famous men, all the earth is a monument, and their virtues are attested not only by inscriptions on stone at home; but an unwritten record of the mind lives on for each of them, even in foreign lands, better than any gravestone."[2] In other words, the good men do shall not perish but be hailed across the face of the earth forever.

For Kennedy, indeed, this is true. We inhabit a world he helped shape. His vision still inspires us when we consider the direction in which our country should move. The image of America that he painted is still our beacon, our guiding hope. Though the public's fascination with all things Kennedy remains strong and real, it is perhaps the recollection of his words that resonates most deeply in the twenty-first century.

Among the most powerful lines in American history continues to be his bold inaugural command: "And so, my fellow Americans: ask not what your country can do for you—ask what you can do for your country." This line—this ethos—captures it all. It sums up all the magic that was—or is—Camelot. It defines us as a people and the places we hope to go. It reminds us that the best way we prove ourselves worthy of past generations is by making ourselves models to future ones.

No doubt, these words will continue to inspire future generations because they stand for the most basic, most central, most important tenet of a successful democracy, and the concept itself is timeless. There will be a day—perhaps it will be today; perhaps it will be tomorrow; perhaps it will be in any number of tomorrows—when a young child, like this author, hears these words for the first time and feels like the whole world has miraculously changed. It only takes a moment—a mere ten seconds—a quickening of one's heartbeat. He may not fully understand the words when he first hears them. He may not know the context in which they were said. But maybe, just maybe, he will feel so moved, so stirred, that he will want to do something with his life that transforms that mantra into practice. Perhaps others will do the same. And if enough people do it—if enough people make those words their own—then the vision of the New Frontier may finally be realized, and we can begin this world over again and make real the generous impulses that form the basis of our national greatness.

APPENDIX

THE LIFE OF JFK

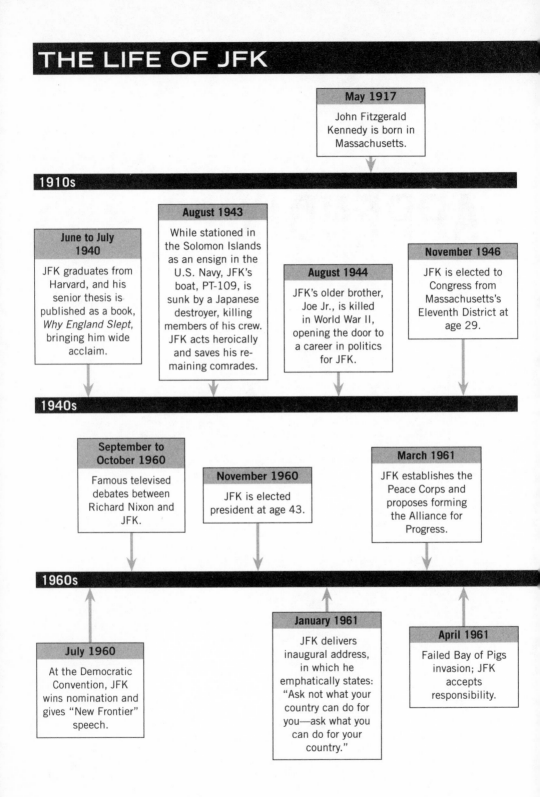

May 1917
John Fitzgerald Kennedy is born in Massachusetts.

1910s

June to July 1940
JFK graduates from Harvard, and his senior thesis is published as a book, *Why England Slept*, bringing him wide acclaim.

August 1943
While stationed in the Solomon Islands as an ensign in the U.S. Navy, JFK's boat, PT-109, is sunk by a Japanese destroyer, killing members of his crew. JFK acts heroically and saves his remaining comrades.

August 1944
JFK's older brother, Joe Jr., is killed in World War II, opening the door to a career in politics for JFK.

November 1946
JFK is elected to Congress from Massachusetts's Eleventh District at age 29.

1940s

September to October 1960
Famous televised debates between Richard Nixon and JFK.

November 1960
JFK is elected president at age 43.

March 1961
JFK establishes the Peace Corps and proposes forming the Alliance for Progress.

1960s

July 1960
At the Democratic Convention, JFK wins nomination and gives "New Frontier" speech.

January 1961
JFK delivers inaugural address, in which he emphatically states: "Ask not what your country can do for you—ask what you can do for your country."

April 1961
Failed Bay of Pigs invasion; JFK accepts responsibility.

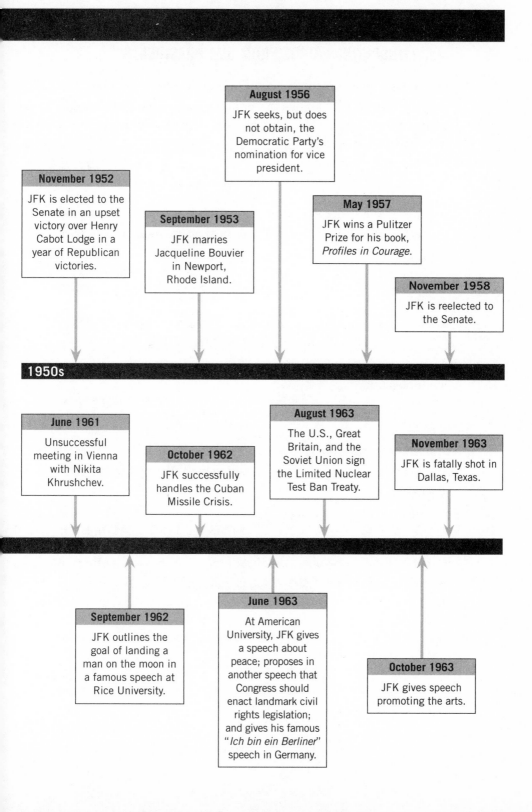

November 1952

JFK is elected to the Senate in an upset victory over Henry Cabot Lodge in a year of Republican victories.

August 1956

JFK seeks, but does not obtain, the Democratic Party's nomination for vice president.

September 1953

JFK marries Jacqueline Bouvier in Newport, Rhode Island.

May 1957

JFK wins a Pulitzer Prize for his book, *Profiles in Courage*.

November 1958

JFK is reelected to the Senate.

1950s

June 1961

Unsuccessful meeting in Vienna with Nikita Khrushchev.

October 1962

JFK successfully handles the Cuban Missile Crisis.

August 1963

The U.S., Great Britain, and the Soviet Union sign the Limited Nuclear Test Ban Treaty.

November 1963

JFK is fatally shot in Dallas, Texas.

September 1962

JFK outlines the goal of landing a man on the moon in a famous speech at Rice University.

June 1963

At American University, JFK gives a speech about peace; proposes in another speech that Congress should enact landmark civil rights legislation; and gives his famous "*Ich bin ein Berliner*" speech in Germany.

October 1963

JFK gives speech promoting the arts.

★ INSPIRING WORDS FROM OUR PRESIDENTS ★

"It may be laid down as a primary position, and the basis of our system, that every Citizen who enjoys the protection of a free Government, owes not only a proportion of his property, but even of his personal services to the defence [*sic*] of it."

—GEORGE WASHINGTON,
Letter to Alexander Hamilton, May 2, 1783

"You will ever remember that all the End of study is to make you a good Man and a useful Citizen. This will ever be the Sum total of the Advice of your affectionate Father."

—JOHN ADAMS,
Letter to John Quincy Adams, May 18, 1781

"A strict observance of the written laws is doubtless one of the high duties of a good citizen, but it is not the highest. The laws of necessity, of self-preservation, of saving our country when in danger, are of higher obligation."

—THOMAS JEFFERSON,
Letter, September 20, 1810

"National honor is national property of the highest value. The sentiment in the mind of every citizen is national strength. It ought therefore to be cherished."

—JAMES MONROE,
First Inaugural Address, March 4, 1817

"Let us at all times remember that all American citizens are brothers of a common country, and should dwell together in the bonds of fraternal feeling."

—ABRAHAM LINCOLN,
Remarks in Springfield, Illinois, November 20, 1860

"I ask patient forbearance one toward another throughout the land, and a determined effort on the part of every citizen to do his share toward cementing a happy union."

—ULYSSES GRANT,
First Inaugural Address, March 4, 1869

"The best results in the operation of a government wherein every citizen has a share largely depend upon a proper limitation of purely partisan zeal and effort and a correct appreciation of the time when the heat of the partisan should be merged in the patriotism of the citizen."

—GROVER CLEVELAND,
First Inaugural Address, March 4, 1885

"Success or failure will be conditioned upon the way in which the average man, the average woman, does his or her duty, first in the ordinary, everyday affairs of life, and next in those great occasional cries which call for heroic virtues. The average citizen must be a good citizen if our republics are to succeed. The stream will not permanently rise higher than the main source; and the main source of national power and national greatness is found in the average citizenship of the nation. Therefore it behooves us to do our best to see that the standard of the average citizen is kept high; and the average cannot be kept high unless the standard of the leaders is very much higher."

—THEODORE ROOSEVELT,
"Citizenship in a Republic" speech, April 23, 1910

"We have learned to be citizens of the world, members of the human community."

—FRANKLIN D. ROOSEVELT,
Fourth Inaugural Address, January 20, 1945

"All Americans must be responsible citizens, but some must be more responsible than others by virtue of their public or their private position, their role in the family or community, their prospects for the future, or their legacy from the past. Increased responsibility goes with increased ability. For those to whom much is given, much is required."

—JOHN F. KENNEDY,
Speech at Vanderbilt University, May 18, 1963

"We must work to provide the knowledge and the surroundings which can enlarge the possibilities of every citizen."

—LYNDON B. JOHNSON,
Inaugural Address, January 20, 1965

"What kind of nation we will be, what kind of world we will live in, whether we shape the future in the image of our hopes, is ours to determine by our actions and our choices."

—RICHARD M. NIXON,
First Inaugural Address, January 20, 1969

"We are creating a nation once again vibrant, robust, and alive. But there are many mountains yet to climb. We will not rest until every American enjoys the fullness of freedom, dignity, and opportunity as our birthright. It is our birthright as citizens of this great Republic, and we'll meet this challenge."

—RONALD REAGAN,
Second Inaugural Address, January 21, 1985

"The old ideas are new again because they are not old, they are timeless: duty, sacrifice, commitment, and a patriotism that finds its expression in taking part and pitching in."

—GEORGE H. W. BUSH,
Inaugural Address, January 20, 1989

"Fellow citizens, let us build that America, a nation ever moving forward toward realizing the full potential of all its citizens."

—BILL CLINTON,
Second Inaugural Address, January 20, 1997

"What is required of us now is a new era of responsibility—a recognition, on the part of every American, that we have duties to ourselves, our nation and the world, duties that we do not grudgingly accept but rather seize gladly, firm in the knowledge that there is nothing so satisfying to the spirit, so defining of our character, than giving our all to a difficult task. This is the price and the promise of citizenship."

—BARACK OBAMA,
First Inaugural Address, January 20, 2009

NOTES

Notes using the abbreviation "PPP–JFK" refer to the Public Papers of the Presidents of the United States: John F. Kennedy, 1961–1963.

Preface
1. John F. Kennedy and Richard M. Nixon, "The First Kennedy–Nixon Presidential Debate" (debate, September 26, 1960), accessed February 17, 2013, www.debates.org/index.php?page=september-26-1960-debate -transcript.

PART I: THE MAN AND THE MISSION

Chapter 1: The Kennedy Promise
1. Thurston Clarke, *Ask Not: The Inauguration of John F. Kennedy and the Speech That Changed America* (New York: Henry Holt and Co. LLC, 2004), 3–4.
2. Daniel Lovering, "JFK's Bomber Jacket Sells for $570,000 at Auction," Reuters, U.S. News on NBCNews.com, February 18, 2013, accessed April 14, 2013, http://usnews.nbcnews.com/_news/2013/02/18/17002967-jfks-bomber-jacket-sells-for-570000-at-auction?lite.
3. Robert Caro, *The Passage of Power* (New York: Alfred A. Knopf, 2012), 585.
4. Martin Luther King Jr., "I Have a Dream," (speech, March on Washington for Jobs and Freedom, Washington, DC, August 28, 1963), accessed February 16, 2013, www.americanrhetoric.com/speeches/mlkihaveadream.htm.
5. Horton Foote, *To Kill a Mockingbird*, directed by Robert Mulligan (Universal Pictures, 1962), motion picture.
6. Ibid.

7. John F. Kennedy, "Radio and Television Report to the American People on Civil Rights" (speech, Washington, DC, June 11, 1963), PPP–JFK, 1963, 468–471.
8. John F. Kennedy, "Inaugural Address" (speech, Washington, DC, January 20, 1961), PPP–JFK, 1961, 1–3.

Chapter 2: Becoming JFK

1. Christopher Matthews, *Jack Kennedy: Elusive Hero* (New York: Simon & Schuster, 2011), 11.
2. Doris Kearns Goodwin, *The Fitzgeralds and the Kennedys: An American Saga* (New York: Simon & Schuster, 1991), 141, 391.
3. Geoffrey Perret, *Jack: A Life Like No Other* (New York: Random House, 2001), 24.
4. Barbara Leaming, *Jack Kennedy: The Education of a Statesman* (New York: W. W. Norton & Co., 2006), 16.
5. Ibid., 18.
6. Herbert S. Parmet, *Jack: The Struggles of Jack Kennedy* (New York: The Dial Press, 1980), 17.
7. Ibid.
8. Matthews, *Jack Kennedy: Elusive Hero*, 441–442.
9. Neville Chamberlain, "Peace for Our Time" (speech, Heston Airport, London, England, September 30, 1938), accessed June 26, 2013, http://news.bbc.co.uk/onthisday/hi/dates/stories/september/30/newsid_3115000/3115476.stm.
10. Alan Brinkley, *John F. Kennedy* (New York: Times Books, 2012), 15.
11. Michael O'Brien, *John F. Kennedy: A Biography* (New York: St. Martin's Press, 2005), 108.
12. Perret, *Jack: A Life Like No Other*, 91.
13. John Buchan, *Pilgrim's Way: An Essay in Recollection* (Boston: Houghton Mifflin, 1940), 47.
14. Leaming, *Jack Kennedy: The Education of a Statesman*, 274.
15. Buchan, *Pilgrim's Way*, 49.
16. Ibid.
17. Ibid.
18. Leaming, *Jack Kennedy: The Education of a Statesman*, 22.
19. Matthews, *Jack Kennedy: Elusive Hero*, 62.
20. O'Brien, *John F. Kennedy: A Biography*, 797.
21. Buchan, *Pilgrim's Way*, 232.
22. David Pietrusza, *1960: LBJ vs. JFK vs. Nixon, The Epic Campaign That Forged Three Presidencies* (New York: Union Square Press, 2008), 6. David Pietrusza noted that JFK was "lucky not to have been courtmartialed for losing" the

PT boat. "'The medal,' JFK's squadron commander officer Lieutenant Alvin Peyton Cluster, a close Kennedy friend, said later, 'was for the survival phase. Not the preceding battle.' Even JFK would admit, 'It was a question of whether they were going to give [me] a medal or throw [me] out.'"

23. Leaming, *The Education of a Statesman*, 180.

24. Deirdre Henderson, *Prelude to Leadership: The European Diary of John F. Kennedy, Summer 1945* (Washington, DC: Regnery Publishing Inc., 1997), 34.

25. Arthur M. Schlesinger Jr, *A Thousand Days: John F. Kennedy in the White House* (Boston: Houghton Mifflin, 1965), 105–106.

26. O'Brien, *John F. Kennedy: A Biography*, 228.

27. Ibid.

28. Ibid.

29. Perret, *Jack: A Life Like No Other*, 172, 197.

30. Matthews, *Jack Kennedy: Elusive Hero*, 73.

31. Ibid., 75

32. Perret, *Jack: A Life Like No Other*, 352.

33. Hugh Sidey, introduction to *Prelude to Leadership: The Post-War Diary, Summer 1945* (Washington, DC: Regnery Publishing Inc., 1997), xxiv–xxv.

34. Schlesinger, *A Thousand Days*, 114.

35. Leaming, *The Education of a Statesman*, 13.

36. Jacqueline Kennedy, interview by Theodore White, November 29, 1963.

37. Paul Woodruff, *Thucydides: On Justice, Power, and Human Nature* (Indianapolis: Hackett Publishing Co., 1993), 40.

38. John F. Kennedy, *Profiles in Courage* (New York: Harper and Brothers, 1956), 48.

39. Ibid., 33.

40. Ibid., 70.

41. Ibid., 72–73.

42. Ibid., 75.

43. Ibid., 111.

44. Ibid., 258.

Chapter 3: A Bold Candidacy

1. John F. Kennedy, "Remarks Announcing His Candidacy for the Presidency of the United States" (speech, Senate Caucus Room, Washington, DC, January 2, 1960), accessed February 17, 2013, www.presidency.ucsb.edu/ws/index.php?pid=25909.

2. John F. Kennedy, "Remarks at the National Press Club" (speech, Washington, DC, January 14, 1960), accessed April 18, 2013, www.presidency.ucsb.edu/ws/index.php?pid=25795.

3. John F. Kennedy, "Speech at the University of Michigan" (speech, Ann Arbor, MI, October 14, 1960), accessed April 20, 2013, www.peacecorps .gov/about/history/speech/.

4. Arthur M. Schlesinger Jr., *Robert Kennedy and His Times* (Boston: Houghton Mifflin, 1978), 210.

5. John F. Kennedy, "Democratic National Convention Acceptance Address" (speech, Los Angeles, CA, July 15, 1960), accessed February 17, 2013, www.americanrhetoric.com/speeches/jfk1960dnc.htm.

6. John F. Kennedy, "Address to the Greater Houston Ministerial Association" (speech, Houston, TX, September 12, 1960), accessed February 17, 2013, www.americanrhetoric.com/speeches/jfkhoustonministers.html.

7. John F. Kennedy and Richard M. Nixon, "The First Kennedy–Nixon Presidential Debate."

8. Christopher Matthews, *Kennedy and Nixon: The Rivalry That Shaped Postwar America* (New York: Simon & Schuster, 1996), 151–152.

9. 1960 Presidential Election Results. Accessed February 8, 2013, http://us electionatlas.org/RESULTS.

10. Brinkley, *John F. Kennedy*, 53.

11. Richard J. Tofel, *Sounding the Trumpet: The Making of John F. Kennedy's Inaugural Address* (Chicago: Ivan R. Dee, 2005), 7.

12. Ibid., 10.

13. Ibid., 10–11.

14. Kennedy, "Inaugural Address."

15. David Halberstam, *The Best and the Brightest* (New York: Random House, 1969), 38–39.

16. William Manchester, *Portrait of a President* (Boston: Little, Brown & Co., 1962), 207.

17. "The Trumpet Summons," *Milwaukee Journal*, January 20, 1961.

18. "A Stirring Beginning," *Los Angeles Times*, January 22, 1961.

19. Arthur Krock, "Inaugural Contrast," *New York Times*, January 22, 1961.

20. William Randolph Hearst, Jr., "JFK Old Enough for Big Job," *New York Journal*, January 22, 1961.

21. Inaugural Address Coverage, *Los Angeles Times*, January 22, 1961.

22. Ibid.

23. Victor Lasky, *The Man and the Myth* (New York: The Macmillan Co., 1963), 500.

24. Robert Frost, "Stopping by Woods on a Snowy Evening," in *The Robert Frost Reader: Poetry and Prose*, ed. Edward Connery Lathem and Lawrance Thompson (New York: Henry Holt & Co., 2002), 106.

PART II: THE NEW FRONTIER

Chapter 4: An Appeal to Our Pride

1. Kennedy, "Inaugural Address."
2. Theodore Sorensen, *Kennedy* (New York: Harper & Row, 1965), 524.
3. Robert Dallek, *An Unfinished Life: John F. Kennedy* (New York: Back Bay Books, 2003), 651.
4. Sorensen, *Kennedy*, 525.
5. John F. Kennedy, "Special Message to the Congress on Urgent National Needs" (speech, Washington, DC, May 25, 1961), PPP–JFK, 1961, 396–406.
6. John F. Kennedy, "Address at Rice University in Houston on the Nation's Space Effort" (speech, Rice University, Houston, TX, September 12, 1962), PPP–JFK, 1962, 668–671.
7. Richard Reeves, *President Kennedy: Profile of Power* (New York: Simon & Schuster, 1993), 139.
8. Kennedy, "Address on the Nation's Space Effort."
9. Cristen Conger, "10 NASA Inventions You Might Use Every Day," accessed June 1, 2013, http://dsc.discovery.com/tv-shows/curiosity/topics/ten-nasa-inventions.htm.
10. Kennedy, "Inaugural Address."
11. Kennedy, "Speech at the University of Michigan."
12. Ibid.
13. Schlesinger, *A Thousand Days*, 607.
14. "Fast Facts," Peace Corps, updated July 16, 2012, accessed May 9, 2013, www.peacecorps.gov/about/fastfacts.
15. John F. Kennedy, "Statement by the President Upon Signing Order Establishing the Peace Corps" (speech, Washington, DC, March 1, 1961), PPP–JFK, 1961, 134–135.
16. Ibid.
17. Reeves, *President Kennedy*, 276.
18. Ibid.
19. "Fast Facts," Peace Corps.
20. Ibid.
21. Ibid.
22. "Education," Peace Corps, last updated July 16, 2012, accessed April 21, 2013, www.peacecorps.gov/about/notable/education.
23. "Peace Corps Interactive Timeline, 1961–2011," Peace Corps, last updated July 16, 2012, accessed April 21, 2013, www.peacecorps.gov/about/history/timeline.

24. Ibid.
25. Schlesinger, *A Thousand Days*, 186–187.
26. Richard Goodwin, *Remembering America* (Boston: Little, Brown & Co., 1988), 149.
27. Ibid.
28. Ibid.
29. Sorensen, *Kennedy*, 533.
30. Goodwin, *Remembering America*, 149.
31. Schlesinger, *A Thousand Days*, 188.
32. John F. Kennedy, "Address at a White House Reception for Members of Congress and for the Diplomatic Corps of the Latin American Republics" (speech, Washington, DC, March 13, 1961), PPP–JFK, 1961, 170–175.
33. Reeves, *President Kennedy*, 73.

Chapter 5: Challenges Abroad
1. Brinkley, *John F. Kennedy*, 66.
2. Ibid., 67.
3. John F. Kennedy, "The President's News Conference of April 21, 1961," PPP–JFK, 1961, 307–315.
4. Brinkley, *John F. Kennedy*, 70.
5. Barack Obama, interview by Charlie Rose, July 12, 2012, accessed February 14, 2013, www.cbsnews.com/8301-503544_162-57471351-503544 /obama-reflects-on-his-biggest-mistake-as-president/.
6. Kennedy, "Special Message to the Congress of Urgent National Needs."
7. Thomas Reeves, *A Question of Character: A Life of John F. Kennedy* (New York: The Free Press, 1991), 300.
8. Ibid.
9. Schlesinger, *A Thousand Days*, 381.
10. Ibid.
11. Reeves, *A Question of Character*, 305.
12. John F. Kennedy, "Radio and Television Address to the Nation on the Berlin Crisis" (broadcast speech, Washington, DC, July 25, 1961), PPP–JFK, 1961, 533–540.
13. Sorensen, *Kennedy*, 594.
14. Schlesinger, *A Thousand Days*, 796.
15. Reeves, *A Question of Character*, 367.
16. Ibid.
17. Schlesinger, *A Thousand Days*, 802.
18. Reeves, *A Question of Character*, 372.
19. Sorensen, *Kennedy*, 687–688.

20. John F. Kennedy, "Radio and Television Report to the American People on the Soviet Arms Buildup in Cuba" (broadcast speech, Washington, DC, October 22, 1962), PPP–JFK, 1962, 806–809.

21. O'Brien, *John F. Kennedy: A Biography*, 668.

22. John F. Kennedy, "Commencement Address at American University in Washington" (speech, American University, Washington, DC, June 10, 1963), PPP–JFK, 1963, 459–464.

23. Ibid.

24. Reeves, *President Kennedy*, 535.

25. Brinkley, *John F. Kennedy*, 130.

26. John F. Kennedy, "Remarks in the Rudolph Wilde Platz, Berlin" (speech, Berlin, Germany, June 26, 1963), PPP–JFK, 1963, 524–525.

27. Ronald Reagan, "'Tear Down This Wall': Speech at Brandenburg Gate" (speech, Berlin, Germany, June 12, 1987), accessed April 24, 2013, www .historyplace.com/speeches/reagan-tear-down.htm.

28. Bill Clinton, "Oklahoma Bombing Memorial Prayer Service Address" (speech, Oklahoma City, Oklahoma, April 23, 1995), accessed February 4, 2013, www.americanrhetoric.com/speeches/wjcoklahomabombingspeech.htm.

29. Barack Obama, "Transcript: Obama's Speech in Berlin," *New York Times*, July 24, 2008.

Chapter 6: On the Homefront

1. Reeves, *A Question of Character*, 330.

2. John M. Murphy, "The Language of the Liberal Consensus: John F. Kennedy, Technical Reason, and the 'New Economics' at Yale University," *Quarterly Journal of Speech* 90, no. 2 (May 2004): 133–162.

3. Reeves, *A Question of Character*, 330.

4. Murphy, "The Language of the Liberal Consensus," 134.

5. Schlesinger, *Robert Kennedy and His Times*, 403.

6. John F. Kennedy, "The President's News Conference of April 11, 1962," PPP–JFK, 1962, 315–322.

7. Murphy, "The Language of the Liberal Consensus," 134.

8. John F. Kennedy, "Commencement Address at Yale University" (speech, Yale University, New Haven, CT, June 11, 1962), PPP–JFK, 1962, 470–475.

9. Murphy, "The Language of the Liberal Consensus," 135.

10. Kennedy, "Radio and Television Report to the American People on Civil Rights."

11. Lathem and Thompson, *The Robert Frost Reader: Poetry and Prose*, 490–491.

12. Evelyn Lincoln, *My Twelve Years with John F. Kennedy* (New York: David McKay Co. Inc., 1965), 295.

13. Sally Bedell Smith, *Grace and Power* (New York: Random House, 2004), xvii.

14. Barbara Leaming, *Mrs. Kennedy* (New York: Simon & Schuster, 2001), 145.

15. Ibid.

16. Ibid., 146.

17. Smith, *Grace and Power*, 255–256.

18. Ibid.

19. Ibid., 255.

20. Schlesinger, *A Thousand Days*, 671.

21. Ibid.

22. Smith, *Grace and Power*, 24.

23. Leaming, *Mrs. Kennedy*, 147.

24. Sorensen, *Kennedy*, 384.

25. Lincoln, *My Twelve Years with John F. Kennedy*, 300.

26. Sorensen, *Kennedy*, 384.

27. Ibid., 389.

28. Robert Frost, "Dedication," in *The Robert Frost Reader: Poetry and Prose*, ed. Lathem and Thompson, 493.

29. John F. Kennedy, "Remarks at Amherst College Upon Receiving an Honorary Degree" (speech, Amherst College, Amherst, MA, October 26, 1963), PPP–JFK, 1963, 815–818.

30. Kennedy and Nixon, "The First Kennedy–Nixon Presidential Debate."

31. Sorensen, *Kennedy*, 473. On a historical side note, the Coast Guard fell under the auspices of the Department of Treasury because, as the nation's first secretary of the treasury, Alexander Hamilton had created the institution. As Hamilton biographer Ron Chernow pointed out, upon his appointment, Hamilton "had to create a customs service on the spot, for customs duties were to be the main source of government revenue." [Ron Chernow, *Alexander Hamilton* (New York: Penguin Press, 2004), 292.] Immediately upon assuming office, Hamilton requested that all of his customs collectors report exact figures of the duties they collected in each state. When the numbers reported to the secretary were flagrantly lower than he had anticipated, Hamilton had an educated suspicion that the smuggling of goods—of course, to avoid paying taxes—had spiraled out of control. Consequently, he wrote to a friend: "I have under consideration the business of establishing guard boats," what Chernow observed to be "perhaps the first allusion to what would turn into the Coast Guard." (Chernow, *Alexander Hamilton*, 292.)

32. John A. Barnes, *John F. Kennedy on Leadership: The Lessons and Legacy of a President* (New York: AMACOM, 2007), 178.

33. Martin Luther King Jr., "Letter from a Birmingham Jail," April 16, 1963, accessed May 10, 2013, www.africa.upenn.edu/Articles_Gen/Letter_Birmingham.html.

34. Reeves, *President Kennedy*, 486.

35. Ibid.

36. Matthews, *Jack Kennedy: Elusive Hero*, 379.

37. Taylor Branch, *Parting the Waters: America in the King Years, 1954–63* (New York: Simon & Schuster, 1989), 780.

38. Reeves, *President Kennedy*, 488.

39. Ibid., 500.

40. Matthews, *Jack Kennedy: Elusive Hero*, 379.

41. Reeves, *President Kennedy*, 515.

42. Ibid., 520.

43. Ibid.

44. Kennedy, "Radio and Television Report to the American People on Civil Rights."

45. Foote, *To Kill a Mockingbird*.

PART III: THE CITIZEN OF TODAY

Chapter 7: The Next Frontier

1. Kennedy, "Special Message to the Congress on Urgent National Needs."

2. Kennedy, "Commencement Address at American University."

3. Associated Press, "America's Competitiveness Ranking Falls Again, Survey Finds," *Daily Finance*, September 5, 2012.

4. Motoko Rich, "U.S. Students Still Lag Globally in Math and Science, Tests Show," *New York Times*, December 11, 2012. "Best Education in the World: Finland, South Korea Top Country Rankings, U.S. Rated Average," *Huffington Post*, November 27, 2012.

5. Jason Kane, "Health Costs: How the U.S. Compares with Other Countries," PBS NewsHour, October 22, 2012.

6. Abraham Lincoln, "House Divided Speech" (speech, Springfield, IL, June 16, 1958), accessed May 13, 2013, www.pbs.org/wgbh/aia/part4/4h2934t.html.

7. Christopher Matthews, "Remarks at Georgetown University" (speech, Georgetown University, Washington, DC, October 25, 2012), accessed May 13, 2013, www.georgetown.edu/news/chris-matthews-talks-making-politics-work.html.

8. Joseph de Maistre, 1811, *Encyclopædia Britannica Online,* accessed February 18, 2013, www.britannica.com/EBchecked/topic/358824/Joseph-de-Maistre/358824suppinfo/Supplemental-Information.

9. John F. Kennedy, "Address at Massachusetts General Court" (speech, Boston, MA, January 9, 1961), accessed May 13, 2013, www.jfklibrary.org /Asset-Viewer/OYhUZE2Qo0-ogdV7ok900A.aspx.

10. Thomas Jefferson, "First Inaugural Address" (speech, Washington, DC, March 4, 1801), accessed May 28, 2013, http://avalon.law.yale.edu/19th _century/jefinau1.asp.

11. Kennedy, "Address on the Nation's Space Effort."

Chapter 8: Profiles in Service

1. "The Presidential Citizens Medal Criteria," accessed April 2, 2013, www .whitehouse.gov/citizensmedal/criteria.

2. Ibid.

3. Barack Obama, "Remarks by the President at Presentation of 2012 Presidential Citizens Medals," (speech, Washington, DC, last modified February 15, 2013), accessed April 1, 2013, www.whitehouse.gov/the-press -office/2013/02/15remarks-president-presentation-2012-presidential -citizens-medals.

4. Richard Nixon, "Remarks at a Ceremony Honoring Roberto Clemente" (speech, Washington, DC, May 14, 1973), accessed April 1, 2013, www .presidency.ucsb.edu/ws/?pid=3844.

5. "The Origins of Veterans Day," U.S. Department of Veterans Affairs, accessed April 1, 2013, www.va.gov/opa/publications/celebrate/vetday.pdf.

6. Ronald Reagan, "Remarks on Presenting the Presidential Citizens Medal to Raymond Weeks at a Veterans Day Ceremony" (speech, Washington, DC, November 11, 1982), accessed April 1, 2013, www.reagan.utexas .edu/archives/speeches/1982/111182a.htm.

7. William J. Clinton, "Remarks on Presenting the Presidential Citizens Medal" (speech, Washington, DC, January 8, 2001), accessed April 1, 2013, www.presidency.ucsb.edu/ws/?pid=64902.

8. Ibid.

9. "Patrisha A. Wright," Disability Rights Education & Defense Fund, accessed April 1, 2013, http://dredf.org/about/staff/wright.shtml.

10. Clinton, "Presenting Presidential Citizens Medal."

11. "Our History," Partnership for Public Service, accessed April 1, 2013, http://ourpublicservice.org/OPS/about/history.shtml.

12. Ibid.

13. Ed O'Keefe, "Partnership for Public Service Founder Wins Presidential Citizens Medal," *Washington Post*, December 12, 2008, accessed April 1, 2013, http://voices.washingtonpost.com/federal-eye/2008/12/partnership_ for_public_service.html.

14. "Roberta Diaz Brinton," USC Neuroscience, University of Southern California, accessed April 1, 2013, www.usc.edu/programs/neuroscience/faculty/profile.php?fid=4.
15. Kennedy, "Inaugural Address."

Chapter 9: Embracing Our Citizenship

1. Kennedy, "Inaugural Address."
2. Kennedy, "Democratic National Convention Acceptance Address."
3. Neil Armstrong, Apollo 11 Transcript, Moon Landing, July 20, 1969, accessed May 13, 2013, www.hq.nasa.gov/alsj/a11/a11.step.html.
4. Declaration of Independence, July 4, 1776, accessed April 24, 2013, www.archives.gov/exhibits/charters/declaration_transcript.html.
5. Barack Obama, "Second Inaugural Address" (speech, Washington, DC, January 21, 2013), accessed June 23, 2013, http://www.whitehouse.gov/the-press-office/2013/01/21/inaugural-address-president-barack-obama.
6. Barack Obama, "State of the Union Address" (speech, Washington, DC, February 12, 2013), accessed June 23, 2013, http://articles.washingtonpost.com/2013-02-12/politics/37059380_1_applause-task-free-enterprise.
7. George W. Bush, remarks at his presidential library dedication, April 25, 2013, accessed May 13, 2013, www.nytimes.com/2013/04/26/us/politics/george-w-bushs-remarks-at-his-presidential-library-dedication.html?pagewanted=all&_r=0.
8. Dwight Eisenhower, "First Inaugural Address" (speech, Washington, DC, January 20, 1953), accessed May 28, 2013, http://avalon.law.yale.edu/20th_century/eisen1.asp.
9. Perret, *Jack: A Life Like No Other*, 197.

Epilogue

1. John F. Kennedy, "Message to Sir Winston Churchill on the 20th Anniversary of the Atlantic Charter, August 14, 1961," PPP–JFK, 1961, 564.
2. Woodruff, *Thucydides: On Justice, Power, and Human Nature*, 45.

SOURCES

Ambrose, Stephen E. *Eisenhower: Soldier and President*. New York: Simon & Schuster, 1991.

Aristotle. *The Politics*. New York: Penguin Books, 1962.

Barnes, John A. *John F. Kennedy on Leadership: The Lessons and Legacy of a President*. New York: AMACOM, 2007.

Beasley, Vanessa B. "Race, Rhetoric, and Risk: Revisiting the History of U.S. Civil Rights." *Rhetoric and Public Affairs* 5, no. 3 (2002): 525–536.

Boller, Paul F. *Presidential Anecdotes*. New York: Oxford University Press, 1981.

Branch, Taylor. *Parting the Waters: America in the King Years, 1954–63*. New York: Simon & Schuster, 1989.

Brinkley, Alan. *John F. Kennedy*. New York: Times Books, 2012.

Bryant, Nick. *The Bystander: John F. Kennedy and the Struggle for Black Equality*. New York: Basic Books, 2006.

Buchan, John (Lord Tweedsmuir). *Pilgrim's Way: An Essay in Recollection*. Cambridge, MA: Houghton Mifflin, 1940.

Butner, David W., and Thomas R. West. *The Torch Is Passed*. New York: Atheneum, 1984.

Campbell, Karlyn Kohrs, and Kathleen Hall Jamieson. *Deeds Done in Words*. Chicago: University of Chicago Press, 1990.

Caro, Robert. *The Passage of Power*. New York: Alfred A. Knopf, 2012.

Chernow, Ron. *Alexander Hamilton*. New York: Penguin Press, 2004.

Clarke, Thurston. *Ask Not: The Inauguration of John F. Kennedy and the Speech That Changed America*. New York: Penguin Books, 2010.

Dallek, Robert. *An Unfinished Life: John F. Kennedy, 1961–1963*. New York: Little, Brown & Co., 2003.

DeSelincourt, Aubrey. *Herodotus: The Histories*. New York: Penguin Books, 1954.

Dillon, Matthew, and Lynda Garland. *Ancient Greece*. New York: Routledge Publishing, 1994.

Ellmann, Richard. *The Artist as Critic: Critical Writings of Oscar Wilde*. Chicago: University of Chicago Press, 1982.

Fairlie, Henry. *The Kennedy Promise*. New York: Doubleday & Co., 1975.

Finley, M. I. *The Ancient Greeks*. New York: Penguin Books, 1963.

Fjelstad, Per. "Restraint and Emotion in Cicero: De Oratore." *Philosophy and Rhetoric* 36, no. 1 (2003): 39–47.

Freeman, Charles. *The Greek Achievement*. New York: Penguin Books, 1999.

Galbraith, John Kenneth. *The Affluent Society*. New York: Houghton Mifflin, 1958.

Goldzwig, Steven R. "LBJ, the Rhetoric of Transcendence, and the Civil Rights Act of 1968." *Rhetoric & Public Affairs* 6, no. 1 (2003): 25–53.

Goodwin, Doris Kearns. *The Fitzgeralds and the Kennedys: An American Saga*. New York: Simon & Schuster, 1991.

Goodwin, Richard. *Remembering America*. Boston: Little, Brown & Co., 1988.

Halberstam, David. *The Best and the Brightest*. New York: Random House, 1969.

Hamilton, Edith. *The Greek Way*. New York: W. W. Norton & Co., 1964.

Hawhee, Debra. "Agonism and Aretē." *Philosophy and Rhetoric* 35, no. 3 (2002): 185–207.

Hearst, William Randolph, Jr. "JFK Old Enough for Big Job." *New York Journal*. January 22, 1961.

Henderson, Deirdre. *Prelude to Leadership: The European Diary of John F. Kennedy, Summer 1945*. Washington, DC: Regnery Publishing Inc., 1995.

Jones, Peter, and Keith Sidwell. *The World of Rome*. Cambridge, England: Cambridge University Press, 1997.

Jordan, John W. "Kennedy's Romantic Moon and Its Rhetorical Legacy for Space Exploration." *Rhetoric and Public Affairs* 6, no. 2 (2003): 209–231.

Kennedy, Caroline. *The Best Loved Poems of Jacqueline Kennedy Onassis*. New York: Hyperion, 2001.

Kennedy, George A. *A New History of Classical Rhetoric*. Princeton, NJ: Princeton University Press, 1994.

Kennedy, John F. *Profiles in Courage*. New York: Harper & Brothers, memorial edition, 1964.

King, Martin Luther, Jr. *Why We Can't Wait*. New York: Signet, 1964.

Knight, John. "What Kind of a President? Kennedy's Words a Profile." *Miami Herald*. January 22, 1961.

Krock, Arthur. "Inaugural Contrast." *New York Times*. January 22, 1961.

Lasky, Victor. *JFK: The Man and the Myth*. New York: The Macmillan Co., 1963.

Lathem, Edward Connery, and Lawrance Thompson. *The Robert Frost Reader: Poetry and Prose*. New York: Henry Holt & Co., 2002.

Lawson-Tancred, H. C. *Aristotle: The Art of Rhetoric*. London: Penguin Books, 1991.

Leamer, Laurence. *The Kennedy Men*. New York: William Morrow, 2001.

Leaming, Barbara. *Jack Kennedy: The Education of a Statesman*. New York: W. W. Norton & Co., 2006.

———. *Mrs. Kennedy*. New York: Simon & Schuster, 2001.

Lincoln, Evelyn. *My Twelve Years with John F. Kennedy*. New York: David McKay Co. Inc., 1965.

Lippmann, Walter. "Kennedy Rejects Ike's Economics." *Denver Post*. January 22, 1961.

Los Angeles Times. "A Stirring Beginning." January 22, 1961.

Manchester, William. *Death of a President*. New York: Harper & Row, 1967.

———. *Portrait of a President*. Boston: Little, Brown & Co., 1962.

Matthews, Christopher. *Jack Kennedy: Elusive Hero*. New York: Simon & Schuster, 2011.

———. *Kennedy & Nixon: The Rivalry That Shaped Postwar America*. New York: Free Press, 1997.

Miller, Warren E., and Santa A. Traugott. *American National Election Studies Data Sourcebook 1952–1986*. Cambridge, MA: Harvard University Press, 1989.

Milwaukee Journal. "The Trumpet Summons." January 20, 1961.

Morris, Edmund. *Theodore Rex*. New York: Modern Library, 2001.

Morrow, Lance. *The Best Year of Their Lives: Kennedy, Johnson, and Nixon in 1948: Learning the Secrets of Power*. New York: Basic Books, 2005.

Murphy, John M. "Crafting the Kennedy Legacy." *Rhetoric and Public Affairs* 3, no. 4 (2000): 577–601.

———. "The Language of the Liberal Consensus: John F. Kennedy, Technical Reason, and the 'New Economics' at Yale University." *Quarterly Journal of Speech* 90, no. 2 (May 2004): 133–162.

Myers, Frank. "Harold Macmillan's 'Winds of Change' Speech: A Case Study in the Rhetoric of Policy Change." *Rhetoric and Public Affairs* 3, no. 4 (2000): 555–575.

O'Brien, Michael. *John F. Kennedy: A Biography*. New York: St. Martin's Press, 2005.

O'Donnell, Kenneth P., and David F. Powers. *Johnny, We Hardly Knew Ye*. New York: Little, Brown & Co., 1970.

Osborn, Michael. "Rhetorical Distance in 'Letter from Birmingham Jail.'" *Rhetoric and Public Affairs* 7, no. 1 (2004): 23–35.

Parmet, Herbert S. *Jack: The Struggles of Jack Kennedy*. New York: The Dial Press, 1980.

Perret, Geoffrey. *Jack: A Life Like No Other*. New York: Random House, 2001.

Pietrusza, David. *1960—LBJ vs. JFK vs. Nixon: The Epic Campaign That Forged Three Presidencies*. New York: Union Square Press, 2010.

Ramsden, John. *Winston Churchill and His Legend Since 1945*. New York: Columbia University Press, 2002.

Renehan, Edward J., Jr. *The Kennedys at War*. New York: Doubleday, 2002.

Reeves, Richard. *President Kennedy*. New York: Simon & Schuster, 1993.

Reeves, Thomas C. *A Question of Character: A Life of John F. Kennedy*. New York: The Free Press, 1991.

Rudd, Niall. *Cicero: The Republic, The Laws*. Oxford, England: Oxford University Press, 1998.

Schlesinger, Arthur M., Jr. *A Thousand Days: John F. Kennedy in the White House*. Boston: Houghton Mifflin, 1965.

———. *Robert Kennedy and His Times*. Boston: Houghton Mifflin, 1978.

Shakespeare, William. *Pericles*. New York: Simon & Schuster, 1968.

Smith, Sally Bedell. *Grace and Power: The Private World of the Kennedy White House*. New York: Random House, 2004.

Sorensen, Theodore C. *Kennedy*. New York: Harper & Row, 1965.

———. *Let the Word Go Forth*. New York: Delacorte Press, 1988.

Strober, Gerald S., and Deborah H. Strober. *Let Us Begin Anew*. New York: HarperCollins, 1993.

Thomas, Evan. *Robert Kennedy: His Life*. New York: Simon & Schuster, 2000.

Tofel, Richard J. *Sounding the Trumpet: The Making of John F. Kennedy's Inaugural Address*. Chicago: Ivan R. Dee, 2005.

Vellacott, Philip. *Aeschylus: The Oresteian Trilogy*. London: Penguin Books, 1956.

Watson, J. J. *Cicero: On Oratory and Orators*. Carbondale, Illinois: Southern Illinois University Press, 1970.

White, Theodore H. "For President Kennedy: An Epilogue." *Life*, December 6, 1963.

———. *The Making of the President: 1960*. New York: Atheneum Publishers, 1961.

Wills, Garry. *Lincoln at Gettysburg: The Words That Remade America.* New York: Touchstone, Literary Research Inc., 1992.

Wood, Gordon S. *The Radicalism of the American Revolution.* New York: First Vintage Books Edition, 1991.

Woodruff, Paul. *Thucydides: On Justice, Power, and Human Nature.* Indianapolis: Hackett Publishing Co., 1993.

ACKNOWLEDGMENTS

PERHAPS THE BEST part of writing a book is having the chance to interact with so many remarkable people along the way—many of whom contributed mightily to making this book a reality.

As an undergraduate student at the University of Pennsylvania, during law school, and continuing throughout this project, I had the great privilege of being mentored by Professor David Eisenhower, whose warm friendship, enthusiasm, and generosity of spirit I could never adequately acknowledge. He has been a dedicated and loyal friend to whom I am most sincerely grateful.

I am likewise indebted to the larger Penn community for the opportunity to have learned from so many distinguished scholars, professors, and peers.

Early in my research, I received meaningful insights and encouragement from Dan Fenn Jr., the founding director of the JFK Library and a staff assistant to President Kennedy in the White House. The late Ted Sorensen, President Kennedy's principal speechwriter, was also kind enough to speak with me about my research during his visit to Penn's campus while I was in school there.

On my trips to the JFK Library in Boston, Tom Putnam, the director of the library, and the staff greeted me cheerfully and offered valuable research guidance. I encourage those who have not had a chance to visit this inspiring institution to do so—it's worth it.

I would like to thank Glenn Yeffeth and the entire team at BenBella for their hard work on this book. In particular, I would like to thank my editor, Debbie Harmsen, whose passion about this book's material and suggestions helped mold my work into the book I wanted it to be—I am thankful for her great vision. Brian Buchanan skillfully shepherded the manuscript through the copyediting phase. I would also like to acknowledge the valuable help I received throughout the entire publication process from Adrienne Lang, Jennifer Canzoneri, Lindsay Marshall, Katie Kennedy, Jessika Rieck, Leigh Camp, Monica Lowry, Amy Zarkos, James Fraleigh, Laura Cherkas, and Debra Bowman.

I received excellent legal counsel from Jonathan Ehrlich and Dan Sirkin, for which I remain most appreciative.

Throughout the publishing process, I was fortunate to be surrounded by amazing friends. At different times, they offered support, encouragement, and help that made the whole process more rewarding than I could have imagined. Thank you to my friends from Wheatley, Penn, Penn Law, Temple Sinai, Willkie Farr & Gallagher LLP, and those from all other walks of life—your friendship means so much to me.

In particular, I would like to recognize Mitch Draizin, Gary Meltzer, and Brian Selander, each of whom made very helpful introductions and cared about this project as if it were their own. My friend Colleen O'Brien read multiple drafts of the manuscript and consistently provided prudent advice. I'm very appreciative of all of their efforts.

I would also like to acknowledge the following individuals: Howard Berrent, Howard Block, Jeff Feldman, Al Felzenberg, Howie Freedman, A. Mark Getachew, Steve Glass, Leah Goldberg, Seth Goldberg, Hannah Gorski, Matt Gorski, Timmy Holland, Casey Lynn,

Adam Rothblatt, Arthur Sherman, Meagan Stacey, Chris Terry, Stefani Wiener, Andrew Wiener, Rebecca Winik, Mike Winik, and the entire extended Freeman family.

My family has always been an endless source of support and enthusiasm. They, too, have lived with this book for some time, and I am profoundly grateful for their inspiration, strength, and more than anything else, their unconditional love.

I am fortunate to have wonderful aunts, uncles, and cousins. My grandparents, Beverly and Eddie Herschenfeld, and Betty and the late Marshall Reich, have always been a significant part of my life. I hope they know that the pride they have in me has always been reciprocal.

One of the great gifts of my life has been having three amazing siblings who are also my best friends. My sister, Leslie, offered brilliant suggestions throughout and was always very generous with her time and willing to help in any way she could. My brothers, Andrew and Jesse, were very enthusiastic about every stage of the book process and gave me great advice whenever it was needed. My siblings share my deep passion for history and a desire to serve the community. They have made my life immeasurably better.

This book literally would not be what it is without Marissa. Words cannot express my love and appreciation for her steadfast support and devotion. At all stages of this book, she inspired me with great ideas, pushed me to dig deeper, and offered creative guidance when I needed it most. Her radiance has lit up my life in countless ways, enhancing this journey—and so much more.

I am supremely grateful to two people who have made everything possible: my parents, Jamie and Danny. No one can choose his or her parents, of course; but if given the choice, I would have a very easy decision. They are the most generous and caring people I know, and everything I am I owe to them. I thank them with love from the bottom of my heart.

Finally, there are two groups of people I wish to acknowledge. Throughout my education, I was fortunate to have had a truly extraordinary set of teachers and coaches—many of whom have become dear friends. Though this work is my own, anything I do bears their fingerprints and I am forever indebted to them. I hope they will take some measure of pride in knowing that they helped make this book—and a good deal more—achievable.

And to all the good citizens of our great republic—the folks who volunteer for good causes, the people who perform charity work, the individuals at home and abroad who protect us and secure our safety and freedom, our civil servants, members of the foreign service, our teachers, those who help others who are less fortunate or are going through difficult times, and those who sacrifice private comfort to help us achieve public gain—you are the backbone of this country and my inspiration for writing this book.

INDEX

ABOUT THE AUTHOR

SCOTT D. REICH is a practicing attorney at Willkie Farr & Gallagher LLP in New York. In 2010, he was appointed by the governor of New York to serve on the College Council of SUNY College at Old Westbury. He serves on the national board of the Union for Reform Judaism, the board of directors of the School for Language and Communication Development, and the board of trustees of Temple Sinai in Roslyn Heights, New York. He has done pro bono work for the Brooklyn Family Court, the New York Legal Assistance Group, and Lincoln Center for the Performing Arts. Reich earned a B.A. in history and communication from the University of Pennsylvania and a J.D. from the University of Pennsylvania Law School, where he was president of his class.